Benefits Management

Releasing project value
into the business

Michael Payne

Project Manager Today
P U B L I C A T I O N S

Project Manager Today Publications
Larchdrift Projects Ltd, Unit 12, Moor Place Farm, Plough Lane,
Bramshill, Hook, Hampshire RG27 0RF

First published in Great Britain 2007

ISBN 978–1–900391–16–0

A CIP catalogue record for this book is available from the
British Library.

Printed and bound in Great Britain
through Print Solutions Partnership, Surrey

About the author

MICHAEL PAYNE

During his professional career as an officer in a technical branch of the British Army, an IT executive with the Guinness Group and a management consultant, Michael has developed a comprehensive understanding of projects, their management and how to release their potential value.

He received formal training in project management while in the Army and went on to be a project manager or senior user on several defence equipment programmes. During this period he was the Ministry of Defence representative to the STARTS initiative, run by the National Computing Centre on behalf of the Department of Industry, and was a major contributor to the STARTS handbook on Software Tools for Application to Large Real-Time Systems.

While with Guinness he was responsible for best practice across the Group in programme and project management and business process re-engineering. He authored a comprehensive company handbook on project management and a guide on process re-engineering within a programme environment.

As a management consultant, Michael has managed a variety of client projects, most involving the introduction of communications or IT systems and re-engineered business processes. He has spent over two years advising international clients on achieving full realisation of business benefits and release of financial value from their projects and has acted as the benefits manager on a number of large, client projects.

Acknowledgements

This book is a personal interpretation and extension of a core methodology developed by Consultica Limited. I am indebted to Jenny Clayton and Richard Beal, the Consultica directors, for introducing me to the methodology, inviting me to join them on assignments applying the method to client projects and for permission to use their original ideas in this book. I am particularly grateful to Jenny for reviewing the manuscript and providing invaluable feedback.

I am also grateful to the many members of client change programmes who have embraced the methodology and supported the use of rigorous benefits management within their projects. I would particularly like to thank Peter Duffy, Jeremy Bamber, Simon Telling, Phil Hughes, Ian Mitchell, Ian Thomas, Derick Carneiro and Bobbie Randles, whose encouragement and support were key to the successful use of the method on their strategically important projects.

I would like to thank Jim Mason for his help in developing some of the ideas on de-duplicating benefits between projects in a change programme.

Finally, my heartfelt thanks to Thomas Rohatsch, David Collins and Fraser Harper for their specialist help during the course of the supply chain project that provides one of the examples in the book.

I would encourage readers who would like help in adopting the ideas in this book to contact:

Consultica Limited
1 Burnsall Street
London
SW3 3SR
UK

Telephone: +44 (0)20 7402 9092

Email: info@consultica.co.uk

Preface

At a recent meeting of project management practitioners someone suggested to me that benefits management was currently a very fashionable subject. I had just completed the drafting of this book and the opinion filled me with foreboding as, to me, 'fashionable' indicated something that is receiving lively but shallow interest, to be replaced at any time by the next fashionable thing. However, on probing the comment it became clear that the group consensus was that the focus of attention in academia and business was beginning to shift from exemplary delivery of projects to achieving a full financial contribution to the business from their implementation; managing a project's benefits to maximise its value to the business in operation was an area of project management that, having arrived, was here to stay.

It would be reasonable to ask why such an important area has been the Cinderella of the project management profession for so long. There are a number of reasons. Project management as we know it today started to develop from the middle of the twentieth century to meet the challenges of an ever more complex world, including the emerging use of computers in commerce and public service. For decades there were increasing instances of projects going dramatically wrong, with costs and timescales spiralling out of control or final deliverables failing to meet user requirements. This rightly resulted in the development of management methods to control the use of project resources and the quality of project deliverables. Over the same period the practice of employing specialist staff took hold and, with it, the concept of a project manager with a well-bounded area of responsibility; that responsibility normally ending with the successful delivery of the project and its handover to the project's clients – users in the business. So, excellence in project management became seen as the ability to deliver a defined project to its clients within agreed costs and timescales and fully fit for purpose. All of these developments have tended to direct attention away from what happens to a project after it has been handed over to its clients.

Project failures still occur but, with improved governance and management systems and wider use of training, they are becoming rarer. However, increasing success in project delivery is beginning to expose the fact that even the most successfully implemented project may not make its expected contribution to the business unless it is properly integrated into the day-to-day operations of the business.

This book has had a lengthy gestation period. It is rooted in events that happened around ten years prior to its completion, when two senior members of a large management consultancy practice became aware that some of their clients were dissatisfied with the returns their businesses were achieving from seemingly well-run projects. They left to form Consultica Limited where, among other things, they developed a method to overcome this erosion of project contribution. Their method was built on some fundamental principles: that projects had to be realistically valued in the first place; that financial contribution had to be derived from project outcomes – what would change on the ground during day-to-day operations as a result of implementing the project; that expected outcomes had to be measured to be sure that they happened as planned; that the client community had to be involved in deriving a project's forecast benefits and in ensuring that they are achieved in operation. Clients that had recognised the problem of fully realising the expected benefits from projects started using the benefits management methodology with help from Consultica practitioners and the method gradually evolved and matured. I became one of Consultica's practitioners and was assigned initially as a member of a benefits management team and subsequently led as the benefits manager for a number of large client projects. During this time I took the method further in some areas, with encouragement from Consultica, to the stage of evolution presented here.

This book is to a certain extent apostolic. Having understood the value of good benefits management and witnessed its strengths in practice, I want the whole world to know about it. I would like to think that the book will result in a general raising of the financial value generated from investment in change; I abhor waste and hope that the book will do its bit towards the elimination of wasted corporate effort. It is targeted at a wide spectrum of readers: from those who have heard about benefits management and wonder if it is something they should be concerned about to those who are committed to the use of rigorous benefits management and want to know exactly how to do it, or do it better.

Good benefits management is characterised by a set of easily understood principles that can be difficult to apply in practice. The purpose of the book is to explain the purpose, relevance and importance of the principles and describe in progressively detailed steps how to plan for and execute the successive activities that together constitute an end-to-end process called benefits management. The book will benefit finance and programme directors with a responsibility for maximising financial return from change initiatives; programme, project and benefits managers and their teams who need to know how to apply effective benefits management; and operational staff with responsibility for the adoption of new ways of working that take full advantage of the capabilities of project deliverables.

Whichever category you fit into, I hope that this book helps you to achieve a greater return from your change initiatives.

Michael Payne

x

Contents

Introducing benefits management

A cautionary tale

A well-known manufacturer of consumer electronics goods decided to invest in a large change programme to improve service levels to its customers – predominantly electronic retail chains and outlets – and thereby improve its market share, sales volumes and profit. The programme, which involved global implementation of a customer relationship management system and reengineered customer-facing processes, was initially deemed to be a success as, indeed, volumes and profits did increase as forecast after the change was implemented. However, the improvement was not sustained and, for no apparent reason, volumes fell back to pre-change levels after about a year. A detailed investigation was carried out and it became apparent that the change programme had not improved the company's market share significantly; the short-term improvement in volumes was more to do with a temporary uplift in the whole market. On further examination it transpired that the reason that the market share had not risen as a result of the change was that customers did not perceive an improved level of service and this, in turn, was because a large part of the sales force had not changed their ways of working in line with the new CRM system and processes. By the time the matter was rectified, through retrospective staff training and incentives, much of the forecast value had been eroded as competitors had had time to catch up with the innovations.

I tell this sorry story to illustrate a situation that is common across a high proportion of enterprises – public organisations and private companies alike – that embark on programmes of change; the situation being that they successfully complete a change project, or programme, but fail to achieve anticipated business benefits from the change. I have called this a situation rather than a problem because, in many cases, the organisations concerned do not recognise the failure. These circumstances are particularly prevalent in change programmes that introduce re-engineered business processes, IT systems or both.

This may appear a strange claim to make at the beginning of the twenty-first century, given that the essentials of programme and project management are widely understood and documented and that programme and project managers tend to be well trained and adhere to good practice. The reason for the disjunction is that project management methods are normally designed to ensure successful delivery of a system or process into the business, where success is measured in terms of delivery to specification, time and budget. There is often an area of confused responsibilities between project delivery and its acceptance by the business, and this is where the damage is done.

There are two sets of activities that, if undertaken properly, will eradicate, or at least minimise, the mismatch between successful project implementation and under-achievement of project benefits; these are change and transition management and benefits management. The first addresses the primary causes of the problem and the second is the diagnostics tool that identifies the size and shape of the problem and signals when it has been resolved. Both of these activities are a joint responsibility between the project team and the project's clients in the business and both tend to be overlooked through being 'the other side's problem'. This book is about benefits management, although the subject of change management will arise from time to time.

Note that I continually talk about projects rather than programmes. The next chapter explains the reasons for this. For now, please accept that everything I discuss is also applicable at the programme level.

What is benefits management?

▶ Definitions

Ask any project manager whether or not benefits management is included within normal project activities and the answer will invariably be yes. However, most people's understanding of benefits management is closer to what I would describe as project financial value appraisal. So let me introduce three terms used throughout the book that have distinct and non-interchangeable meanings. The terms are 'outcomes', 'benefits' and 'financial impact' and I cannot avoid giving you a formal definition, supported by an example, for each:

- **Outcome**. This has two meanings, depending upon the context. At the macro level, desired outcomes are the strategic changes that a programme is designed to fulfil; such as 'improved customer service' or 'reduced cost of goods sold'. At the micro level, outcomes are the changes to day-to-day operations that project outputs cause.

- **Benefits**. Measurable improvements resulting from outcomes. Thus, for a project output 'an improved sales forecasting process', a consequent outcome 'to improve accuracy of sales forecasts' would lead to a benefit 'to reduce safety inventory levels by four stock days'.

- **Financial impact**. The improvement in business financial performance that results, directly or indirectly, from achievement of one or more benefits. Continuing the previous example, the financial impact of reducing safety stocks by four days is 'to reduce working capital by the cost of four days of stock and to reduce annual running costs by 9% of the capital saved through reduced cost of cash and reduced storage and handling costs'.

Benefits management is a process that defines the potential business benefits and financial impact of a project and ensures that these are achieved in practice.

▶ Objectives

This book, then, is about following a rigorous benefits management process with the aim of achieving two main objectives:

- Identifying and defining the real benefits that should accrue to the business if a project is implemented, and deriving the potential financial value of the project to the business from these benefits.

- Ensuring that identified benefits are achieved and that the forecast financial impact is released into the business.

Precise, full and realistic benefit definition is the key to forecasting the financial impact of projects accurately and ensuring that the financial value is released into the business.

Who should read this book

Experience working with a number of companies has led me to the conclusion that a majority of them not only fail to achieve the value they are expecting from change projects but also fail to realise the extent to which this is happening. I have written this book in an attempt to expose the problem and offer a way of overcoming it. Towards this end, it would be valuable to:

- Chief executives and finance directors who want to understand the discontinuity between successfully delivered projects and unimproved bottom lines.

- Strategy and programme directors who need to ensure that there is a consistent view of benefits across a change programme, with no double-counting of value between projects.

- Project business sponsors and gatekeepers who want to ensure that forecast project value is achievable and achieved.

- Project managers who need to understand the resource implications and advantages of including robust benefits management within their project activities.

- Benefits managers who need to understand the principles of sound benefits management and how to apply them.

- Function leaders within organisations who want to play their part in ensuring that the business benefits in full from delivered projects.

- Academics and students concerned with best project management practice.

There is much that each of these groups of people can take from the book. However, it is written principally for practising or aspiring project or programme benefits managers and most of the following chapters of the book are specifically addressed to them.

What the book covers

The contributions of the remaining chapters of the book are shown in the panel below.

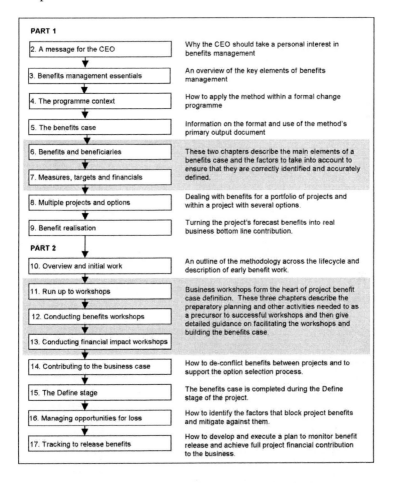

PART 1

2. A message for the CEO	Why the CEO should take a personal interest in benefits management
3. Benefits management essentials	An overview of the key elements of benefits management
4. The programme context	How to apply the method within a formal change programme
5. The benefits case	Information on the format and use of the method's primary output document
6. Benefits and beneficiaries 7. Measures, targets and financials	These two chapters describe the main elements of a benefits case and the factors to take into account to ensure that they are correctly identified and accurately defined.
8. Multiple projects and options	Dealing with benefits for a portfolio of projects and within a project with several options.
9. Benefit realisation	Turning the project's forecast benefits into real business bottom line contribution.

PART 2

10. Overview and initial work	An outline of the methodology across the lifecycle and description of early benefit work.
11. Run up to workshops 12. Conducting benefits workshops 13. Conducting financial impact workshops	Business workshops form the heart of project benefit case definition. These three chapters describe the preparatory planning and other activities needed to as a precursor to successful workshops and then give detailed guidance on facilitating the workshops and building the benefits case.
14. Contributing to the business case	How to de-conflict benefits between projects and to support the option selection process.
15. The Define stage	The benefits case is completed during the Define stage of the project.
16. Managing opportunities for loss	How to identify the factors that block project benefits and mitigate against them.
17. Tracking to release benefits	How to develop and execute a plan to monitor benefit release and achieve full project financial contribution to the business.

It's just more overhead, isn't it?

The principles, tools, techniques and resource requirements described in the book can be viewed in two ways:

- A powerful methodology that, applied rigorously but sensibly, will help you achieve more financial benefit from the projects you are implementing – in many cases to a significant degree.

- Yet another overhead on both your change programme and your day-to-day operations; sapping the resources you need to get on with what is most important – running the business and maximising profits (or whatever strategic objectives of your organisation).

Which of these views prevails will depend very much on your attitude of mind. But, in truth, both are valid. The question then is whether the pain of introducing and resourcing another management process is justified by the improvements it will bring.

Let us look at a typical example. First, please accept the premise that rigorous benefits management will never add more than five per cent to the overall cost of a project or programme – often much less; this will become clearer later in the book. Now look at the numbers in the panel below:

> A well implemented medium-to-large-scale project has an overall project cost of £10M and forecast business value payback of £4M a year; £20M total over a 5 year period. Let us assume that the project would deliver 70% of the forecast benefits, a typical return for projects without rigorous benefits management; only providing a modest return on investment (ROI) after 5 years.
>
> If the benefits management regime described in this book had been applied, it might add up to £0.5M to the project cost. As a result of doing this, we can conservatively expect that benefits will increase to at least 85% of expected value; an increased return of £600k a year, giving an additional £3M of value over 5 years.

For simplicity I have ignored NPV calculations. Either way, rigorous benefits management shows a significantly better ROI than the project itself.

How to use this book

There are really only two significantly different ways of using this book:

- Use it as a guide and handbook for introducing and undertaking benefits management within your business. If this is what you want to do, there is sufficient detail provided to allow you and your business to do this without any external assistance. However, you – or someone in your business – will need to read and understand the book from cover to cover.

- Use it as a vehicle to persuade yourself, or others in the business, of the need to introduce rigorous benefits management and then engage an external specialist to help you do this.

> I am reminded of a section in Richard Stutely's splendid book on writing a business plan[1] headed 'Don't trust consultants'. As a consultant myself, I found this a bit harsh. However, I know what he means. An engaged consultant should be confined to guiding you on the method, facilitating workshops and supporting the production of benefits cases. The benefits case itself must be created and owned by your business, otherwise it just won't work, however well drafted and presented.

If you take this route, you may get away with reading only this chapter. However, I would recommend that you at least read most of the book under these circumstances as you will want, as an 'intelligent client', to be sure that the external help knows what it is doing.

The book is divided into two parts. The rest of Part 1 defines the benefits management process – and its importance – from the viewpoints of a CEO and a benefits management practitioner. It then describes the elements of a benefits case in detail, covering the factors that need to be taken into account when developing them. Part 2 gives a step-by-step account of applying the end-to-end benefits management process across the project life cycle. The diagram below shows which activities within the method need to be undertaken for different types of project, and where to find the details.

Method activities	Types of project			Pages in book	
	Simple	Multi-option	Multi-option within program	Techniques	Application
Create strawman benefits case		□	□		145 – 158
Feasibility benefits workshops	□	■	■	45 – 73	169 - 207
De-duplicate benefits			■	77 – 81	216 – 232
Select preferred option		■	■	82 - 88	232 – 240
Define benefits workshops	■	■	■	45 – 73	249 – 264
Contribute to business case	■	■	■	86 – 88	240
On-board benefits coordinators	■	■	■	90 – 93	266 – 270
Conduct benefit risk workshop	■	■	■	93 – 100	273 – 287
Selecting benefits to track	■	■	■	101 – 104	289 – 293
Create benefit tracking plan	■	■	■	104 – 115	294 – 299
Track benefits	■	■	■	112 - 119	300 - 307

■ Essential activity   □ Possibly needed activity

Figure 1.1 – Where to find descriptions of activities needed for different types of project

Why this method?

Assuming that you are still with me, you will by now, I trust, be persuaded to the advantages of using a rigorous benefits management process to achieve greater business benefit from your investment in change. However, you may already use, or be familiar with, other approaches to benefits management; so why would you need to adopt, or change to, the method described in this book? The final section of this chapter is an unashamed pitch for this method. I make it not for any self-seeking purposes but because I am genuinely convinced that the method I describe is the only one I know that has all the characteristics needed for full success in business benefit release.

The characteristics that differentiate the method and give it strength are listed below:

- A realistic and honest bottom-up approach to defining benefits.

- Unambiguous separation between the identification of benefits and derivation of their financial impact on the business.

- Involvement and buy-in from project clients in the business from an early stage in its life cycle.

- Potential benefits and their financial impact used to help shape sensible decisions on implementation options.

- Clarity over the relative beneficial contribution from a number of projects within the same change portfolio.

- Emphasis on tracking physical change rather than financial improvement.

- A continued focus on the final objective – to release into the business the full potential benefit from investment in change.

▶ Basis of benefits

An understanding of project outcomes – what will change within normal operations as a result of project implementation – is fundamental to the use of this benefits management method. Such an understanding of how business activities and people's actions and behaviours will change is the starting point for the identification and description of bottom-up business benefits. This implies not only a thorough understanding of the capabilities of the project being implemented but also knowledge of the local business conditions wherever the project is being implemented. A full understanding of project capabilities is probably not possible until towards the end of the Define stage and some assumptions will have to be made. Nevertheless, this bottom-up approach to benefits should start at the beginning of the Define stage.

▶ Separating benefits from value

Traditionally, a project's financial value is assessed in one step, using a variety of estimation methods. For example, a project capability to automate an order-to-cash process may be calculated directly by applying a number of financial assumptions, fundamentals and multipliers. This traditional method has a major weakness in that the only way of checking that the benefit has been realised is to measure that its forecast financial impact has been achieved. Thus, in this example, one might expect the unit cost of selling to reduce (among other possible financial improvements). However, measuring the contribution that this project makes to reduced cost of selling, in the face of external factors and other internal initiatives that will almost certainly be under way in this part of the business, is highly problematical.

In the method described in this book, you identify how new project capability has outcomes that will physically affect business processes and people's activities and behaviours and thus impact operational performance; you then find ways of measuring these changes. Only then do you attempt to ascribe a financial impact to the changes. The advantage of this approach is that an audit trail is constructed between introducing capability and achieving improved financial performance, with several points at which achievement of forecast change can be measured in a way that is directly attributable to the project concerned.

▶ Business involvement and buy-in

Project benefits and their financial impact are developed with representatives from the business communities that will be most affected by the project, the project's clients. This is first done at workshops held during the Feasibility stage – relatively early in the project. There are a couple of minor downsides to this approach: the first being the additional internal overhead of engaging a dozen or so business people for two days and the second being that it is difficult to persuade people who will be accountable for achieving the benefits to set themselves stretched performance improvement targets. However, these downsides can be militated against and are far outweighed by the advantages of early business involvement; informed local knowledge and realism built into the benefits case that the business will readily sign up to rather than challenge when the business case has to be approved for the next project stage or for final implementation.

▶ Shaping implementation options

Towards the end of the Feasibility stage of the project a number of decisions have to be made: what will be the organisational or geographical cover of the project; what development and implementation methods will be used; which parts of a modular system will be implemented where? At the same time, the first iteration of the bottom-up benefits case will be developed; a benefits case that assesses benefits by region or country and by implemented module, where appropriate. Thus a detailed picture of which parts of a project will deliver benefit (and acceptable ROI), into which parts of the business, is drawn.

An example of the use of this methodology to shape option selection occurred in a company that planned to implement an advanced logistics planning system in each of its four geographical regions. The system comprised six separate modules and would be implemented to allow logistics planning across clusters of countries. A benefits case was developed for each region with local business input. The relative contribution of each module was assessed for each identified benefit in each cluster of countries. It transpired that a full implementation footprint in every region gave an inadequate ROI and the selected option became a partial implementation (some clusters more partial than others) that provided a good overall ROI, while meeting the most pressing needs of each cluster and meeting the global aspirations for improved logistics.

▶ Benefits within a portfolio

One of the advantages of the method is that it avoids confusion and argument over which projects within a portfolio are contributing which benefits. This may not always be an issue, particularly where the different projects are addressing exclusively different business processes, or where the portfolio of projects is being managed within a formal change programme (see Chapter 2). However, having clear water between all projects is rare. Take, for example, the case of one company that was implementing an ERP consolidation and replacement project, a new management information system, a logistics planning system and a customer relationship management system. Nearly all of the main business processes were impacted by at least two of these projects – in some cases three. Where there are areas of overlap between projects, it is an articulation of exactly what changes on the ground each project will cause that allows an assessment of the relative contribution of each to be made. This assessment is easier in companies that have codified their standard business processes as well as, of course, the usual codified financial structure.

▶ Emphasis on physical tracking

The method takes two post-implementation steps to ensure that benefits are realised:

- The first step is to put in place a mechanism for tracking changes in process characteristics, people's activities and operational performance that project implementation is forecast to make.

- The second step is to take remedial action where tracking reveals a shortfall in anticipated changes.

By 'tracking' I mean taking periodic measurements of relevant activities and outcomes that will indicate the expected changes. One of the skills needed to use this method successfully is to choose measurements that will not only confirm the expected changes but that will give a good lead as to what is going wrong when benefits fail to materialise. This requires a degree of foresight into likely barriers or risks to benefits achievement; a need that is systematically addressed by the method.

▶ Realisation of benefits

Benefits work in projects often focuses on deriving the potential financial benefit of the project to the business, to support the business case, and then stops. Many projects are implemented successfully and yet end up being a disappointment to the business because they fail to live up to expectations. In a good number of these projects it is not so much that potential benefits have been overstated (although this is all too often the case) but more that, for a variety of reasons, they have just failed to materialise. The method recognises this and much of the benefits work happens after the project has been implemented, to ensure that the business interacts with the project's capabilities in a way that realises all the benefits and maximises the project's value to the business.

CHAPTER TWO

A message for the CEO

The problem facing CEOs

Organisations are run by people and people are humans, with all the human frailties. Even the most senior people in your organisation are likely to be driven, at least in part, by personal motivation. So, what does that have to do with benefits management? Actually quite a lot – at both ends and the middle of the project life cycle.

Let's take a look first at your portfolio of change programmes and individual projects. Why are they as they are? Have they been selected such that their combined effect is to help achieve the top-level objectives that represent your organisation's vision? Or are there elements of personal championing, following perceived industry fashion or falling under the spell of persuasive third party systems sales executives? How can you know for sure?

Now let's look at the programmes that are in progress. You receive regular reports that the various projects within the programme are running to time and budget and are on track to deliver to specification. This may or may not be true – there are ways of hiding the fact that a programme is going off track and it is not uncommon for a project manager to do this, in the belief that the problems can be put right before the next reporting period. Denial of problems is a natural manifestation of the instinct for self-preservation or, in this case, preservation of the project in trouble. Even if the project is on track, how can you be sure that its deliverables will indeed achieve forecast benefits? It is not rare for a part of a project to be abandoned towards the end of its delivery phase to bring it back on track financially or on time; how do you know whether or not a significant proportion of the benefits were dependent on the part that has been cut out?

Finally, consider the programme that has been completed, or at least partially delivered. You may be informed that the delivery was successful and that business benefits are now streaming in. Again, this may or may not be an accurate reflection of reality. No one will consider it in their own best interests to report a project that has failed to deliver expected benefits; and benefits can be very difficult to pin down and are easy to spin.

These issues may appear to be of secondary importance in the face of other matters that may be concerning you: protecting your business against mounting risk, meeting annual sales and profit targets and resolving shareholder anxieties. They should not be brushed under the carpet. Huge investments in change are routinely made by private and public sector organisations and accepting a rate of return of less than fifty per cent of that expected – not at all exceptional – is akin to throwing away a significant proportion of the investment budget and may be at least as damaging to the business as the occurrence of a major unprotected operational risk.

The solution for CEOs

The glib answer to these problems is to ensure that you have an effective project benefits management system in place but there is more to it than that. There are a number of specifics that the CEO should ensure are addressed:

- The need for programmes to be benefit-driven from the outset.

- Understanding the factors – both generic and specific to your organisation – that can suppress the achievement of project benefits

- Ensuring the right role and effective reporting lines for the benefits manager

- Mandating the development of fact-based benefits cases for all projects

- Mandating the use of benefits cases to check the achievability of benefits during project development and to track the achievement of benefits after the project has been delivered.

▶ Benefit-driven programmes

All too often, programmes are initiated, and projects selected, before an attempt is made to define programme benefits, which is usually left until a business case is first needed for a project stage approval.

The correct planning sequence is to start with the organisation's vision and the key objectives that need to be met to achieve it. Objectives will normally require some improvements in operational performance, which themselves become the end benefits that a change programme should strive for. Various techniques are then used to identify the projects that will, via a network of intermediate benefits, achieve the end benefits that directly support achievement of the organisational objectives.

You should adopt this planning approach in order to avoid the vested interests of senior programme and project staff and to ensure that your investment in change directly supports your organisation's vision and key objectives.

▶ Factors leading to loss of benefits

The important thing here is that you recognise that the human condition will almost inevitably lead to a reduction in business benefits from projects unless something is done about it. For this reason, we do not call these risks, because 'risk' implies a degree of uncertainty whereas these factors are almost inevitable. Instead, we use the term Opportunity for Loss (OfL). OfLs can arise from disbenefits (aspects of change that are seen as disadvantageous by some stakeholders), resistance to change, personal prejudices or the desire to hide failure that we discussed earlier.

The CEO's role in overcoming OfLs is to take nothing at face value and to arrange that audit aspects of benefits management are dealt with outside the change programme structure. OfLs need to be identified and managed from the outset of a project or programme, and throughout its life cycle.

▶ Role and position of the benefits manager

There will be people within the programme and project organisations –
possibly called business change managers – who undertake benefits
management activities; particularly creation of benefits cases. But there is a
need for a programme-independent role which encompasses the
responsibilities of benefits management educator, advisor and auditor.

This company-wide role might be called the Benefits Facilitator, or Group
Benefits Manager or a similar title. The important point is that the role should
report directly to a board member; the strategy or finance directors would be
appropriate reports. In this way, many of the OfLs described above can be
brought to light and dealt with in an objective way, free of the vested interests
that can blight the release of benefits.

▶ Mandating the development and use of benefits cases

The benefits case is an explicit expression of the business benefits that will
accrue from a project that is correctly delivered and embedded into the
business. It is written in such a way that makes it possible to check, during
development, that the benefits are achievable and, after delivery, that the
benefits are achieved. Your organisation's rules for project governance
probably already include the requirement to present a business case at major
project approval stages; the rules should be extended to include the
requirement for a realistic and objective benefits case as an essential
component of the business case.

The rules should also make it mandatory that:

- Project teams check, at each major stage, that the project design and
  implementation will still enable the forecast benefits.
- The business tracks the benefits to ensure that they are realised in
  practice.

These activities need to be overseen by your Group Benefits Manager.

CHAPTER   THREE

Benefits management essentials

Introduction

You know, or suspect, that your projects, though well managed, are not living up to their promise in terms of ROI. You are persuaded by the argument that good benefits management will make the difference. Where do you go next?

Before delving into detail, or making expensive commitments, it is important that you understand the overall shape of benefits management. How does it manifest itself in practice? What is its scope? Who needs to be involved? The benefits management method of this book can be described in terms of a number of critical elements: benefits management processes conducted within an organisational framework mandated by the leadership team and supported by a collection of tools and techniques, as illustrated below in Figure 3.1:

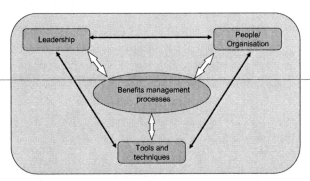

Figure 3.1 – Critical elements of a benefits management environment

The paragraphs that follow describe benefits management in a nutshell by explaining each of these critical elements.

Leadership

Introduction of benefits management will be resisted by many as a chore or an imposition, particularly in organisations where project success is measured in terms of deliverables (on time, within budget, meeting specification) rather than on evidence of achieving benefit from effective change. Such resistance can only be countered by visible and enduring support from the top. If the leadership team is seen to be deeply concerned with achieving full operational and financial benefit from change initiatives then this will affect the behaviours of everyone in the organisation.

The leadership team can influence a successful transition to benefit-driven change in many ways. The most obvious are to appoint a company-wide benefits manager with appropriate authority, to mandate the inclusion of benefits management for all projects and to demonstrate its importance through communications and reward.

People and Organisation

There are two elements of benefits management organisation: inside individual projects and in the wider business. The extent of this organisation depends on the size of the business and the intensity of its change programme. Figure 3.2 opposite shows one possible outline structure of the organisation for an international company with a busy change programme.

An alternative, programme-centric organisation is shown in the next chapter. You may feel that the organisation shown at Figure 3.2 is somewhat daunting. I should quickly explain that:

- The organisation serves the needs of a large company with global operations and change programmes.

- Only the two highlighted roles – Group Benefits Managers and project business change managers– are dedicated to the task of benefits management, and the latter role also incorporates the project responsibilities of business change and transition management. The others are roles that require part-time participation – normally no more than ten per cent of their time for a finite period – from individuals already existing in the business.

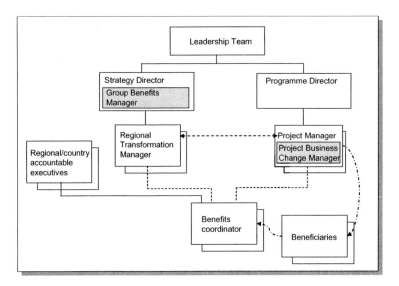

Figure3.2 –Organisation for benefits management in a large company

Let me briefly introduce the key roles within this organisation.

▶ Group Benefits Manager

The Group Benefits Manager is the business's benefits management guru, responsible for ensuring a correct and consistent approach to benefits management across all projects, auditing the veracity of benefits cases, the verification of benefit achievability and the tracking of benefit achievement.

▶ Project business change/team

I am going to call the business change manager a project benefits manager, to signify that I am talking about the benefit management aspect of the role as opposed to change or transition management. The benefits manager is the guardian of benefits management methodology within the project, under guidance from the Group Benefits Manager, and is the primary driver in ensuring that an honest and robust benefits case is developed and that the business is properly prepared to undertake benefit tracking and to take any necessary remedial action to ensure full benefits realisation. In a very large project, the benefits manager may need to be supported by one or two team members.

▶ Regional Transformation Manager

The organisation shown assumes there to be a senior executive in each regional business unit's leadership team with overall responsibility for business transformation; including prioritizing of the regional change programme and monitoring its achievement of business value. If so, this executive is well placed to oversee the benefit tracking activities of all benefits coordinators within the business unit. If such an executive does not exist explicitly, then the region will need to nominate a member of its leadership team, or direct report, to take on these responsibilities.

▶ Accountable executives

These project clients are normally functional executives within the business who have a role to sign off the forecast project benefits and their value and be accountable for the achievement of these benefits once the project has been successfully delivered into the business. They are not part of the project organisation although they may well be on a project steering committee at some level.

▶ Benefits coordinators

Benefits coordinators are also in the business although they have some project responsibilities. This is a part-time role, ideally carried out by performance or finance analysts within the business; this preference is more to do with the inherent skills of such individuals than with their day-to-day role within the organisation. Their project role is to coordinate all benefit tracking activities after the project has gone live and alert the accountable executives to any issues arising from the tracking or its results.

▶ Beneficiaries

Beneficiaries are those members of the business whose activities will be impacted once the project goes live; it is the beneficiaries who will do things differently as a result of using project deliverables, the assumption being that this different 'doing' will improve operational performance and release financial value. Beneficiaries are very rarely members of the project team but are staff members rooted in day-to-day operations; however, some of them will participate in project-sponsored benefits workshops and be involved in the exercise to track benefits.

Processes

The benefits management method is primarily defined by a number of consistent sub-processes which are joined together to form an end-to-end process. The end-to-end process may vary, depending on the nature of the project itself, but will always follow a few key principles and include the core sub-processes. Most of this book is spent describing the processes and the characteristics, tools and techniques that are associated with them. Here I am introducing them to you in outline only.

At the highest level there are five sub-processes that describe the end-to-end process, as shown at Figure 3.3; the highlighted boxes indicating core sub-processes:

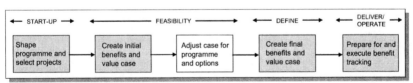

Figure 3.3 – Top-level benefits management sub-processes

The diagram also shows in which project stage each top-level sub-process normally sits. It is worth looking at the next process level down to get a better feel for the activities carried out in each project stage.

▶ Programme and project initiation

The main activities to develop a benefits-led programme are shown at Figure 3.4 below:

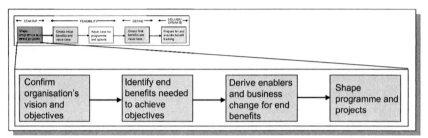

Figure 3.4 – Activities for initial benefits-led programme development

The initiation stage is outside the scope of this book and its activities are only alluded to. Readers who wish to examine these sub-processes further are advised to consult Gerald Bradley's book on benefits realisation management[2,] in which the subject is covered in detail.

▶ Initial benefits case

The figure below illustrates the activities to develop the initial benefits case:

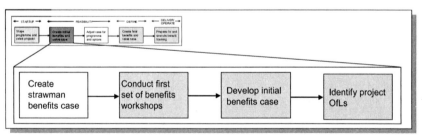

Figure 3.5 – Activities for initial benefits case development

An initial benefits case is developed to support project Feasibility stage activities; this benefits case misses out detail not needed at this point of the project and would typically be to an accuracy of plus or minus thirty per cent. The heart of this sub-process is the holding of a number of business-orientated benefits workshops to develop a bottom-up benefits case. There may be a need for the benefits manager to create a strawman benefits case prior to holding the workshops but this is not always necessary. The project level OfLs are identified and a mitigation plan put in place.

▶ Benefits case adjustments

Adjustments may need to be made to the initial business case to allow for possible benefits duplication with other projects and to derive the financial benefit of different implementation options to help select a preferred option. These activities in this sub-process are shown below.

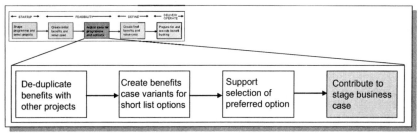

Figure 3.6 – Activities for benefits case adjustments

Three of these activities are not shown as core as it is not always the case that a project is vying with others in a programme, or of a nature where options need to be individually valued. The fourth activity is included as an adjustment because it requires the addition of a time element to the benefits case to be able to input to the stage net present value (NPV) calculations.

▶ Final benefits case

The final benefits case is produced once the preferred project option has been selected and defined in greater detail. The activities to achieve this final version are similar to those for the initial benefits case, as illustrated in the diagram opposite, but the result is a benefits case complete in all detail and to an accuracy of typically plus or minus ten per cent. The project deliverables are examined to ensure that they will still enable the forecast benefits.

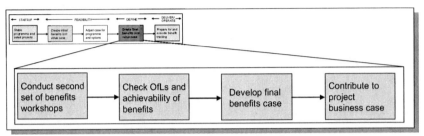

Figure 3.7 – Activities for final benefits case development

▶ Benefit tracking

The final set of activities undertaken within the project environment is shown in the diagram below:

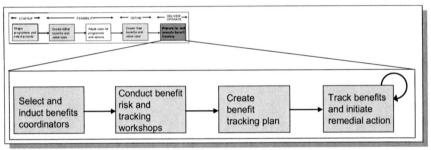

Figure 3.8 – Activities for developing and executing benefit tracking

The primary purpose here is to develop a benefit tracking plan that can be executed under the control of benefits coordinators after the project team has been dissolved. To achieve this, a risk assessment has first to be conducted so that, among other things, a tracking plan can be designed that focuses on the benefits most at risk. As we shall see later, the benefits risk assessment is separate from the high-level OfL assessment and of any project risk assessment and is conducted by a different set of people.

Benefits are tracked until all blockages to their release have been overcome through remedial action and full potential project benefits have been realised.

Tools and techniques

I do not advocate any specialist software tools to support the benefits management process. However, adroitness with word processor, spreadsheet and presentation software packages is essential and a desktop relational database package can be useful when undertaking benefits management for a large, complex project or programme. Life can be made very much easier if tailored templates are used within these packages; all of these are described in detail in the book.

Most of the techniques used relate to ways of extracting the required benefits information from business users in a workshop or interview environment. Mastering these techniques requires a thorough understanding of the principles of benefits management. The book describes these techniques, the principles behind them and how to apply them, in some detail.

CHAPTER FOUR

The programme context

Introduction

The majority of this book is concerned with benefits management at the project level, whereas current thinking places the focus of benefits management activity at the programme level. The reasons that I have chosen to concentrate on project-level benefits management are that:

- Not all organisations create programme structures to carry out change but all change initiatives are conducted within projects.

- Most of the activities of the method described in the book are carried out at the project level, whether or not the projects are part of a wider change programme.

The programme-centric view of benefits management is well outlined in the OGC book *Managing Successful Programmes*[3]. This chapter describes how the method would be used within the OGC's programme framework and maps and explains differences between the principal products of the two approaches.

Advantages of a programme approach

There is no doubt that any organisation undertaking a number of simultaneous or overlapping projects and associated activities, all contributing to a strategic goal, or set of goals, will be best served by managing these activities within a formal change programme structure. When this is done, there is a core of management effort available to ensure that the right projects are initiated, delivered in the right sequence, to optimise the use of resources towards the organisation's goals.

A programme structure also provides the opportunity to improve the way in which benefits management is conducted. A programme of change implies that there are strategic-level outcomes required of the programme if it is to achieve the organisation's strategic goals; some of these outcomes may require the outputs from two or more projects. Consider the example in the panel below.

One required output from a change programme was to improve customer satisfaction through a more responsive and reliable order promising and delivery process. Two projects within the programme were needed to achieve this desired outcome: one to implement advanced proactive supply chain planning processes and the other to implement an improved customer relationship management system.

The programme approach allowed these two projects to be coordinated and synchronised so that the desired outcome was achieved quickly and optimally. Centralised benefits management ensured that the operational and financial benefits of the outcome were understood at the programme level, avoiding disputed or overlapping benefits claims between projects. Tracking of these benefits was also undertaken at the programme level; without a programme structure there would have been a need for two sets of project-level benefit tracking activities.

I need to inject a word of caution here. Individual projects deliver outputs, the effects of which have outcomes within the day-to-day operations of the organisation. These project-level outcomes combine to contribute towards the programme's desired strategic outcomes (as illustrated in the example above). To define the benefits of these strategic outcomes, some benefits identification, definition and analysis work will need to be carried out at the project level, in association with the project team members who fully understand the capabilities of the project's outputs. Having said this, all of the techniques, templates, workshops and analytical tools described in this book are equally applicable at the programme and project level. In the former case, benefits workshops, would be run, and benefits cases developed, for tranches of projects rather than individual projects (see later section in this chapter on Programme-level workshops).

Organising for programme-centric benefits

The OGC suggests the organisation in Figure 4.1 for large or complex programmes.

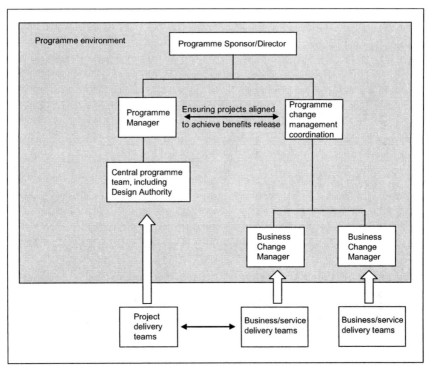

Figure 4.1 – Organisation for a large, complex programme

I will discuss the role of business change manager in the next section. For now, you need to know that the role incorporates responsibility for benefits management.

The idea is that each business change manager is responsible for change within a specific business area. So, for instance, using the examples contained in this book, there might be three such roles covering the business areas of Sales & Marketing, Supply Chain and Finance & Control. Arguably, for my example projects which deliver capability globally, you might need 12 business change managers; three covering each business function in each of four global regions.

In fact, the benefits management organisation that I have suggested for large global projects (Figure 3.2) is a compromise in which two central functional benefits managers (one covering Sales & Marketing and the other Supply Chain and Finance & Control) complement four regional transformation managers, who provide a local cross-functional business perspective. This compromise reduces the number of benefits-related resources for global programmes from 12 to six managers.

The other difference between the two organisational structures is that the business change managers in the OGC organisation are drawn from the business area and have ongoing operational responsibilities that include embedding change into the organisation. In Figure 3.2, the regional transformation managers are drawn from the business, while the benefits managers are project roles who, in a complex programme, would be the equivalent of the change management coordination team.

Whichever model is used, the same overarching need to provide a solid alignment between project delivery and benefits realisation applies.

Role of business change manager

The role of business change manager is central to the OGC programme organisation. The role encompasses the responsibilities of change management, transition management and benefits management. Bringing these three responsibilities together in one role is extremely sensible as all three aspects are inextricably linked; change and transition are business issues and their effective management is essential if the outputs from projects within the programme are to be translated into successful programme outcomes and benefits.

I have not combined these roles in the book for one reason only; the book focuses solely on benefits management – change and transition management are book topics in their own right. Despite this, you should assume that wherever I refer to the benefits manager in the book (which I do a lot) it could equally mean 'the business change manager undertaking his or her benefits management responsibilities'.

Programme-level workshops

Workshops held with the business community are a central component of the benefits management method described in this book; several chapters describe how to plan, prepare for, and conduct, these workshops. There can be a large number of such workshops; for instance, for the global implementation projects that provide the examples for this book, the number of workshops required (discounting the effect of multi-function projects – see Figure 11.9 and accompanying text) is summarised in Table 4.1 below.

Project stage	Workshop	Level	Quantity
Feasibility	Benefits Financial impact	Region	4 4
Define	Benefits Financial impact	Region	4 4
Execute	Risks Benefit tracking	Country/ cluster	25 25

Table 4.1 – Benefits management workshops for a global implementation

Whether or not benefits are being addressed at a programme or project level, the number, type and conduct of the workshops will be the same for each instance. Where benefits are being addressed at the project level, the project is the instance. The number of instances for programme-level benefits management will depend on the shape of the programme. Figure 4.2 overleaf explains this.

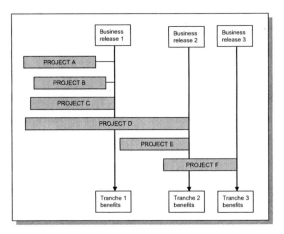

Figure 4.2 – Grouping of projects into programme releases/tranches

In this example a programme has a portfolio of six projects (Projects A through F) and these have been grouped such that they deliver three tranches of benefits over time – each tranche sometimes referred to as a business release. The grouping is typically planned so that all projects that contribute to a desired strategic outcome are scheduled to deliver their outputs at around the same time. In this way, business benefits are released soon after the completion of individual projects and full advantage is taken of those benefits that can be released early in the programme. The text panel on the second page of this chapter illustrates an example of two projects that should be grouped to deliver an early business benefit.

When projects are grouped to deliver benefits in tranches, the end-to-end benefits management process is applied to each tranche rather than to individual projects. Thus there would be three sets of benefits workshops and benefit tracking activities rather than six. Of course, the number of workshops within each set will depend upon the functional and geographic spread of the projects within each tranche and may vary from tranche to tranche.

To develop the programme benefits case, the benefits cases developed for each tranche are summarised and collated into one single benefits case.

Principle benefits management products

The OGC's programme framework includes a number of products developed to help manage and control the programme. Two of these are specific to the benefits management process:

- Benefits profiles
- Benefits realisation plan

A benefit profile is developed for each identified programme benefit and describes:

- What the benefit is and what its dependencies are
- When the benefit will be realised and how measured
- Which projects contribute to the benefit and what project outcome leads to the benefit
- Who is responsible for realising the benefit.

The benefits realisation plan summarises the schedule for benefits release, identifies milestones for the conduct of programme benefits reviews and provides details of change and transition activities needed to ensure full benefits release.

The method described in this book also creates two primary benefits management products. These are different from the OGC products but they map closely and cover the same ground. The products used in this book are illustrated at Figure 4.3.

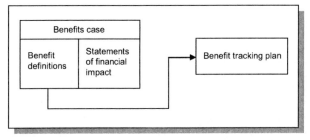

Figure 4.3 – Primary benefits management products

The individual benefit definitions within the benefits case are very similar to the OGC's benefit profiles, except that details of when measurements are to be taken, how and by whom are not included.

The benefits case itself is split into two parts:

- The first part defines each individual benefit in terms of the outcomes that cause it, the measures and targets that define the associated forecast operational changes and performance improvements, and the roles responsible for benefits realisation.

- The second part defines the financial impact of groups of benefits within the benefits case by applying business logic to translate achievement of target operational performance improvement into consequent business financial performance improvement.

The tracking of benefit release is defined at a later date in the project life cycle and is derived from the benefit definitions and an assessment of the risks to benefits release. This separation between benefits definitions, financial impact of benefits and benefit tracking details is necessary within the methodology because the financial impact of benefits is required well before it is possible to complete tracking details. This need is fully explained in later chapters.

These products are equally applicable at the programme and project level. For practical purposes, separate products would be produced for each tranche but these could readily be combined into a single set of programme products.

CHAPTER FIVE

The benefits case

Introduction

The benefits case forms the hub of the benefits management methodology and almost all activities within the benefits management end-to-end process touch the benefits case in some way; either contributing towards its creation or using it as an input to the activity.

This chapter will help you become familiar with the benefits case: its positioning within the method, its composition, its uses and how it might look. Familiarity with the benefits case will greatly help your understanding of the chapters dealing with the techniques used to develop the benefits case and with the step-by-step activities followed to create and use it.

Benefits case workflow

The benefits case is never set in stone. It is a living document that is developed over much of the project life cycle and may need to change even after its encapsulation in the project's Project Initiation Document (PID). This does not mean that the document itself is free-form; indeed, it is an important project document that must be subject to version control and change management much as any other key project document-based deliverable. Within this controlled environment, the benefits case is published in various stages of development; but for the most straightforward projects at least twice for project governance approval.

The benefits case is the most important document produced as an output of the benefits management process but is not the only one. Figure 5.1 overleaf shows all the primary documentary outputs of the methodology and at what stage within the method's workflow they become available.

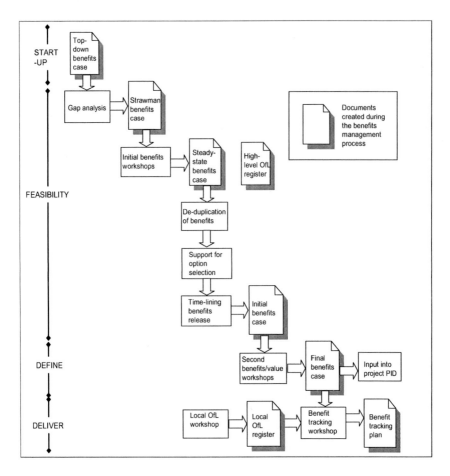

Figure 5.1 – Benefits management principal documents and workflow

The strawman benefits case is an optional extra, as I shall explain later. The simplest of projects may only need one set of benefits workshops and one published benefits case; most will need at least two.

The benefit tracking plan, another essential output of the method, needs the benefit case as an input to the process of creating it.

Benefits case composition

The benefits case is, in essence, a descriptive list of all the benefits that a project is forecast to deliver, with their associated financial impact. Each benefit is qualified by a number of attributes. The schema at Figure 5.2 shows the relationship between these various elements and attributes.

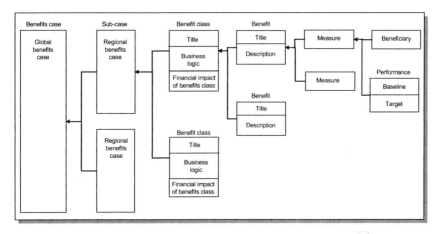

Figure 5.2 – Benefits case schema

▶ Benefits

The heart of the benefits case and the benefits schema is the individual benefit. Associated with each benefit are a definition of the benefit and its attributes of measure, beneficiary and performance. There may be a need to identify more than one measure for each benefit; the reasons for this are discussed in Chapter 5. For each measure there is a beneficiary and an improvement target set against a baseline performance of the measure.

▶ Benefits classes

Benefits are clustered together to form benefits classes. There are a number of ways of doing this but, in general, clustering is done on the basis that a single piece of business logic can be used to derive a financial impact based on reaching the improvement targets set for all the benefits in the class.

▶ Sub-cases

Each project implementation instance will have a number of benefits classes which, together, form a benefits sub-case. Figure 5.2 calls these instances 'Regional benefits cases', which is an appropriate name for a globally implemented project. However, in a smaller-scale project implemented in one country, the sub-case instances could be, for example, factories or distribution centres; it depends very much on the design, scope and scale of the project. With some projects there will be no need for division into sub-cases. Note that where there are separate sub-cases, such as the regional benefits case example of the diagram, even though the benefit descriptions and measures may be the same in each sub-case, the target performance improvements and class financial impacts may be very different for a variety of local reasons.

▶ Project benefit case

Finally, the regional – or other type – sub-cases are grouped together to form a total project benefits case. This final grouping is normally described in terms of a summation of regional financial impacts by benefit class. Of course, this final step is not needed where there is just one benefits case covering one project implementation instance.

Use of the benefits case

The benefits components described in the previous section can be summarised into two high-level parts, as illustrated in Figure 5.3.

List and definition of benefits, with associated measures, targets and beneficiaries.	List of benefit classes, with associated business logic and financial impact.

Figure 5.3 – Primary high-level components of a benefits case

This is an artificial split, in that the benefits case is not presented in this format – even though the two elements can be readily distinguished within the formats produced. These two elements are used in different ways, separately or together, as illustrated in Figure 5.4.

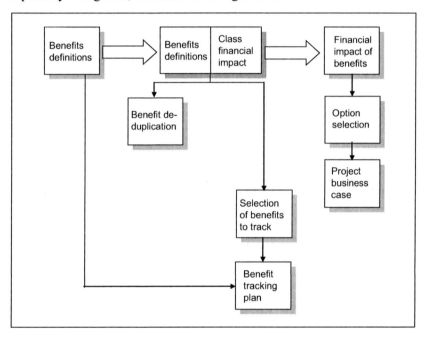

Figure 5.4 – Parts of the benefits case used as inputs to benefits management activities

The main points to draw from this illustration are that:

- Financial impact is derived from benefits definitions

- The financial element is mainly used to support option selection and the project business case

- Once the benefits to track have been selected, knowledge of the financial impact of benefits is not needed to carry out benefit tracking

Format of the benefits case

There is no fixed format for the way that benefits cases are presented, although there are elements that must be included; largely those shown in Figure 5.2.

To conclude this chapter I illustrate the benefits case formats that were used for the two global projects that provide most of the examples in the rest of the book. The two look very different – possibly because the first example was developed in an MS Excel spreadsheet and the second in an MS Access database.

For both projects we did produce a separate financial summary for convenience. This summary for the supply chain planning project is shown below at Figure 5.5.

	Asia Pacific		Americas		Rest of World		Europe		Total	
	Revenue	WC	Revenue	WC	Revenue	WC	Revenue	WC	Revenue	WC
Revenue	2.75		1.58		0.50		2.00		6.82	
COGS (RM)	1.24		0.04		0.20				1.49	
COGS (Conversion)	1.43		0.81		0.60		1.72		4.56	
COGS (Strategy)										
Cost to deliver	2.93		0.25		0.30				3.48	
Inventory	0.28	5.53	0.07	0.74	0.40	4.50	0.46	9.15	1.20	19.91
Total	8.6	5.5	2.7	0.7	2.0	4.5	4.2	9.2	17.5	19.9

Figure 5.5 – Value summary for a supply chain planning project

Figures 5.6 and 5.7 show part of the benefits case for two different projects. The first is a supply chain planning project and the second a management information system (MIS) project.

Apart from the different formats, you will notice that the MIS project benefits case is more detailed. This is because it is the result of the second series of benefits workshops, while the supply chain case is at the end of the first series of workshops. These differences will be explained later in the book.

Value bucket	Benefit	Performance targets	Business logic	Financial target	Baseline assumption	Min Rev	Min WC	Max Rev	Max WC
Revenue	Support customer intimacy: -Collaborative forecasting -- VMI implementation	-improve forecast accuracy from ~ 45% to 70 to 80% -- Reduce customer inventory by 3 to 5% p.a.	Increasing customer service through better intimacy, promise and delivery. This leads to a reduction in lost sales and lost customers and will make it easier to attract new customers with a better service offer.	0.5 to 1.5%	Gross margin less cost of secondary transport: 306.4 - 32.9 = $US274M	1.37		4.13	
	Enable better offer to the customer	Provide promise within 1 hour of customer request							
	Deliver in full, on time, every time	-33% over base case -- Reduce number of IFOT related complaints by 50%	Value opportunity of these benefits is improved sales						
	Inform customers of delivery delays	- 100%							
COGS (RM)	Reduce manufacturing complexity	Reduce RM storage costs and increase bulk discounts for a total value of $0.3M to $0.5M	Need to establish a judgement call on the impact of improved forecast on RM procurement prices (particularly additives and packaging)	$0.3M to $0.5M reduction in base oils associated costs	Total RM COGS = $522M. Assume additives plus packaging are 3/7 of this, or £224M.	0.86		1.62	
	Improve medium and long term RM forecast	Improve additives forecast by ?? % (need view of current accuracy)	Put placeholder assumption of 0.25 to 0.5% improvement for additives and packaging costs	0.25 to 0.5% reduction in additives and packaging costs	Financial benefit is this figure plus the cost reduction associated with base oil purchases				
		Improve packaging forecast by ?? % (as above)							
COGS (Conversion)	Improve accuracy and efficiency of plant scheduling	Increase blending/filling efficiency by 5 to 10%. Reduce plant labour costs by 2 to 5%	Overall value is reduction of labour costs, which comprise 60% of manufacturing costs	2 to 5%	Manufacturing costs are $25.1M; of which labour costs are $15M. 2 to 5% reduction is worth $0.3M to $0.75M	0.30		0.75	
COGS (Regionalization)	Enable forecasting and demand planning at a regional level	Free up 10 to 20 country supply chain managers		10 to 20 SC managers	Fully costed SC managers are $60k p.a	0.6		1.2	
Cost to deliver	Improve secondary transport scheduling	Reduce primary and secondary transport costs per litre/mile moved by 5 to 10%	Overall transportation costs reduced by 5 to 10% on like-for-like basis	5 to 10%	Transportation costs are: -Primary $6.2M -Secondary $32.9M - Total $39.1M	1.95		3.91	
	Improve primary transport scheduling								
	Reduce administrative cost of invoice processing	Target to be produced							
Inventory	Reduce inventory through better forecasting and planning	Reduce FG stock days by 2 to 5 days	WC value id number of stock days reduced times value of 1 day's stock. Also a 5% revenue saving in cost of servicing WC	2 to 5 days stock	Value of stock held in the region is $101M; representing 64 stock days. One stock day is worth $101M/64 = $1.58M	0.16	3.16	0.39	7.89
					TOTALS	5.24	3.16	12.00	7.89

Figure 5.6 – Benefit case for supply chain planning project after first (Feasibility)) series of workshops

Benefit class: Reduce lost sales

Benefit: Better focus sales effort to problem customers

Description: Identify waivering customers through trend analysis of monthly sales data and either drop unprofitable customers or focus sales effort to reverse negative trends.

Measure: Number of waivering customers

Beneficiary details for this measure:

Title	Country	Number	Baseline	Target
Country Sales Manager	Malaysia	6	10%of customers	5% of customers after a year
Country Sales Executive	Malaysia	65	10% of customers	5% of customers after a year

Measure: Number of unwanted customers

Beneficiary details for this measure:

Title	Country	Number	Baseline	Target
Country Sales Manager	Malaysia	6	3% unwanted customers	2% unwanted customers
Country Sales Executive	Malaysia	65	3% unwanted customers	2% unwanted customers

Benefit: More proactive management of IFOT problems

Description: Customer contacts will gain early knowledge of delivery problems and proactively minimise impact on customer

Measure: % of IFOT instances where sales person can warn customers

Beneficiary details for this measure:

Title	Country	Number	Baseline	Target
Country Sales Manager	Malaysia	6	Nil	95%
Country Sales Executive	Malaysia	65	Nil	95%

Benefit: Manage the causes of Credit Notes better

Description: Analyse the reasons for Credit Notes over time and between different sales units and apply root cause analysis to identify remedial action to reduce instances of Credit Notes

Measure: Number of credit notes per invoice

Beneficiary details for this measure:

Title	Country	Number	Baseline	Target
Country Sales Manager	Malaysia	6	30 per 6k invoices	50% reduction
Country Sales Executive	Malaysia	65	30 per 6k invoices	50% reduction

Figure 5.7 – Benefits case for one benefit class of MIS project after second (Define) series of workshops

CHAPTER SIX

Benefits and beneficiaries

Introduction

This and the next chapter discuss the factors that need to be taken into account when identifying and defining the elements of a benefits case. In this chapter I cover benefits and beneficiaries. I have also used this chapter to discuss the characteristics to look for when selecting beneficiaries to attend benefits workshops.

Benefits

The word 'benefit' has a specific meaning within this benefits management method; it is a measurable improvement in operational performance resulting from a project outcome. We have seen that a project's benefits case is a collection of such benefits, each being fully described with a definition and associated attributes of measures, targets and beneficiaries. Here, we are just concerned with the definition part of the benefit description.

▶ Anatomy of a benefit

Before discussing how to draft a good benefit definition it is worth examining its make-up in some detail. There are three parts to a definition, as illustrated in Figure 6.1 below:

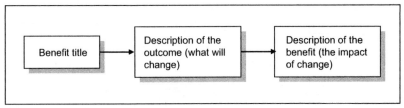

Figure 6.1 – Elements of a benefit definition

Benefit title

There is little to say about the benefit title other than that it should be clear, concise and able to convey the essence of the benefit while standing on its own. The reason for this need is that there will be many report formats where the benefit title is listed without the support of its description. The title should convey the beneficial impact of an outcome rather than the change itself. Thus:

> Improve sales forecast accuracy

is a more meaningful benefit title than

> Reinforce the sales forecasting process with an advanced forecasting tool

Titles also need to be distinct and unambiguous. A full project benefits case may contain several dozen separate benefits and, in a list of these benefit titles, each must be identifiably distinct from all of the others.

Description of the outcome

You might be tempted to think that the important element of the benefits description is the beneficial impact of change rather than the change itself; after all, even the benefit title is focused on the impact of change. However, as we shall show later, an understanding of the outcome is crucial to the method.

Take an example of the introduction of a management information system, where one of the benefits is:

> Reduce the effort needed to produce reports

The outcome description might be:

> 'Performance analysts currently spend a significant proportion of their time creating report templates, chasing for data from several business sources, compiling reports, resolving data anomalies and answering follow-up queries from the leadership team. Introduction of the MI system will speed the task of designing report templates and will automate data submission and report compilation without the need for manual intervention by performance analysts. Many of the leadership team queries will be eliminated and those remaining will be answerable with much less effort.'

Note that this is a full description of the outcome but only in qualitative terms; quantitative elements are addressed later.

Description of the benefit

It is not essential to separate out the two descriptive elements (the outcome and the benefit) physically but I would recommend that they are separated for two reasons:

- Deliberate separation ensures that both descriptive elements are specifically covered.

- Separation can make it easier later on to identify appropriate lead and lag measures.

Again, the description of the benefit is presented in qualitative terms rather than quantitative terms.

Continuing the example of the last section, the impact of the benefit of reducing the effort to produce reports might be described thus:

> 'Automation of the report production process will greatly reduce the time currently spent by performance analysts on manual report production. The effort released will be used to reduce the number of performance analysts and, for those remaining, more time will be spent analysing data and advising the leadership team on performance issues while reducing the number of hours spent on unpaid overtime.'

▶ Defining benefits

You have seen what constitutes a good, complete, benefits description. Here I cover the techniques used to aid their completion. This is probably the least structured technique within the method, yet it is a pivotal step that forms the bedrock of the benefits management process. The main aspects of this technique are the exhaustive identification of all potential benefits and the need to define each benefit in terms of what will change on the ground (the outcome) and with what impact on operational performance (the benefit).

Identifying benefits

It is unlikely that all potential benefits will be identified in one pass. This should not present a problem as there are several opportunities for developing and reviewing the list: while drafting the strawman benefits case and in the various benefits workshops held during the Feasibility and Define stages.

The initial list of benefits will be created by the benefits manager from a good knowledge of project aspirations and deliverables (in the early part of the Feasibility stage, project aspirations may be all there is to go on but by the beginning of the Define stage project deliverables should be well understood). The initial list should provide a good start but workshop delegates are likely to come up with more, once they know the details of project deliverables, because of their understanding of the project's impact on the local business environment.

During benefits workshops an early session should be devoted to brainstorming potential benefits; either on a blank canvas, to be checked later against the benefits manager's list, or as an exercise to build on the strawman list of benefits. The resulting brainstormed list then needs to be normalised to eliminate duplicates and adjust remaining benefit titles. Possible adjustments include ensuring a consistent syntax (starting with an active verb), the correct focus on the impact of change and the necessary distinctiveness and lack of ambiguity mentioned earlier.

Once the list of benefits has been established, follow-on sessions will address benefit definitions, measures and targets. These sessions will increase the delegates' understanding of the benefits and, once they are finished, it is well worth reviewing the benefits list for completeness.

Defining the outcome

The outcome description may have been first drafted by the benefits manager as part of a strawman benefits case. However, to define the change accurately there has to be knowledge of the current business environment and of the project's capabilities. Using a somewhat simplistic analogy, to define the nature and extent of the ripple you need to know about the pebble and the pond. An accurate definition of an outcome can therefore only be achieved through a partnership between the project team members, who understand the pebble, and the local business community, who are familiar with the pond.

It is easy to underestimate the need for a description of the outcome or to lose focus and start drifting into a description of its beneficial impact. A useful technique to overcome these problems is to ask workshop delegates to close their eyes metaphorically and think through exactly what will be different in the day-to-day processes and people's activities and behaviours associated with the benefit being described.

The outcome description needs to be at a level of detail similar to the example in the previous section of this chapter.

Defining the benefit

One of the greatest difficulties in defining the benefit is putting a boundary around the definition. To explain this, I want to introduce a concept here that we will discuss in greater detail later; that of the chain of events impacted by change. For any benefit there are potentially three major change points: the physical changes on the ground (the outcome), the resulting operational performance improvement, and the consequential change in financial performance. The link between physical change and operational performance is normally clear but some degree of business logic is usually needed to establish the link between operational and financial performance change.

The element of the benefits definition dealing with the impact of change should be limited to a description of the knock-on effects of the changes on the ground that lead to improvements in operational performance. The temptation that needs to be resisted is to include elements of business logic in this description. A blurring between these elements makes the tasks of deriving the financial impact of change and selecting appropriate measures far more difficult to complete.

Again, the example in a previous sub-section (Description of the benefit) shows the level of detail appropriate for this element of the benefit definition and illustrates the bounded nature of the description, dealing only with the knock-on effects leading to operational performance improvement.

Grouping benefits into benefit classes

Grouping benefits into classes is not an essential activity within the methodology until we start to derive the financial impact of benefits. However, this grouping adds valuable structure to the benefits list and is another activity that can lead to the unearthing of further benefits. I therefore recommend that grouping should take place at the end of the workshop session dealing with the identification of benefits.

There are no hard and fast rules as to how benefits should be grouped, nor any uniquely correct solution. The following paragraphs contain pointers that will help the selection of an appropriate grouping of benefits into classes.

Nature of the benefits class. The title of a benefit class is likely to focus on improved financial performance, rather than the operational focus of individual benefits. Examples of typical benefits classes are 'Increase sales revenues' and 'Reduce manufacturing costs'.

Benefit class structure. It is extremely useful to align benefits classes with the financial structure of the parent organisation. This does not mean that all of the organisation's financial sub-categories should be represented in the list of benefits classes, nor do all the benefit class titles need to align with sub-categories at the same level in the organisation's financial hierarchical structure.

Relationship between benefits and classes. All of the benefits within a class should contribute to the financially-related improvement of the class. So, all the benefits within a class called 'Reduce distribution costs' should contribute, directly or indirectly, to a reduction in the cost of distribution.

Numbers. The number of benefit classes will depend on the scope of the project and the number of benefits. Typically, there will be between two and six benefits in each benefits class.

Anomalies. There may be a benefit that uniquely contributes to one type of financial improvement. In this case, the benefit will form a class of its own. Conversely, a benefit may contribute towards more than one type of financial improvement. Here, the benefit should either be split and reworked as two separate benefits or be duplicated and appear in both relevant benefit classes.

Beneficiaries

▶ Identifying beneficiaries

Every person in the organisation whose work will be directly impacted by a project, and whose actions and behaviours can in turn affect the release of project benefits, is a beneficiary of that project. For a global implementation within an international company we could be talking about literally thousands of project beneficiaries.

To a certain extent, identification of beneficiaries falls out of well-defined benefits; if a benefit is fully defined, the roles that will be responsible for achieving the benefit should become fairly obvious. During early benefits work, beneficiaries will probably be identified by role title only. Later, the final benefits case will identify beneficiaries by role and location. Finally, when drafting the benefit tracking plan, beneficiaries whose activities are to be measured will be named.

▶ Selecting beneficiary representatives

Selection of a representative group from the host of beneficiaries to attend benefits workshops is less straightforward. Within the method, benefits workshops are critical to the creation of a sound benefits case; these workshops will only be successful if the delegates have the right attitude and, between them, the full depth and span of local knowledge of the part of the business affected by the project (or by all the projects within a programme tranche).

Nomination of workshop delegates must be decided by the local business that is hosting the workshop – probably by a combination of the transformation manager, accountable executives or functional directors and the local project manager (the latter to ensure no clash of resource allocations between benefits workshops and other project activities). However, local nominations must be steered by the needs specified by the benefits manager. The following factors will shape the benefits manager's wish list:

Numbers

There is no ideal number of delegates to benefits workshops but experience has shown that any number between eight and 12 will work well; this number not including workshop facilitators or other project team members.

Coverage

Between them, the delegates should have good knowledge of all the business processes and operational (beneficiary) roles that will be impacted by the project. If it would take significantly more than 12 delegates to achieve this coverage then serious consideration should be given to running a series of two or more workshops. Splitting workshops may anyway be a sensible thing to do if the project covers two or more very different functional areas – say sales and supply chain. However, beware missing out on potential cross-functional synergies; if separate functional workshops are held it is worth having one or two representatives on each from the other impacted function.

Seniority

Delegates must be drawn from potential beneficiaries which, for most projects, will rule out the most senior members of the organisation. Nevertheless, it is good to have a mix of seniority levels so that different viewpoints can be heard on the matters being discussed. There is a danger here that more junior delegates may feel inhibited from contributing opinions by the presence of senior members of the organisation; this can only be resolved through sensible nomination of named delegates, taking individual personalities into account.

Attitude

Although debate, challenge and even some cynicism can be stimulating, extreme attitudes to the project – either positive or negative – in any delegate can jeopardise the work to be completed during the workshop. Again, it needs sensible local nomination to avoid this possibility.

Other attendees

As well as the delegates to the workshop – the eight to 12 representative beneficiaries – others will be needed to make the workshops successful. There should be one or two facilitators – the benefits manager will probably be one of them – and at least one subject expert from the project team; this last to answer the inevitable detailed questions that will arise about the project deliverables and capabilities.

Measures, targets and financials

Introduction

Having described the project's outcomes and benefits in clear qualitative detail, you now need to apply some quantified yardsticks to be able both to derive a financial value for the project and to assess real progress towards full benefits realisation once the project goes live.

This chapter deals with these quantifiable elements of the benefits case. In summary:

- One or more measures are selected that will give a true indication of the state of the performance characteristics associated with each benefit.

- Targets are set for each measure to reflect a joint project and business area belief in the level to which performance can be improved as a result of project implementation.

- A forecast financial impact is derived, by applying business logic and financial baseline fundamentals to the assumption that all benefit performance improvement targets are achieved.

Measures

The subject of measures is complex and multifaceted and it is quite easy to get lost in the detail and end up selecting and defining measures inappropriate to their purpose. The techniques used ensure that measures identify solid links between the things that change on the ground and the resulting improvements in operational performance; between cause and effect and between lead and lag changes. The techniques also find solutions to benefits that at first appear immeasurable. Note that I have not used the term 'intangible'; the method does not recognise the concept of intangible benefits – if a benefit cannot be seen, touched or measured in some way it is probably not a benefit at all.

Before we start to discuss the different types and categories of measures, you need to be quite clear about what they are designed to do.

▶ Purpose of measures

There are two reasons for defining measures for each benefit:

- As a step towards defining the financial impact of the benefit case.
- As a means of tracking the release of benefits after the project has been handed over for day-to-day operation.

Aiding derivation of financial impact

As we shall see in a later chapter, derivation of the financial impact of each benefit class starts with the premise that each of the benefits within the class achieves a target level of operational performance improvement. A target implies that the improvement will be measurable on a sliding scale – rather like a specific temperature on a thermometer. Continuing the analogy, the graduations on the thermometer have to be defined before the target temperature point can be set. Similarly, a forecast improvement in operational performance requires a metric and a corresponding target level.

To give an example, the target performance improvement associated with the benefit 'Improve distribution efficiency' might be to reduce the cost of secondary transportation by a certain percentage. But for this target to be meaningful and have an associated financial value it must be measurable in a relevant way; in this example we want to measure improvement in efficiency, which implies unit rather than total costs; so the metric might be the transportation cost per kilometre tonne moved. Thus the forecast project benefit can be translated into a specific, measurable figure through the selection of an appropriate metric which, in turn, is amenable to financial manipulation.

Tracking the release of benefits

One of the main advantages of the method is to be able to confirm that forecast benefits have been achieved or to highlight the need for appropriate remedial action if benefits are blocked. To reach this level of assurance, we may need to be able to probe individual benefits at more than one point in the chain of events subject to change.

So, particularly for benefits at risk, we select measures that will allow us to see where along the chain of events a breakdown in expected change has occurred. I show an example of this later in the chapter.

▶ Characteristics of measures

There are different types of measure, as we shall see in the next section, and some of these have specific-to-type characteristics. There are also some common characteristics; all measures need to display these characteristics, described below, if they are to meet the dual objectives described in the previous sub-section in a reasonable way.

Relevant

Measures must accurately reflect the change they are designed to monitor. In other words, would measurements taken before and after project implementation faithfully represent the change that they are attempting to monitor? This may sound obvious but, in fact, considerable care is needed to ensure that selected measures are truly representative. It is much easier to select appropriate measures if the change they are designed to monitor is fully understood and accurately described in the benefit definition.

Separable

Measures must represent only the forecast change of the benefit in question and tune out any external factors. Take the previously illustrated simple example of using the metric 'Cost of transportation per kilometre-tonne moved' to measure a benefit of improving distribution efficiency. Measuring costs relative to the quantities of goods and distance moved avoids potentially distorting external factors such as an increase or decrease in tonnage moved (due perhaps to changes in market conditions) or a change in customer delivery locations. This selectivity needs to account not just for possible external factors but also benefits being claimed by other projects impacting the same business process. Again, this may need considerable care to ensure an accurately targeted measure.

Practical

The task of selecting measures starts a long time before the project goes live and benefit measures start to be taken. Despite this, it is important to select measures from the outset that are not merely academic but can be taken in practice.

Affordable

Right from the outset I have stated that rigorous benefits management brings with it a project cost overhead which is justified by a greatly increased overall return on project investment. The last thing you want to do is to fritter away this financial advantage by mounting a very costly monitoring and measurement exercise. One way to reduce the cost of measurement is to select, where possible, metrics that are already being collected as routine business key performance indicators (KPIs). For benefits not covered by such KPIs, measures should be selected with cost of measurement in mind.

Non-intrusive

Project beneficiaries are inevitably busy members of the organisation who will have little spare capacity to get involved in extensive benefits measurements. Where possible, it is preferable to take an automated approach to measurement taking. For instance, if we want to measure the usage levels of a new system it is better to use the system's own statistical tools to gather the information than to conduct user surveys. Where questioning beneficiaries cannot be avoided, this should be done through the use of questionnaires designed to extract the information with the minimum of effort on the part of beneficiaries.

▶ Types of measure

Measures differ in type in two ways:

- Their position along the chain of events impacted by the change.
- Their relationship to the change they are designed to monitor.

Measures along the chain of events

The chain of events subject to change is shown schematically in Figure 7.1 below:

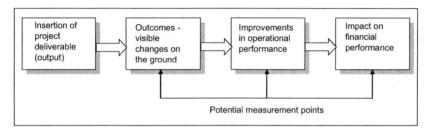

Figure 7.1 – The chain of events impacted by change

The figure illustrates that there are three points at which a measurement could be made and, in some cases, this is exactly what you do. However, there are several reasons (that we will cover later) why a measurement of the impact of a benefit on financial performance cannot realistically be made and we tend to focus on measuring the changes on the ground and the consequent improvements in operational performance.

The first obvious question to ask is why do you need to take measurements at two or three points along the chain of events when perhaps one carefully positioned and selected measure will tell you all you need to know about the release of a particular benefit? Well, sometimes such a strategy does work but Figure 7.2 overleaf helps to show why a single measure is unlikely to meet the dual objectives of benefits measurement.

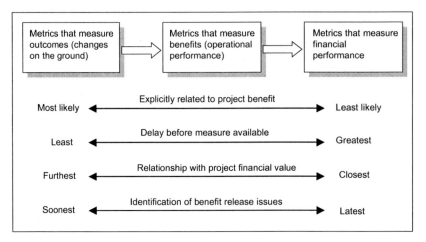

Figure 7.2 – Comparison of measure characteristics along the chain of events

A summary of these comparisons highlights the differences between the three types of measure.

Measures of outcomes:

- Will give you the fastest indication that forecast beneficial changes are on track and the earliest opportunity to take remedial actions where necessary. They are also the type of measure most likely to indicate the causes of benefit blockage when they occur.

- Are most likely to reflect changes resulting directly from the project implementation rather than any other factor.

- Are of little use, on their own, in deriving or measuring the financial impact of benefits.

Measures of improvements in operational performance:

- Play a useful, often essential, part in deriving the financial impact of benefits and assessing whether it has been delivered.

- Need to be treated with some caution as it can be difficult to attribute the whole of a performance improvement to the project in question.
- Will probably lag behind measurement of outcomes but provide good collateral evidence that benefits release is on track.

Measures of improvements to financial performance:

- May not be measurable for weeks or months after measured changes in operational performance.
- Are extremely difficult to attribute wholly to the project under examination.
- Give the most direct indicator of financial performance improvement when the attribution problem can be overcome.

This summary suggests that the dual objectives of setting measures and taking measurements – deriving financial value and tracking forecast benefits – are unlikely to be met, for any one benefit, by the deployment of a single measure; and this is the case in reality.

Relationship of measures to change

In an ideal world, one direct measure would entirely capture the change that it is designed to monitor; whether an outcome or a consequent change in operational performance. Unfortunately, reality seldom meets this ideal and we often need a more complex measurement structure to be able to fully monitor the expected change. As a rule, measures that monitor change in operational performance are likely to be straightforward while measures that monitor outcomes that lead to improvement in operational performance are likely to be more complex.

There are four types of measure that, when applied correctly, should provide as complete a monitoring of change as is desired. These are:

- Direct measures
- Partial measures
- Surrogate measures

- Transferred benefits

Direct measures

These are the measures that are able singly to capture the complete change in question – more likely with operational performance change than changes on the ground.

Partial measures

As the name implies, these are measures that individually capture only part of the change being monitored. If full monitoring of a forecast change is needed, then it will be necessary to select and deploy two or more partial measures.

Surrogate measures

Despite what I have said about all benefits being measurable, sometimes there are reasons why direct measurement of the contributing changes is not practicable. In this case you should look for a surrogate measure, where you monitor some other factor that is known to correlate well with the inaccessible change in question.

Transferred benefits

This might be called the 'non-measure'. It applies when a capability provided does not result in a beneficial change within the project's scope but enables or supports some other project. In this case, your project provides the support and in return is credited with a proportion of the relevant benefit of the enabled project; any measurement of the benefit is conducted within the management of the other project's benefits.

▶ Examples of different measure types

Some of the concepts in the previous section are not easy to imagine in isolation. These examples should bring the measure types to life.

Outcomes and performance improvements
An international drinks company significantly increased its portfolio of

products through the acquisition of two competing companies. Along with the new companies and products, the acquiring company inherited additional sales teams and sales processes. The company decided to initiate a project to rationalise and improve customer-facing processes; the re-engineered processes would be supported by a new customer relationship management (CRM) system.

One of the benefits of the project was that sales representatives would have constant access to up-to-date information on their customers: buying history, credit ratings and arrangements and payment status; this would lead to more informed discussions with customers that would result in better payment patterns. Of course, there were many other benefits associated with improved processes and information, but we focus here on improving payments.

So, what would be the outcomes driving this benefit? Well, the most immediate change would be the sales representatives' access to, and usage of, the new CRM system; something that can be measured directly from built-in system tools. Obviously, if representatives fail to use the system the benefit will be stillborn.

The next thing that will change will be the way that representatives talk to their customers as a result of better information. This is much more difficult to measure and, if we wish to do so, would probably require before and after questionnaires to be completed by a sample of representatives. Instead, it might be better to measure the average repayment history of all customers in each representative's portfolio. This will not measure what has changed on the ground from the representatives' perspective but it does reflect how customers' payment behaviours change as a result and is a metric that the company's management accounting systems can readily produce. Furthermore, improving customer payment patterns is, in fact, the operational performance improvement that this benefit seeks to achieve.

So, in summary, the outcomes will be sales representatives' use of the new CRM system and the improved focus of their discussions with their customers; the resulting operational improvement will be a reduction in customer debt. In this case, a decision could be made to limit measurement to CRM usage levels and customer debt days. A comparison of changes in the average debtor days of all customers of each sales representative, coupled with a mapping of that representative's CRM usage against his or her success at improving customer debtor days, will give an accurate insight into which representatives to question about their new customer-facing behaviour if the benefit fails to materialise.

Direct and surrogate measures

Let us examine more closely the benefit description example illustrated in the last chapter. In summary, this concerned the implementation of a global MI system that, among other things, would greatly reduce the manual effort made by performance analysts to produce routine monthly, and ad hoc, performance reports; allowing some reduction in numbers, better quality performance analysis and a reduction in unpaid overtime worked. The first outcome will be a significant reduction in the hours needed to produce monthly reports. This change can be monitored by a straightforward direct measure, albeit one that is somewhat intrusive as it requires the completion of before and after questionnaires and activity logs by a sample of analysts (more of these techniques in Chapter 9).

Let us then focus on one of the secondary changes – reduction in overtime worked. Again, this is a directly and easily measurable change; particularly if the organisation already tracks daily hours worked by individuals. The problem arises when we seek the next step in this chain of events. A diagram of the whole chain of events for this benefit is shown in Figure 7.3 below:

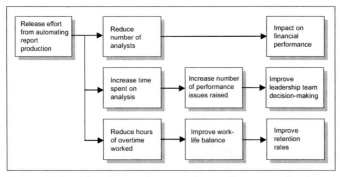

Figure 7.3 – The chain of events changed as a result of automating reports

It is worth noting, in passing, that the diagram illustrates a concept that I have only touched on until now. This is that the first change on the ground does not always lead directly to a performance improvement; rather, the first change enables a further change which in turn leads to a performance improvement. It is not unknown for a third change along the chain of events before we get to the performance improvement.

So, it can be seen that the company has assessed that there is a link between reducing excessive overtime and increasing staff retention rates, and the linking change is an improvement in work-life balance. Work-life balance is a quality of staff satisfaction that could be measured through a well-targeted staff survey; but most organisations would be loath to mount additional surveys to those already planned and the timing of the latter may not meet the need for timely project benefit tracking. So we need a more accessible way of monitoring the impact of reduced overtime on the community of analysts. There is the possibility of a surrogate measure here – a known correlation between levels of staff satisfaction and sickness and absence rates. If these levels are monitored routinely by HR (common in many organisations), and there are no other factors that might significantly affect staff satisfaction in the same timeframe, then changes in sickness and absence levels would be a reasonable surrogate for the measurement of work-life balance.

Setting targets

Setting targets is about forecasting the degree of change that will occur on the ground and the level of consequential performance improvement. However well the benefits have been defined and however appropriate the chosen measures, there will nearly always be a need for some business judgement in setting targets. Techniques used here are designed to reduce the elements of judgement to a minimum and to help those having to make judgement calls to arrive at realistic assessments.

▶ The importance of target setting

The task of setting targets against each of the measures that have been chosen to illustrate achievement of benefits is one of the most straightforward in concept but one of the most difficult to undertake in practice. Add to this that target setting is an absolutely critical step towards both the derivation of project financial value and to the achievement of full release of benefits in operation, it makes it probably the highest risk task within the method.

The most essential target from a financial impact perspective is the target improvement in operational performance. However, setting targets for the measured outcomes is also an important step; when set well, they pave the way for accurate performance improvement targets and provide a yardstick against which to monitor whether project benefits are likely to be achieved or not.

One of the strengths of the method is early involvement of the business community to gain a realistic insight on locally achievable benefits and to get early business buy-in. Setting targets is a step for which it is vital to involve the appropriate people from the business. But this also has attendant risk as there will be a built-in resistance, from those who will be responsible for achieving project benefits, to set targets above their comfort zone; left to their own devices they would inevitably set unchallenging, conservative target levels of improvement.

So, great care is needed in facilitating the target setting section of benefits workshops. We will speak more about facilitation in Part 2; here I want to cover the techniques you can use to aid this facilitation.

▶ Techniques to aid target setting

There are a number of ways that you can help benefits workshop delegates to think beyond their comfort zone. Before I describe these, you need to understand this comfort zone that we have to break out of. Beneficiaries attending the workshops will be involved with the business processes that the project is addressing. Some delegates will operate a part of the process and others will be responsible for the performance of the whole process; the latter will be the ones asked to propose process performance improvement targets.

Under normal circumstances, there are three areas of experience and belief that process owners will have:

- Experience of making small process improvements; often through their own initiatives.

- Belief that they have exhausted all avenues of improvement and that the process is operating at near optimum performance – particularly if KPIs associated with their process compare well with those of the same process in other parts of the organisation.

- Belief that, while quantum levels of process improvement may theoretically be possible, the conditions for such improvement do not apply within their part of the business.

For such entrenched process owners it can be extremely painful to face the idea that their process is significantly under-performing.

Here are some techniques to help overcome resistance to bold target setting.

Knowledge of project capability

Before targets are set, it is essential that delegates have as full an understanding as possible of the project, its capabilities and its potential impact on the business process in question. This will all have been covered in the earlier benefit definition part of the workshop but it is worth summarising again the main points when setting targets.

Benchmark evidence

While it is inappropriate to use benchmarks of best industry practice to establish potential performance levels, they can be very powerful in opening delegates' eyes to what has been found achievable in other organisations. Benchmarks are always open to the criticism that the circumstances in which they were achieved were very different from those that apply in this business. To overcome this criticism it is useful if the benchmarks have been published by a respected industry association (rather than by the system vendor), apply to a similar business, and the environment in which they were achieved is known and describable. The benchmark should be associated with the implementation of a similar system or other improvement as that of the project which is being addressed in the benefits workshop. In this case, the benchmark should be quoted as an absolute value rather than a percentage improvement. For instance, if the project is about implementing advanced supply chain planning tools and re-engineered processes, it is better to quote a best practice figure for reducing the number of days stock held to, say, 10 days rather than quoting a 40 per cent reduction in cost of inventory, as percentage improvements depend upon starting positions, which will inevitably be different between organisations.

Working outwards

Always start by setting targets for the immediate outcomes, then for the knock-on changes and finally for the performance improvement. Estimating the likely size of the changes on the ground is less controversial than estimating performance improvement but, once set, these will establish a firm base from which to derive performance improvement targets. Going back to the supply chain benchmark example of the last paragraph, if you can first establish the degree to which sales forecast accuracy, inventory visibility and speed of reaction to unexpected demand can be improved, then it becomes much easier to set a challenging target for reduced stock holding.

Bracketing

When it comes to the moment of truth of agreeing a level of performance improvement, despite all the preparation described above, the responsible manager can find it difficult to offer a specific figure or percentage improvement. A way round this impasse is to ask the delegates to suggest the maximum and minimum levels of improvement that could be achieved. They may still be cautious about proposing a stretched maximum and reintroducing the industry best practice benchmark can be a useful incentive at this point. Once these boundaries have been agreed, further discussion should allow the maximum and minimum figures gradually to move closer together. When this step has been exhausted it merely remains to agree a target that will probably be around the midpoint between the final maximum and minimum figures.

Instilling partnership

This technique probably sounds somewhat brutal and needs to be used with caution to avoid distorting targets beyond that which is realistically achievable. In essence, it is to make it clear to delegates that the project will not survive without a satisfactory ROI and that such an ROI is unavoidably dependent upon a forecast project financial value based on substantial performance improvement. Of course, this will only work if the consensus among delegates is that they really want the project to be implemented in their part of the business. Assuming that this is the case, target setting takes on the nature of a pact agreed between the project team and the local business; in exchange for delivering the project and its capabilities, the business agrees to maximize the opportunities presented and offers challenging targets based on this understanding. It is vital not to overdo this, as the last thing you want to do is to set targets that are unrealistically inflated and unachievable.

Deriving the financial impact

Information for the project's benefits case is completed with the step to derive the financial impact of benefits. This step is both important and difficult and is awarded a separate workshop of its own.

▶ Sources of value

The starting point for deriving financial impact is a list of benefits clustered into benefits classes and with at least benefit descriptions and performance improvement measures and targets fully defined. Figure 7.4 overleaf illustrates the primary inputs for derivation of financial impact. The figure illustrates some important points:

- Financial impact is derived for each benefit class, not for individual benefits.

- The essential input from each benefit class is the performance improvement target associated with each benefit within the class.

- It is rarely possible to derive the financial impact associated with a benefit class without applying some business logic.

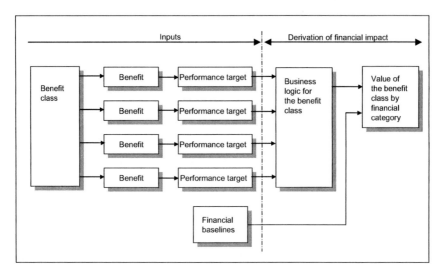

Figure 7.4 – Essential elements of value derivation

- The outcome of business logic can only be converted to financial value if the organisation's financial baselines are available to the required level of granularity.

- Most organisations will want the project's financial contribution to be split into the various financial categories that will receive value. For this reason we try to cluster benefits such that the classes align with the relevant sections of the organisation's financial hierarchical structure.

▶ Business logic

I have referred to business logic several times already in the text without being specific about exactly what it is. Now the time has come when I can avoid it no longer; so I will attempt to put some definition around the expression (see panel opposite) and then illustrate it with an example or two.

> **What is business logic?**
>
> The business logic associated with a benefit class starts with the premise that the performance improvement target for each of the benefits in the class is achieved and then attempts to answer the question 'what impact will this have on the finances of the business?'.
>
> In some cases this is an extremely easy question to answer, requiring virtually no logic at all. In others, the logic may have to be quite complex or convoluted to arrive at an answer to the question.
>
> Bear in mind that the business logic itself provides not the financial value of the benefit class but a formula that applies to the whole business class from which a value can be derived by plugging in one or more financial baseline figures.

Let us illustrate this with some examples.

Simple business logic example

Take the benefit class of 'Reducing stock levels' associated with the project to implement advanced supply chain planning tools and processes. We will assume that there was only one benefit in this class and target setting gave this benefit a performance improvement target of reducing the number of days of stock held by, say, four days. In this case the only calculation needed would be to derive the financial value of one day's stock and multiply it by four to give the financial value of the inventory reduction. But this calculation is just the application of two baseline figures – the total current value of stock held and the number of days of stock held; logic does not come into it even if simple mathematics does. Of course, if this class had more than one benefit, each contributing to the desire to reduce stock levels, then some logic may be needed to arrive at a composite stock-day reduction figure. For instance, separate benefits might reduce the levels of raw materials, work in progress in the factory and finished goods in the distribution supply chain. In this case the combined figure for stock-day reduction is unlikely to be a simple addition and some business logic will need to be applied. Reducing stock levels do also provide an annual saving in the cost of holding and handling stocks but I need not go into that here.

More complex business logic example

Again, we revisit the example of the introduction of an MI system that will reduce the hours spent by performance analysts in producing routine monthly and ad hoc reports. We have already agreed that there will be three benefits in this class; reducing numbers of analysts, improving the quality of performance advice and thus the quality of decisions made by the leadership team and improving work-life balance for the remaining analysts and thus improving staff retention rates (see Figure 7.3). I have seen two entirely different approached to business logic for similar benefit classes in value workshops I have facilitated:

- In the first approach there was no question of staff savings and an average figure was arrived at for the financial equivalent of the hours released; interestingly, this was set at twice the hourly cost of the analysts concerned as this was considered a conservative figure for the higher value work that the (happier) analysts would now undertake. The rest of the logic was just creating the formula, using the number of analysts and the hours released for each, giving a financial value once hourly analyst costs were plugged in.

- The second approach, where staff reductions were made, applied separate business logic to each of the benefits to arrive at a combined formula.

There is seldom a single, correct approach to business logic and the one selected will depend as much on the consensus feelings of the delegates as to any preconceived ideas on the approach held by the facilitator. To see this example to completion I have laid out the business logic for the first approach in the panel opposite.

An example showing one approach to deriving the financial impact of increasing the time available to performance analysts to carry out higher value work:

> The primary financial value of this benefit class is the ability to switch analysts from data gathering to higher-valued analysis or project work. To this end, a conservative assumption has been made that each additional hour of analytical work generates a value to the company of twice the hourly cost of employing the analyst. The additional value of reducing the overtime worked by analysts has not been costed, although it will result in material benefit to the company.
>
> In the regional headquarters, 2 analysts will reduce overtime worked and be able to spend 40% more of their time doing analysis. This means that each will contribute added value equivalent to 80% of their employment cost doing higher value work, giving a total of 160% of the cost of a regional headquarters analyst.
>
> In each country in the region, the 4 performance analysts will each reduce their overtime from 30 hours to 10 hours a month and will be able to divert 40% more of their time to analysis and process improvement works. Thus each will contribute added value equivalent to 80% of their employment cost doing higher value work. Value for the country is therefore 320% of the cost of a country analyst and for all 12 countries in the region is 3840% of the cost of a single country analyst.
>
> Average fully loaded cost for all analysts in the region is $US20k p.a. giving a value for this class of $US(1.6 + 38.4)*20k, or $US800k.

CHAPTER EIGHT

Multiple projects and options

Introduction

We have discussed so far the techniques used to develop the elements of a benefits case. There may have been many benefits workshops carried out to reach this stage. Take for instance the real example of benefits workshops associated with the global delivery of an MI system for an international lubricants company. In this case the project had a wide functional scope which required pairs of workshops (for benefits definition and financial impact derivation respectively) for three separate functions within each region; six workshops per region. It was decided to hold workshops in two regions only and then extrapolate the results to the other two regions. This was still 12 workshops held, that could have been 24 if it had been deemed necessary to hold workshops in all regions (as it transpired, this approach caused more problems than it solved and, with hindsight, it would have been better to have held the 24 workshops across all regions).

We now have nearly all the source material we need to support:

- The selection of options
- Engagement with other projects to ensure no duplication of benefits and
- Production of the benefits section of an initial business case.

I have combined these three elements from the end-to-end process into one chapter because, as we shall see, they are inextricably linked. Before we examine each in turn, I want to talk briefly about sequencing.

▶ Sequencing

Output from the workshops is in the form of steady-state benefits and financial contributions (benefits viewed at the stage when they are delivering peak annual value), with a granularity showing financial contribution by benefits class and region – assuming a global implementation. This format is sufficient to inform the activity of de-duplicating benefits with other projects.

The benefits case will then need some additional work to support the selection of a preferred option. This may need an assessment of the relative financial contribution made by each country in a region and by each element of a modular system.

Finally, a time dimension will need to be added so that the benefits case can contribute meaningfully to the net present value (NPV) calculations to determine the project ROI.

So, an ideal sequencing of activities to develop benefits workshops' output into the input needed for the business case would be:

- Assemble a global steady-state benefits case.

- De-duplicate the benefits case with other projects within the programme or portfolio of change projects.

- Add further granularity to the benefits case to support selection of a preferred option.

- Add a time dimension to the benefits case of the preferred option and present it for inclusion in the stage business case.

A variation to this sequencing will be needed if project governance wishes to use comparison of ROIs to help select a preferred option. In this case the time dimension will be added at the same time as the granularity of financial contributions by country and module.

▶ Steady-state benefits case

There is little to say at this stage about the initial compilation of a steady-state benefits case. As we shall see in Part 2, the formats of outputs from benefits workshops are such that creation of a single project steady-state benefits case becomes a mechanical process of collation and summarisation.

De-duplicating benefits

If a project is part of a large portfolio, whether in a formal programme or not, it may be progressing alongside a number of other projects at a similar stage of development. This being the case, the opportunities for projects to claim the same or overlapping benefits will be numerous. Identifying all the touch points and potential benefit conflicts between a number of projects can be a nightmare under these circumstances and you will need to add some structure to simplify the task. Of course, if the portfolio is within a formal programme then the likelihood of overlapping benefit claims will probably not apply (see Chapter 4).

Assuming that benefit overlap is a real possibility, the factor that allows us to introduce conflict management structure is that, in almost every case, duplication of benefits occurs when two or more projects are impacting the same business process and delivering value into the same bucket in the organisation's financial structure.

So, for instance, if two projects are impacting the process of maintaining inventory and the associated benefits of each are contributing respectively into the 'Cost of goods sold' and 'Cost of inventory' financial buckets, then they will not be claiming the same benefit. If, on the other hand, they both contribute to the same financial bucket then there is a good chance that a benefit is being wrongly duplicated. I say 'a good chance' because there is no certainty that two projects delivering benefits from the same business process into the same financial bucket are in conflict; they may well be delivering complementary benefits.

▶ Identifying potential benefit duplication

The first thing you will need to do is to present a summary of the project benefits that shows each benefit positioned in a matrix of business process against financial bucket. I shall show how to do this in detail in Part 2; for now, the schematic in Figure 8.1 shows what I mean:

		Financial bucket 1	Financial bucket 2	Financial bucket 3
Business process 1	Benefit 1	✓		
	Benefit 2		✓	
Business process 2	Benefit 3	✓		✓
	Benefit 4	✓		

Figure 8.1 – Association of benefits with business processes and financial buckets

The diagram illustrates some points about individual benefits within a single project:

- Benefits very rarely impact more than one business process but there may be more than one benefit associated with a single business process.

- Benefits may contribute to more than one financial bucket – although, when they do, it is sometimes better to split them into two benefits if possible.

Producing this format is only useful if the following conditions apply:

- The same hierarchy of financial categories, or buckets, applies across all projects in the portfolio (this is only likely to be an issue in the rare case of a portfolio or programme spread across two recently merged companies that have yet to harmonise their financial structures).

- The organisation has a codified structure of business process definitions or a blueprint process map. If this is not the case, it may well be worth a large programme producing its own process model; this will almost certainly be needed anyway if the programme involves an element of process design or re-engineering.

- All projects within the programme produce a process/finance matrix for their benefits, using the organisation's standard process and financial structures and definitions.

The first step towards de-conflicting benefits is to produce a master programme process/finance matrix onto which are posted the benefits from all projects within the programme. This can be done in several ways and is an activity that should be led from the programme office; by the programme benefits manager (or business change coordinator) if one exists. It is possible to lead the activity from within one of the projects but this would be a somewhat unfair overhead on the project concerned.

Once the master matrix has been produced, it is a relatively straightforward exercise to identify all the touch points between projects; basically, wherever there is more than one tick in a cell of the matrix.

▶ Resolving potential benefit duplication

The next step is to examine the identified touch points to see whether a duplication of benefits, or something worse, is happening. Before going into this, I want to make a claim on behalf of the method which I will then attempt to justify overleaf.

A claim for benefits management

If all projects within a programme use a rigorous and consistent benefits management process, it will be impossible for benefits to be duplicated.

The basis for this claim is that the method first ensures that the project outcomes are accurately reflected in the benefit description and then ensures an auditable link between the outcome and the financial impact of that change (via the chain of events and business logic). So, the only way that the projects could be claiming the same benefit would be if they were both causing the same outcome (more of which later).

So, back to our examination of the touchpoints between projects – best conducted bilaterally between the benefits managers of the two projects concerned (unless it is a touchpoint between three or more projects, in which case more benefits managers will be involved). What are they likely to discover during this examination? Normally, one of three findings:

- The two projects are addressing different, unconnected aspects of the business process and each benefit exists in its own right. A simple check is needed to ensure that the combined financial contribution of the two benefits is realistic.

- The projects are providing complementary improvements to the business process, in which case a careful review of the respective outcomes and associated chains of events needs to be made to eliminate any overlap in the values claimed by the two projects.

- The projects are, indeed, attempting to cause the same outcome, in which case it is not just the benefits that are overlapping and changes to the scope of one or both of the projects must be made.

An example of each of these possible outcomes should help in their understanding:

Separate benefits

Two supply chain projects in a drinks company were claiming to improve throughput in the bottling plants. There was no conflict in the benefits, as one project was improving schedule planning to maximise use of capacity while the other project was making mechanical improvements to the bottling line to increase capacity. However, a check had to be made that the sum of the improved throughputs claimed by the two projects would be feasible in practice.

Complementary benefits

A lubricants company had two global projects, which I have previously introduced, progressing together through the Feasibility stage; one to improve customer-facing services and the other to improve supply chain planning. Both projects were claiming the benefit of the ability to promise a firm delivery date within minutes of receiving a customer's order. It transpired that the changes made by both projects were necessary to provide the capability claimed in full; the supply chain advanced planning tool provided the data on forward availability of goods and the customer-facing CRM tools allowed customer-facing staff to access and manipulate the data to give customers an immediate answer. One of the projects had to revise its benefit description and reduce the financial contribution claimed for it.

Conflicting benefits

The same supply chain project was planned for implementation in a region that was also planning the introduction of a replacement ERP (Enterprise Resource Programme) transactional system. Both projects claimed to be improving the sales forecasting process, with similar outcomes, knock-on effects and consequent financial impact. The problem here was that both projects were making process improvements enabled by the new systems they were introducing; the ERP project was providing better data to support forecasting and the supply chain project was providing an advanced planning tool, also to support forecasting. The matter was resolved through programme-level arbitration that decided that as the process was of a planning rather than transactional nature its improvement should be led by the supply chain project. This resulted in a reduction in scope for the ERP project and the avoidance of significant confusion within the business community, as well as elimination of duplicated project effort and claimed benefits.

Whatever the outcome of these examinations, it is essential that they are followed through where some conflict has been found. This means that, as a minimum, one or more benefits cases will need to be adjusted; either in the benefit description or in the business logic. Either way, the programme benefits manager will need to be satisfied that any benefit duplication has been resolved. In the case requiring a change in the scope of a project the programme director and the project governance board of the affected project will also need to be involved.

Supporting option selection

When a project starts and its objectives have been clarified, it is quite normal for there to be some widely different proposals for meeting the objectives. However, these extremes tend to get eliminated during Start-up or early in the Feasibility stage, leaving more subtle differences between the remaining options. If significantly different options remain then each option will need its own separate benefits case. If, however, the remaining options reflect minor variations on a single technical and business process solution it should be possible to support option selection from a single benefits case.

There is little to say about the case where separate benefits cases are needed. The need must have been identified, and the differences between the options well documented, before the benefits workshops are held. The most economic way of developing twin benefits cases during workshops is to complete the case for one option and, at the end of each workshop session, identify the differences in the benefits and their attributes for the alternative option or options. It is likely, given that the objectives of all options are the same, that many of the benefits will be common between options.

I want to concentrate on the more usual occurrence of selecting between similar options, where the variations are typically between what parts of a system are implemented where. I go into some detail on how to do this in Part 2, using a supply chain example. I use the same example here to help illustrate the principles and techniques.

First, let us look at the scenario. This involves the same supply chain project that we have seen several times already. The project was to implement an advanced planning system and improve associated supply chain planning processes in all of the company's four regions.

The drivers for option selection were:

- A desire of the company to differentiate itself by becoming world class in customer service; including reliability and flexibility in product availability and delivery.

- A need to influence the cost of goods sold downwards.

- Limitations on the funds available year-on-year for project implementation.

Output from the benefits workshops was collated into regional benefits cases, giving the qualitative details on each benefit that we have previously discussed and a single regional financial contribution figure for each benefit class. Table 8.1 below illustrates what the financial summary of a regional benefits case might look like for this example. This summary represents the full financial granularity available at this point in the process.

Benefit class/ financial bucket	Regional peak benefitsvalues	
	Annual ($USM)	WC ($USM)
Revenue	2.6	
COGS (RM)	3.8	
COGS (Conversion)	1.3	
Cost to deliver	2.3	
Inventory	0.4	7.9
Total	10.4	7.9

Table 8.1 – Example project regional value summary

The acronym COGS in the list of impacted financial buckets stands for 'Cost of goods sold', RM stands for 'raw materials' and WC stands for 'Working Capital'. Note that the figures shown represent either the peak values of forecast annual benefits or the total value of a one-off benefit (such as the one-off cash saving of an inventory reduction shown here). At this stage, benefits contributions are based on the assumption that all modules of the advanced planning system (APS) will be implemented across the whole region. Initial calculations in this scenario show that the cost of full implementation in the region is too high while the ROI is likely to be too small; so we need to examine ways of improving these figures.

The system to be implemented is made up of six different modules, each of which enhances a specific supply chain process and can, up to a point, be installed independently of the others. The financial contribution to the region of each individual module will depend upon its relative contribution to the financial impact of each business class. Similarly, the value of installing some or all of the system modules in each country, or cluster of countries in some cases, will depend upon the comparative contribution from that country or cluster to regional supply chain value drivers such as volumes manufactured, warehoused and distributed to customers. There may be other non-volumetric factors that would need to be overlaid to reflect a more accurate division of country contributions, such as relative capacity for improving a particular supply chain process.

Having said that one of the method's strengths is that it develops benefits bottom-up, I am now advocating a top-down approach to achieving this necessary added level of financial granularity. I make no apologies for this; the process of adding this granularity will not affect the validity of the overall bottom-up value case and it is a cost-effective way of apportioning contributions to support option selection. My only proviso is that the factors chosen to drive the apportionment must be sensibly chosen and carefully applied.

We will go through this process in detail in Part 2; for now I will cover the things that need to be considered in calculating and using the apportionment. In the scenario I have described we would end up with apportionment tables looking like those of Table 8.2 below and Table 8.3 opposite:

Proportion of value contributed by each APS module							
Benefit class/ financial bucket	Improve:	(DFM) Demand forecast management	SMP (Supply master planning)	SDP (Supply distribution planning)	PS (Plant scheduling)	STS (Secondary transport scheduling)	OPF (Order promising & fulfilment)
Revenue	Customer satisfaction	0.17		0.17		0.33	0.33
COGS (RM)	RM Purchasing	0.75	0.25				
COGS (Conversion)	Manufacturing	0.17	0.17		0.67		
Cost to deliver	Logistics	0.17		0.17		0.67	
Inventory	Inventory levels	0.40	0.20	0.20	0.10	0.10	

Table 8.2 – Example apportionment of module value contribution

Proportion of value contributed by each cluster/country							
Benefit class/ financial bucket	Driver:	Cluster A	Cluster B	Country 1	Country 2	Country 3	Count
Revenue	Volume sold	0.62	0.38				
COGS (RM)	Value of RM purchases	0.58	0.42				
COGS (Conversion)	Volume produced			0.15	0.12	0.0	
Cost to deliver	Transportation costs			0.17	0.10	0	
Inventory	Stock-days held	0.65	0.35				

Table 8.3 – Example apportionment of country value contribution

How did we decide what the relative contributions should be? The method differs for the two types of apportionment:

- The contribution of each system module needs a deep understanding of how each module contributes to the improvement of supply chain processes and the relative contribution of improved processes to benefits class financial value, by financial bucket. This estimation of relative module contribution is best carried out by the system and process subject experts on the project team, together with the benefits manager.

- The contribution of each country, or cluster of countries, depends on their relative contributions to the appropriate current financial drivers; the only tricky bit here being to choose the driver most suited to the particular benefit. So, for instance, if the benefit class of improving customer satisfaction results in a percentage increase in volumes sold, then the country share of total current regional sales volume is the driver for this revenue-related benefits class. Local knowledge will be needed to identify any other factors that may affect the volume-driven, or any other, apportionment.

A word here about why we have based geographical apportionment partly by country and partly by cluster. This is a peculiarity of how advanced planning systems are likely to be implemented but could apply to other types of system. One of the benefits of implementing advanced supply chain planning systems is that they allow some planning functions to be carried out at an aggregated level; however, plant and transport scheduling tend to be point solutions that need to be applied at plant or country level respectively.

Once the apportionment tables have been completed they can be applied to the basic regional value case (Table 8.1) to produce a table giving financial contribution by benefit class, module and country or cluster. It is then a relatively easy task to run various 'what-if' scenarios, cutting modules from countries where they provide comparatively little value, and thus shaping options that have acceptable ROIs. Again, I will demonstrate how this is done in Part 2.

The time dimension

One factor we have not yet considered is the time element of benefits release. Very few benefits will release financial value to the business from the day the project goes live and some can take 18 months or more to come through. Even when benefits start to give a financial return, it can be several quarters before their peak contribution is reached.

The time span considered for NPV calculations differs from company to company; typical spans considered are five years or 10 years from the start of major project investment – normally from the start of the Deliver stage of the project. Over this time, particularly if the 10-year time span is used, some benefits will start to tail off. For example, take a benefit that improves the company's standing among its customer base, compared with its competitors, by introducing some innovative customer service. The resulting competitive edge cannot be expected to remain for more than a year or two, after which time competitors will have started to play catch-up.

The time element of benefits must therefore be taken into account when calculating the project's NPV, ROI and other financial indicators. Time variations will depend both on the build-up and tail-off effects described above and on the scheduling of project implementation; it is not unusual for a global implementation to take two years or more and some financial return will start coming through from early 'go-lives' well before full implementation is completed.

The revised financial contribution table created for option selection already has the granularity needed to cater for different country-by-country implementation dates. You just need to add the build-up and tail-off effects to have the financial element of the benefits case fully prepared for inclusion in the project NPV calculations. For this, we will need another table, as illustrated in Table 8.4 below:

APS module	Rate of benefits release after "go live"			
	Q1	Q2	Q3	Q4
Demand forecast management		0.3	0.7	1.0
Supply master planning		0.3	0.7	1.0
Supply distribution planning	0.5	1.0	1.0	1.0
Plant scheduling		0.5	1.0	1.0
Transport scheduling	0.3	0.7	1.0	1.0
Order promising & fulfilment	0.3	0.7	1.0	1.0

Table 8.4 – Example of differential build-up of benefits

I have chosen here to link the delays with the APS modules being implemented. The reason for doing this is that, even within individual country implementations, there will be different go-live dates for each module – by several months in this example. It then becomes easier to associate benefit build-up delays with go-live dates on the benefits timeline. However, this does introduce an over-simplification, as the build-up of financial contribution for each benefit class is, in reality, associated with the benefits within the class rather than with the modules that enable the benefits. We overcome this oversimplification partly by allowing for it in the assessment of the build-up rate associated with each module and partly in the way the benefits timeline is modelled in the financial spreadsheet (shown in Part 2). Anyway, I contend that the resulting financial model is at least as faithful to reality as the flat-rate case on which it is based. It would be possible to model the build-up effects in a more representative way but I do not consider that the extra effort required to do so would add value to the exercise.

Note that the build-up is shown quarter by quarter, even though NPV calculations are normally based on annual figures. Quarterly figures are needed to illustrate differences in the build-up of benefits in different implementation options and can readily be converted to annual figures for NPV calculations; again, you will see this in action in Part 2.

Rate and timing of tail-off of benefit value are less precise than build-up rates; they can be quoted as annual reductions in financial contribution and can be associated directly with the relevant benefits class rather than with the modules that enable the benefits within the class. This implied inaccuracy does not really matter as tail-off happens much later in the 10-year span than build-up effects and therefore has a much smaller impact on the NPV.

The business case

Most large companies will have mandated standards for programme and project governance and this will no doubt include the format of end-of-stage documentation such as the business case. There is therefore little point in including a format for the benefits section of a business case in the method; indeed, it is designed to be sufficiently flexible to fit with any form of corporate documentation. For those open to suggestion as to what this section should include, I offer the following pointers.

Apart from contributing to NPV calculations, it would be quite normal for the benefits section of the business case to include:

- A brief description of the benefits approach taken during the stage

- A textual summary highlighting the qualitative findings on benefits

- A table quantifying the steady-state financial contributions by region and benefits class

- A table or diagram showing the year-on-year non-discounted project financial profile for benefits over the NPV years

- A short description of the benefit work to be completed during the next stage, with resource implications

- Possibly the full benefits case in an appendix.

CHAPTER NINE

Benefit realisation

Introduction

This last chapter of Part 1 reflects a significant shift in the nature of project benefits work. Up to now you have been concerned primarily with the development of a benefits case from which a project's financial contribution could be derived in a way that supported both the selection of a preferred option and the building of business cases that enabled the project to proceed successfully through Feasibility and Define stage gates towards project delivery. You are now concerned with the techniques used to prepare for, and conduct, benefit tracking; the flavour changes from deriving a financial value to be contributed by project benefits to ensuring that this value contribution becomes a reality on the ground.

You have already engaged the business, particularly during the various stage benefits workshops, but now that involvement becomes more intimate. Also, for global implementations, the focus of attention moves from the regional headquarters to country clusters, individual countries and system implementation instances. As with benefit work conducted during the Feasibility and Define stages, much of the material we need is generated (at least during the Deliver stage of the project) during benefits workshops; again, at country or cluster level rather than the previous regional workshops. I will, as ever, cover the details of how these workshops are scheduled and conducted, and the format of their output, in Part 2.

Before starting to discuss the techniques associated with benefit tracking, I want to cover the appointment of benefits coordinators. This is a relatively short topic but it must be addressed and brought to a satisfactory conclusion before the other Deliver stage benefits activities start. You can also consider the appointment of benefits coordinators as the watershed between benefits definition and realisation.

Benefits coordinators

▶ Benefit coordinator role

Before we talk about the sort of people you need as benefits coordinators, and how to go about getting them, you need to understand what the role entails. Of course, as I suggested in Chapter 1, if the company has already established a permanent network of benefits coordinators then this section may be of passing interest only; however, it is in any event important for you as a benefits manager to understand the role.

In a large, global implementation there may have to be two levels of the role – regional and country. The demands of each of these roles are similar in some areas and different in others. I will start with the role of the country benefits coordinator and then describe the additional tasks of the regional benefits coordinator.

▶ Country benefits coordinator

The most important fact to remember is that benefits coordinators are not in any way responsible for the achievement of benefits (other than as project beneficiaries in their normal business roles) but they are the primary agents in ensuring that benefit tracking is conducted according to plan. To carry out this responsibility successfully, benefits coordinators need to be masters of the benefits tracking plan and the documents from which it was generated – the (in this case) country benefits case and the benefit risks register and control document. This responsibility defines the activities that the benefits coordinator must lead or support during preparation for, and execution of, a benefit tracking plan.

Preparation for benefit tracking

Preparation for benefit tracking will either be led by the country benefits coordinator, with guidance and support from the regional benefits coordinator, or will be undertaken by you (as the project benefits manager) with support from the benefits coordinators. Which, will depend largely on timing; you will need to conduct the first few country benefits workshops to establish the necessary generic procedures, templates and questionnaire formats. Once these have been properly tested and documented then the benefits coordinators in subsequent countries can be trained to take over these activities. Either way, it is essential that the benefits coordinator is closely involved with the production of documents needed to conduct benefits tracking. The activities are to:

- Organise and run a benefit risk workshop with local beneficiaries and, with the output, produce a benefit risk register and control document.

- Similarly organise and run a benefit tracking workshop and produce, as a result, the country benefits tracking plan.

- Discuss these outputs with the relevant country function leaders and get their support for any resources that will be needed to implement the tracking plan.

- Brief the beneficiaries who have been nominated for tracking activities (such as recording measurements or completing questionnaires) and ensure that they understand what is required of them and that they are willing to participate.

Conducting benefit tracking

Whether or not the benefit coordinators led or supported the preparation for tracking, they will definitely lead the actual conduct of tracking, albeit closely monitored by you if they are overseeing the tracking of benefits in the first country or two to be implemented. The activities they will lead are to:

- Monitor that tracking is taking place according to the tracking plan, collecting and collating measurement results and submitting summary tracking reports to country function leaders and the regional benefits coordinator.

- Ensure that remedial actions listed in the benefit risk control document are taking place and monitoring that they are having the desired effect.

- Identify issues from the tracking activities – either problems with tracking or indications that benefits are being blocked – and bring these to the attention of those responsible for their resolution.

- Own the country benefits case, benefit risk register and control document and benefit tracking plan and update them as necessary.

▶ Regional benefits coordinator

The regional benefits coordinator has three principle responsibilities:

- Act in the same way as country benefits coordinators for the tracking plan that applies to the regional headquarters.

- Collate regional tracking summary reports for submission to the regional transformation manager and appropriate regional function leaders.

- Monitor that the regional network of benefits coordinator is functioning properly and provide guidance and support to country benefits coordinators.

This list of responsibilities can cause some problems for the regional benefits coordinator because implementation of the project within the regional headquarters is often quite late in the regional implementation schedule; thus being asked to provide guidance to country benefits coordinators before having had personal experience of activities such as running benefit tracking workshops. The way round this difficulty is for the regional benefits coordinator to shadow the benefits manager when preparation for benefit tracking is being carried out in the first one or two countries in the region.

▶ Selecting benefits coordinators

What are the skills and characteristics needed to make a successful benefits coordinator? The main ones are ability to:

- Be organised, methodical, structured and tenacious in their work.

- Engage comfortably with, influence and be respected by their superiors and peers within the organisation.

- Be numerate and analytical.

- Understand well the area of the business covered by the section of the tracking plan for which they are responsible.

- Have the capacity to allocate 10 per cent of their working hours to the benefits coordinator role for a period of up to two years without adversely affecting their normal responsibilities.

As I suggested in Chapter 1, performance analysts make ideal candidates for the benefits coordinator role as they inherently share most of the characteristics listed above. Of course, this is not to say that only performance analysts can fill the role successfully but others with the required characteristics may be more difficult to find.

Having identified suitable candidates for the role, how can you secure their nomination? I suggest that the surest way is to secure the support of the relevant function leader, whether at country or regional level. This means that function leaders need to be briefed on their personal responsibilities for the achievement of benefits and the importance of the tracking mechanism to ensure that benefits are achieved. This briefing needs to be given at the beginning of the period in which the project engages with the country for delivery.

Opportunities for loss

Firstly, it really is important to differentiate the activities of managing opportunities for loss of project benefits from those of managing project risks. Why is this important? Partly because the two sets of activities are undertaken by different people in a different timescale; managing OfLs and the consequent risks to benefits release will probably continue long after the project has been successfully implemented and the project team has move on to other things. More importantly, it is essential that no one within or outside the project ever has the bright idea that these two activities might be merged; as I stated in Chapter 2, OfLs need to be managed outside the programme environment – at least initially. Finally, it is equally important that the objectives of the two sets of activities are understood to be distinctive and different by anyone concerned with the project and its assimilation into business life.

But what makes OfLs so different that they have to be dealt with separately? Well, project risks typically deal with those things that can get in the way of successful project delivery. OfLs can, however, be totally divorced from project risks and still be a threat even if the project is delivered perfectly. Figure 9.1 below provides an analogy:

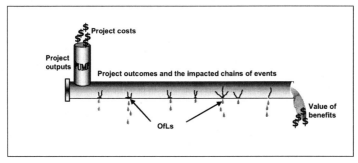

Figure 9.1 – The nature of opportunities for loss (OfLs)

In this analogy the pump represents the project outputs, fed with dollars, and the pipe represents the successive outcomes along the chains of linked events caused by the project to produce a stream of benefit value. If the pump and pipe are sound then, over a finite period of time, the stream of benefits will deliver financial contributions to the business that outweigh the dollars fed in – giving an excellent return on investment (ROI). If however the pipe is leaky, the benefit stream will reduce to a trickle and the project will not reach even an acceptable ROI. Many water companies, and their customers, will recognise this analogy only too well.

Continuing the analogy, the holes in the pipe causing the leaks are the OfLs; they are losses of benefit that will almost certainly happen if we do nothing about them. So, unlike project risks, the nature of OfLs is an erosion of a forecast outcome; project risks tend to be concerned more with project stoppages, overruns or overspends (I use the word 'tend' advisedly because I know there are many exceptions to this general rule). This part of the method is all about identifying the holes, dealing with those that can be plugged before the pump is turned on and carefully monitoring those remaining for leakage.

Identifying opportunities for loss

▶ Relationship between OfLs and risks to benefits

An OfL is a general risk to the achievement of a project's collective business benefits; there is not usually an exclusive mapping between an OfL and the risks to individual benefit. In fact, most OfLs will affect several benefits; albeit that the severity and likelihood of the impact of an OfL may vary from benefit to benefit. Conversely, a single benefit may potentially be impacted by more than one OfL; again, with various degrees of severity and likelihood. There may therefore be a many-to-many mapping between many of the OfLs and benefit risks associated with a particular project.

The mapping between OfLs and benefit risks will, in many cases, not be immediately obvious. The mapping has to be identified and documented as part of the OfL management process for two reasons:

- Knowing the number and value of benefits impacted by a specific OfL will support the assessment of that OfL's severity, which will help determine the way it should be managed.

- Knowing the number and severity of OfLs that may affect a specific benefit will help the assessment of whether that benefit should be actively tracked.

▶ Defining OfLs

The whole business of identifying OfLs, assessing their importance and deciding what to do about them is an inexact science, best achieved through brainstorming and consensus in a workshop environment. The way of doing this is covered in Part 2.

What does an OfL look like? When completed, it comprises the elements illustrated in Figure 9.2 overleaf:

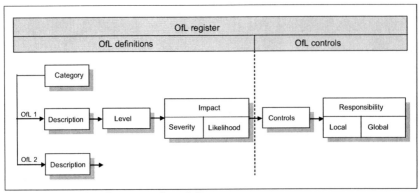

Figure 9.2 – The elements of an OfL

Points to note are:

- OfLs are grouped into categories that initially help the identification process and subsequently add structure that aids OfL management.

- In a global implementation, OfLs will have an impact at different levels (typically, regional and country levels). The 'Level' attribute defines which level or levels the OfL impacts.

- The elements to the left of the vertical dotted line are those that define the OfL and to right are the control elements associated with the OfL.

Examples of a list of OfL categories and OfL definitions within a category, respectively illustrated in Tables 9.1 and 9.2 opposite, are taken from a project to implement a business-wide data warehouse and management information system:

OfL categories
Usability and interpretation
Erosion of effort saved
Behaviours
Expectations & motivation
Change management, training & communications
Business policies
Limitations in implementation
Standards, mapping and data input
Maintenance

Table 9.1 – An example list of OfL categories

Srl	OfL	Level	Impact		
			Likelihood	Severity	
	Standards, mapping and data input				
29	Misinterpretation of MI data by users - through misunderstanding or insufficient accessibility of global standards	B	H/M	H/M-L	
30	Incorrect mapping due to misunderstanding of global standards, leading to erroneous data in data warehouse	B	L	H	

Table 9.2 – An example of OfL definitions within an OfL category

Coding in this table means:

- Level: C, country; R, region; B, both
- Impact: L, low; M, medium; H, high

The reason for the somewhat ambiguous impact assessment codes shown in the table is that the example is an extract from an OfL register that was collated from the outputs of three different functional OfL workshops. Many of the OfLs identified were common across the workshops but their assessed impact levels differed – possibly because of different viewpoints between delegates from, say, the sales and finance functions.

Readers who are familiar with standard risk management methods will recognize the format of Table 9.2. In fact, despite the distinct differences between the nature of project risks and OfLs, the methods of deriving them are very similar.

▶ Establishing OfL controls

Having identified OfLs, you need to decide what to do about them. Much will depend upon how threatening the OfL appears to be. Again, we use a traditional risk management technique to decide where to focus management attention. The technique is best explained graphically, as shown in Figure 9.3 below:

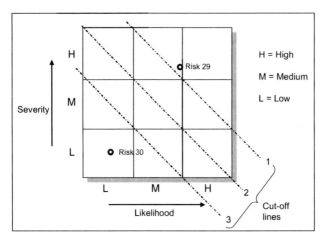

Figure 9.3 – OfL impact matrix

Each OfL, having been assessed for severity and likelihood, will have a position on the impact matrix. The two OfLs from Table 9.2 are shown here but, of course, a complete matrix would be populated with many more OfLs; so much so that it may be necessary to complete a separate matrix for each OfL category to avoid a too confused picture.

The matrix is then divided by a diagonal line; OfLs to the top and right of the line will be actively managed while those to the bottom and left of the line will be ignored, or just monitored. The position of this diagonal line is fairly arbitrary; three possible options are shown on the diagram as cut-off lines 1, 2 and 3. Which of these, or other, positions is selected depends on a number of factors:

- **The centre of gravity of the OfLs' positions on the matrix**. For instance, if most OfLs have been assessed as High or High–Medium in both severity and likelihood, then cut-off line 1, or higher, is likely to be chosen.

- **The number of OfLs identified and the organisation's capacity for OfL management**. The organisation may feel that it is capable of actively managing only, say, 25 OfLs in each country. In this case the diagonal will be slid into a position such that it isolates the top 25 risks.

- **The nature of the organisation**. Some organisations are more prudent and risk-averse than others. This factor may influence the positioning of the cut-off line; the more risk-averse the organisation the further to the left and bottom will be the cut-off line (perhaps cut-off line 3 or lower).

The outcome from this selection process will be a list of OfLs to be actively managed. Incidentally, this does not mean that OfLs not selected should be deleted; they should remain on the OfL register as they could become more significant at some later stage.

For each of the selected OfLs we need to identify one or more controls. These controls will differ in nature but normally would describe one of three types of action; that is, actions taken to:

- Pre-empt or minimise the possibility of the OfL occurring.

- Minimise the impact of the OfL, should it occur.

- Put metrics in place to monitor whether an OfL occurs; deferring a decision on how to cope with such an occurrence until it happens.

These possible control types are listed in order of preference; costs permitting, it will always be better to eliminate an OfL than just to watch for its occurrence.

Table 9.3 below continues the examples of Table 9.2 and Figure 9.3 and shows the controls for benefit risks serials 29 and 30.

Srl	OfL	Controls	Local responsibility	Central responsibility
	Standards, mapping and data input			
29	Misinterpretation of MI data by users – through misunderstanding or insufficient accessibility of global standard definitions	Strong user awareness programme for understanding of standards. Ensure training/induction covers standard definitions and where they can be found. Health warning on reports.	Project team (pre go-live) Functional leaders (BAU)	Global Standards Manager
30	Incorrect mapping due to misunderstanding of global standards; leading to erroneous entries in data warehouse	Need to establish single regional point of responsibility for data mapping integrity. Make sure organisation/ resource available to ensure reliable mapping of new data elements.	Data Manager	Global Standards Manager

Table 9.3 – Examples of OfL controls

The controls show what has been decided to be done to mitigate the OfL who is responsible for executing the control within the country and who has regional or global responsibility for the technical appropriateness of the control.

Benefit tracking plan

I have confidently claimed that one of the method's principal strengths is its ability to achieve full benefits release from project implementations; or at least a lot fuller than other methods are able to. There are three things needed to turn this claim into reality: the support of the local leadership team, carefully selected and well trained benefits coordinators, and a high-quality benefit tracking plan. To achieve such a tracking plan requires good inputs – the country benefits case and OfL register – and a carefully executed process. There are aspects of the tracking plan that can be quite difficult to resolve, perhaps encouraging a half-hearted approach to its completion. I hope to show you that such an approach will lead to ambiguity in the plan, severely jeopardising its ability to steer the tracking of benefits with the necessary degree of accuracy.

There are two main steps to developing a benefit tracking plan:

- Selecting the benefits to be tracked.
- Defining the way that each selected benefit will be tracked.

▶ Selecting benefits to track

The first obvious question is: why not just track all benefits? This is an option but, bearing in mind that we want to avoid a measurement regime that is too costly or intrusive, it is one that is rarely chosen; this is definitely a case where less is more. I will not bother to examine the opposite extreme of not measuring any benefits at all but instead suggest that the number of measurements should be kept to a minimum – just enough to meet the objectives of the exercise.

At this point we should remind ourselves what it is we are trying to achieve in developing and executing a benefits tracking plan. The objective is to monitor that the outcomes expected from project implementation, which will lead to the achievement of performance improvement and financial contribution, do actually happen in practice. The two telling phrases here are 'changes actually happen' and 'achievement of financial contribution'. You will still meet your objectives if you restrict your measurements to those benefits where there is some doubt that the outcome will happen and the change in question is a lever to material financial contribution.

In practice you will consider a few more factors when assessing whether to include a benefit in the tracking plan. The factors are:

- Risk level
- Value
- Doability
- Cost
- Intrusiveness

Taking account of all the factors listed can make the task of selecting benefits to track quite complex. You can reduce this complexity by recognising that some of the factors apply to the benefits while others apply to the measures associated with those benefits. Thus you can split the task into two steps; the first to determine which benefits should be tracked and the second to look at the suitability of the measures for each of these benefits.

First-pass selection of tracked benefits

For the first step you consider only the risks and value associated with each benefit to decide which are candidates for tracking. There is no need to be too precise in this exercise and you can continue to use the simple categorisation of Low, Medium and High in quantifying both risk level and financial contribution.

If you have made a good job of the OfL register, you will have identified all the potential hazards to achievement of benefits, with their levels of severity and likelihood; all you have to do is identify which OfLs impact which benefits. This is a painstaking exercise but it is not difficult. It needs to be carried out methodically rather than intuitively as the results showing which benefits are affected by the most and the least number of OfLs can be surprising. An acceptable way of limiting the exercise is to consider only those OfLs that have been selected for active management. It then becomes a simple judgment exercise to assess the combined impact of the OfLs that affect each benefit and set the risk level for that benefit.

The relative financial contribution of each benefit is assessed from the benefits case, as it applies to the country in question. In particular, you need to remember that, in some cases, an apparently high-value benefit actually generates most of its financial contribution from changes within the regional headquarters rather than at the country level.

Once you have completed this assessment of risk and financial contribution against each benefit it is a simple exercise to make an initial selection of benefits to be tracked. I suggest that, despite what I have said about minimising the scope of tracking, you should not be too cavalier at this stage in eliminating benefits from the list. However, any benefit with a low assessment for both financial contribution and risk level can be cut out and you can put a big question mark against benefits with a medium/low or low/medium assessment.

Selection of tracking measures

You next need to look at the proposed measures for each of the benefits provisionally selected for tracking. For each of these measures you will need to assess:

- **Type**. This is not really part of the assessment but a check that you know how the measure will be taken; whether from the system, some other automated KPI, a questionnaire or activity log or an interview. This knowledge will help you assess the measure against some of the other factors.

- **Appropriateness**. You need to satisfy yourself that the proposed metric will really measure the change that you need to monitor. This should be no more than a check, as this characteristic should have been addressed at the time that the benefits case was being finalised during the Define stage.

- **Doability**. Can the metric actually be measured in practice? Again, this should have been covered during the Define stage but it is sometimes difficult to find the appetite to think these aspects through during the earlier project stages. Also, Doability may be a local issue, varying from country to country. For instance, I have previously mentioned a metric of 'kilometre-tonne moved'; but in some countries, particularly where transportation is undertaken by less sophisticated third party carriers, these statistics are simply not available, however appropriate the measure.

The two attributes of Appropriateness and Doability are not graded, just given a simple 'yes' or 'no'. A measure needs to be both appropriate and doable to be considered further.

- **Cost**. This relates to the financial cost of establishing the measurement mechanism and taking measurements. I should say additional cost, because the cost of KPIs that are already in place in the organisation is not relevant.

- **Intrusiveness**. This assesses the amount of time and effort that beneficiaries need to put in to complete a measure. It is particularly relevant to measures that require the completion of questionnaires.

This can be difficult to assess for the first country, as the questionnaire may not yet have been designed; however, you should know enough about the questions to be answered to take a reasonable stab at whether intrusiveness will be high or medium (it is unlikely to be low in this case).

Once you have done the assessment for each proposed measure you can reassess the provisional list of benefits to be tracked. This reassessment may result in two types of changes:

- Benefits that were marginally required in the provisional tracking list can be eliminated if their measures are difficult (not appropriate or doable, or highly costly or intrusive).

- Where there are no, insufficient or impractical measures for benefits that are firmly required to be tracked, then new measures will need to be identified and defined.

Once the entire selection process is completed you will have a confirmed list of benefits to be tracked and measures that will be used to track them. This list forms the basis for development of the benefit tracking plan.

Developing the tracking plan

From a list of benefits to track, and measures to be used to track them, you need to develop a plan that will, standing on its own, steer the country benefit tracking exercise in a precise and unambiguous way. What do you need in the plan to achieve this degree of precision? Figure 9.4 opposite illustrates the components of a tracking plan for one benefit to be tracked:

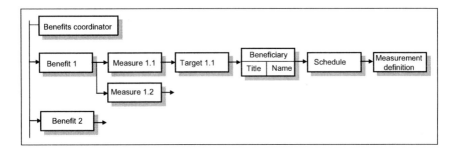

Figure 9.4 – Elements of a benefit tracking plan

Let us examine the meaning and purpose of each of these elements (other than the name of the benefit and its measures that we covered in the last section):

- **Benefits coordinators**. The name of the benefits coordinator is particularly important where a project needs more than one coordinator in each country. The example we have been using in this and the previous chapter – a global MI implementation – is a case in point where three benefits coordinators were needed in each country to cover the functional scope of the project. The position of the benefits coordinator's name in the list identifies which benefits he or she is responsible for.

- **Target**. This is the absolute figure, or percentage increase, that defines the amount by which the thing being measured is expected to change, as defined in the benefits case. It does not add anything useful to the tracking exercise but is required to help the benefits coordinator to analyze, from successive sets of measurements, whether benefits are being realised.

- **Beneficiary**. These columns list the title and name of all the individuals tasked with taking measurements, or overseeing the taking of measurements. For any one measure there may be one named beneficiary or several, depending on the nature of the measurement; this difference will have been identified in the benefits case. It is important to include both the beneficiary's title and name as it is more than likely that the individuals filling named roles will change over the tracking period.

- **Schedule**. This defines when each measurement is to take place. It will probably specify the period during which a baseline measurement is to be taken and then the frequency of subsequent measurements. It will not give an end date as this will depend very much on how soon the associated benefit is seen to have reached its full potential.

- **Measurement definition**. Human nature suggests that if there is a wrong way to interpret how to take a measurement then this will be taken by at least some of the beneficiaries. The definition therefore has to be sufficiently clear, precise and detailed that any potential ambiguity is avoided.

The workshop run to develop the tracking plan will need to concentrate its attention on three of the plan elements: the list of beneficiaries, tracking schedule and measure definition. Factors to consider for each of these elements are discussed in the following paragraphs.

▶ Selecting beneficiaries

The benefits case informs us whether single or multiple beneficiaries are associated with each measure, and from which day-to-day roles. If a single beneficiary is involved there should be little problem in identifying him or her by name, as the role will almost certainly be unique to one person. For instance, the beneficiary role might be the logistics manager, of which there is only one in each country.

Where the measure is associated with a role filled by several, or many, people, things get a bit more complicated. As I have said in several places, the aim is to involve as few a number of people as possible in the benefit measurement process while still achieving the objectives of benefit tracking. I want to look at three examples from the global MIS project that will illustrate the thought processes needed to achieve the right balance. The examples come from three different benefits of the MIS project:

- Reducing the effort needed to produce reports.

- Increasing gross margin by increasing up-selling to customers.

- Improving the management of discretionary spend.

Reducing the effort needed to produce reports

This benefit applies to the country performance analysts, of which there are about four per country (actually, the benefit also applies to some other in-country roles, but I want to keep the example simple). The measures for this benefit were: hours spent producing reports and analyzing operational performance; the number of instances of performance advice submitted to function leaders; the number of hours spent on overtime and staff satisfaction levels, monitored through the surrogate metric of sickness and absentee rates. All but the last measure required the beneficiary to complete logs covering a month of activity; once in the month before implementation and then on two further occasions over a period of six months. The decision here was that, as the sample was small and the measurement activity not difficult for the people involved, all four beneficiaries in each country would participate in the measurement exercise.

Increasing volumes through improved up-selling

This benefit results from the sales force having constant access to more up-to-date, comprehensive and granular data on their customers' buying patterns. This allows them to make insightful comparisons between customers, leading to better informed discussions with them on the benefits of taking a higher-value mix of products. There is an average of 60 sales staff in each country, divided into six sales teams; each team focusing on a different market sector. The measures for this benefit were: usage levels of the MI system by individual sales executives; the number of informed discussions with customers (by which was meant discussions that included the compelling case, provided by the MI system, for higher value product mixes as experienced by other similar customers); the value per volume of the total sales within each sales executive's customer base. In this company, 'intrusive' took on a whole new meaning when applied to the sales force, and it was always going to be difficult to gain their cooperation in benefit tracking. Of course, system usage and changes in customer buying patterns were metrics that could be produced automatically but there was a strong feeling that potential behaviour issues among the sales force could block this benefit and the benefit itself had significant financial value attached to it. The decision was taken to investigate the 'informed discussions with customers' measure through a questionnaire. A sample of 10 sales executives was chosen; six were the complete sales team considered most at risk, including the team leader, and the other four selected from the other sales teams. In this way, a reasonable readily managed sample was achieved and the intrusiveness contained.

Improving the management of discretionary spend

One of the benefits of the new MI system results from the availability of details for expense and similar discretionary budgets that are under the control of country function leaders. Previously, data on discretionary spend against budget had taken two or three months to come through but now the data is available to function leaders very soon after expense items are committed. The benefit is based on the belief that function leaders' confidence in the figures, and their ability to control them, will lead to expense budgets being more tightly set and cash from forecast under-spends released earlier for other use. The changes make cash management a more efficient process. The key to the benefit is the function leaders' perception and whether this would improve their attitude to hoarding cash in budgets. In this case, usage of the MI system discretionary spend reports could be monitored automatically and indications of an improvement in cash management would come from the established management account reporting system. However, it was felt important to understand whether any improvement in cash management was due to function leaders' confidence in the figures presented to them. Each country has four function leaders and it was decided to interview them all before, and four months after, the system was implemented to detect any change in attitude and behaviours. This was full sampling in a fairly intrusive way but was justified because of the importance of gaining the understanding and because the four interviewees in each country, although very senior, all had a personal interest in ensuring that benefits were achieved and seen to be achieved. Of course, because of these factors, the interviews had to be carefully structured to retain as much objectivity as possible.

What I have tried to show here is that the selection of beneficiaries to participate in benefits measurement is not necessarily a straightforward task and each instance needs to be thought through on its own merits. In every case it is important to weigh the degree of intrusion against the need for accurate and representative measurements.

▶ Setting schedules

As with beneficiary selection, there are two aspects to the task of scheduling measurements; one simple, one less so. The simple decision is whether or not a baseline measurement is required for the measures of each actively tracked benefit. In some cases the baseline will be known. For instance, if you have chosen to measure improved work-life balance by measuring changes in sickness rates, largely chosen because HR already record these figures at the level of granularity required (by named individual by month, say) then it is most likely that the baseline figures are already available; perhaps the only issue here being to ensure that the measurement definition is harmonised with the way that sickness levels are recorded by HR. As a general rule, measures that are met by existing KPIs will not need a special baseline measurement for benefit tracking purposes. In most other cases a specific baseline measurement will be needed – particularly where the target is represented by a percentage improvement on current performance, rather than an absolute figure. This should be taken before, and as close as possible to, the local project go-live date. Care needs to be taken when the measure in question takes a protracted period to complete; such as the month of activities to be logged by performance analysts to establish the number of hours spent producing reports and doing analysis. Ideally this measurement would be taken over the calendar month immediately preceding the go-live date.

It is more difficult to decide when to start post-implementation measurements and how often to repeat them. To do this sensibly you need to understand the rhythm of each change being measured. You already have some assessments to help in this understanding – the delays to benefits release that were forecast when completing the Define stage benefits timeline. To take this understanding further you need to extend these forecasts to produce an imaginary timeline profile for each change being measured and select suitable measurement points along this timeline. Take, for example, the forecast benefits release timeline shown in Figure 9.5:

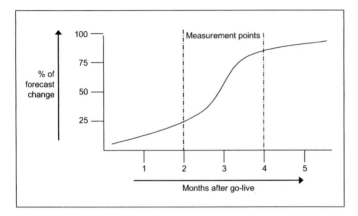

Figure 9.5 – Profile of a typical measured change over time

Here, it can clearly be seen that the two measurement points shown, at two and four months after go-live, would make good sense. Of course, you want to see what is happening as soon as possible but, if changes happen as forecast, any measure taken before the two-month point would be inconclusive. Similarly, a measurement after the four-month point would not register any significant further change. We will discuss what might happen in reality later in this chapter.

If this process of schedule setting is followed for each measure, you will find a number of timeline profiles of a similar shape but with quite different timeline scales (I am not suggesting that these profiles have to be actually drawn up but merely understood). A completed tracking plan will therefore have different measurement schedules for many of the measures included in the plan.

▶ Defining measures

The emphasis here is on 'defining', as the measures have already been identified and named. The definitions must be sufficiently precise that they are totally understandable and unambiguous to someone who has not been involved in their formulation. This does not necessarily require a lengthy description (although it might) as we shall see in the examples illustrated by Tables 9.4 to 9.6.

Benefit	Measure	Measurement definition
Reduce debtor days	Number of debtor days	Debtor days calculated by the absorption method

Table 9.4 – Example 1: A measure definition referring to an existing company standard

In this example, the only potential confusion was that the company had a number of ways of measuring debtor days. However, they had all already been defined for global use by the finance department. The tracking plan had therefore merely to refer to the relevant definition to avoid ambiguity.

Benefit	Measure	Measurement definition
Improve price management to optimise customer margins	Number of optimising actions taken as a result of availability of new MI	See sales force questionnaire

Table 9.5 – Example 2: A measure definition referring to a questionnaire

Here you are looking for a subjective response; which of the beneficiaries' pricing optimisation actions have been prompted by better data from the MI system? The tracking plan refers to a questionnaire that has been drawn up for the selected beneficiaries.

Benefit	Measure	Measurement definition
Better focused sales effort to problem customers	Number of wavering customers	Quarterly sales by customer down by 10% or more compared with the same quarter in the previous year

Table 9.6 – Example 3: A measure defined for the tracking plan

Here the problem was that 'wavering customers', although a term understood by the sales force, had not been previously defined. The term had therefore to be defined specifically for the tracking plan. The definition was framed in a way designed to highlight customers whose buying performance was declining rather than showing seasonal blips.

Questionnaires for benefit tracking

It is likely that a number of the measures within a tracking plan will require personal information from beneficiaries. The proportion of such measures, compared with those where the measurement is an existing KPI or is system-generated, will depend on the type of project. Certainly in an MIS project, where many of the benefits rely on beneficiaries acting in a different way because of the information now available to them, a significant proportion of measures will need the most intrusive type of beneficiary involvement. Given that one of your aims is to conduct the benefit tracking exercise in an as non-intrusive way as possible, you need to find a way of getting this information from beneficiaries in a straightforward and painless manner that still remains objective, consistent and unambiguous.

An answer to this challenge is the questionnaire, which will certainly ensure consistency and, if carefully designed and administered, can also avoid ambiguity and at least minimise subjectivity and intrusiveness. There are a few different types of questionnaire:

- General questionnaires
- Activity logs
- Decision logs

- Targeted questionnaires

Depending on circumstances, some of these questionnaire types can be combined into one.

▶ General questionnaire

These are questionnaires designed to elicit perceptions on a system's usability and usefulness; so called because they are not targeted at any specific role or group of roles but can be applied to any beneficiary. They are not usually designed to get responses on a specific measure in the tracking plan and are, perhaps, not of great value on their own. However, they can provide very useful diagnostic tools when combined with one or more of the other types of questionnaire.

▶ Activity and decision logs

Logs seek some daily (or possibly weekly) information over a period; typically a month. Thus one or more beneficiaries are asked to make an entry on each day of the logging period in one or more data rows. An example of part of one of these logs is shown in Table 9.7 below.

Activity (hours)	Mon 18	Tue 19	Wed 20	Thu 21	Fri 22	Sat 23	Sun 24	Mon 25	Tue 26	Wed 27	Thu 28	Fri 29	Sat 30	Sun 31	Mon 1	Tue 2	Wed 3	Thu 4	Fri 5
Data gathering																			
Data analysis and preparation of reports																			
Investigation of anomalies																			
Total hours spent in data-related activities	??	??	??	??	??	??	??	??	??	??	??	??	??	??	??				
Total hours worked	??	??	??	??	??	??	??	??	??	??	??	??	??	??					
Number of hours overtime																			

Table 9.7 – Example of part of an activity log

Here, performance analysts are asked to record the number of hours spent daily on producing reports and undertaking analysis. The reason that a period of a month is chosen is that the reporting cycle is repeated monthly. With this type of questionnaire it is essential to include a carefully worded instruction sheet.

It is helpful to all concerned if this type of questionnaire can be delivered electronically and the completed questionnaires returned in the same way. Apart from providing an easy delivery mechanism, electronic questionnaires can more easily be collated and can incorporate a degree of validation. So, for instance, if a beneficiary attempts to enter a value outside the possible range of answers, the error can be trapped and corrected at source. It is not a difficult task to build such validation into questionnaires and logs built in modern spreadsheet applications.

▶ Targeted questionnaires

Sometimes there is no avoiding a measure that is based on personal perceptions; we have already discussed one such measure, which concerned the confidence levels felt by function leaders, in the expense expenditure reports presented to them. At the time, it was decided to probe the changes in confidence levels, and how they altered behaviours in the management of discretionary budgets, in a series of before and after interviews. The solution could just as easily have been to issue targeted questionnaires or to combine questionnaires with interviews. There are pros and cons to both approaches. The targeted questionnaire may appear to the subjects to be a more remote (and uncaring) way of getting the information from them. However, it has the advantage of allowing careful composition in an attempt to minimise subjectivity and inconsistency from the information received.

The term 'targeted' applies more to the recipients of a questionnaire that to its content. It may well be that there is a requirement to extract information on more than one measure from the same set of beneficiaries. If the scheduling of these different measures can be harmonised, there is an advantage in combining the questions for all such measures into one targeted questionnaire.

I have suggested more than once that careful drafting of questionnaires can avoid subjective answers, even when the questions concerned involve highly personal matters such as personal confidence levels. How do you do this?

The simple answer is to avoid asking the direct, isolated question. A deeper look at the example above should help here. Take the question:

> What is your confidence level, on a scale of one to 10, in the monthly expense account figures presented to you?

Answers to this question would inevitably be inconsistent, highly subjective and generally unhelpful. To improve this state of affairs, you first need to understand what might be undermining function leaders' confidence in the management accounts. Is it that figures might be fundamentally inaccurate or that they are so out of date at the time of presentation that they cannot support sensible budget management? Assuming that the latter is the issue, the question itself could more usefully be split and rephrased:

> Question 1. How useful do you find monthly management accounts as a tool to help you manage your discretionary budgets?

> Question 2. Is there any way in which the management account statement could be improved to help you manage your discretionary budget more closely?

Note that we have not asked the question:

> When do you receive management account statements and how up to date are they?

This is information that we know, or can find out from other sources, and to ask the question of the function leaders would be both unnecessary and irritating. We should only ask those questions that we cannot get answers to in any other way (such as personal perceptions).

There is no reason why those questioned should not be prompted to ensure that they answer the right question. For instance, in this example, a statement could precede the questions above in which the expected benefit – tighter discretionary budget setting and earlier release of uncommitted cash in a forecast under spend situation – is explained.

Analyzing tracking results

At the moment of go-live, with the project implemented, tested and handed over to the business, work begins to ensure that project benefits are realised. There are three main aspects to this work:

- Managing risks to benefits by ensuring that benefit risk controls are being executed.

- Watching for trigger points that might require a review of the benefits case.

- Conducting benefit tracking and analysis and initiating remedial action where necessary.

The first two bullets describe relatively mechanistic activities. Similarly, the conduct of benefit tracking is largely an issue of procedures and reporting formats that I shall cover in some detail in Part 2. This section focuses on the one remaining activity that needs some discussion on techniques; analysis of the results of tracking.

When tracking measurements are returned to the benefits coordinator they will be viewed within a very precise context; that is, set against their associated baseline measurements and the rate of change compared with that expected on the forecast profile of change against time. This is probably not easy to visualise; so let us look at an example from the MI system project.

I will use the example of the benefit to reduce the effort needed to produce reports. You will recall that the two most direct changes of this benefit were reduction in the hours per month spent by performance analysts in producing reports and a consequent increase in the hours they spend undertaking analysis. It was forecast during the Define stage that these changes would start to happen in the month after go-live but that they could take up to six months to reach full value. And, of course, the baseline and final figures for both forecast changes were known. In fact, the start and end figures were different for different analysts (particularly between those based in countries and those in the regional headquarters), so I shall confine the example to country-level benefits, where the two timeline profiles looked like those in Figure 9.6 below:

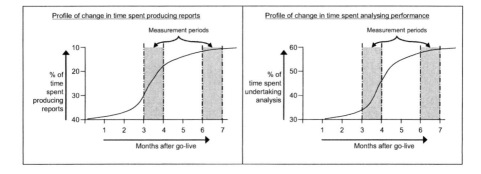

Figure 9.6 – Profiles and measurement points for direct changes from the benefit 'Reducing time spent producing reports'

The two profiles are similar in shape, albeit with different vertical measurement scales. The main difference between them is a lag of about a month, with increased time spent on analysis occurring after the reduction in time spent producing reports.

When the benefit tracking plan was developed during the Deliver stage, it was decided that the post-implementation measurement months for both these changes would start three and six months after project go-live. Arguably, the change associated with reducing hours spent producing reports could have been measured one month earlier but it was decided to harmonise both measurements so that they could be included on the same activity log, thus reducing intrusiveness.

When completed logs were returned at the end of month 3, the benefits coordinator expected the average time spent producing reports to have dropped from 40 per cent to about 25 per cent and the average time spent undertaking performance analysis to have increased from 30 per cent to about 40 per cent. What they actually found was that time spent producing reports had only dropped, on average, to 32 per cent and that there had been no significant increase in the time spent undertaking analysis.

So what can you deduce from these results? There are two basic causes for results such as these, best illustrated in Figure 9.7 below:

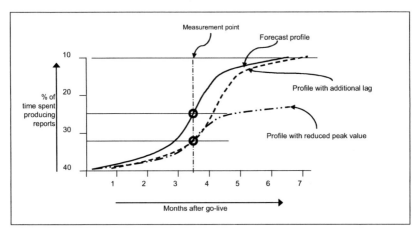

Figure 9.7 – Possible causes of poor measurement results

What the diagram shows is that a worse-than-expected result may be because the change being investigated is happening slower than had been forecast or because the peak value of the change caused by the project is going to be lower than that forecast. Either of these anomalies may be because of incorrect target setting and timeline profiling during the Define and Deliver stages or, more likely, because some unexpected factor is blocking either the rate or extent of change (or both).

The situation was sufficiently threatening to the release of forecast benefits that the beneficiaries concerned – primarily the performance analysts and their senior management 'customers' – were interviewed, even though to do so was not included in the benefit tracking plan. Findings from these interviews were:

- The performance reports that had been designed by the project team did not meet all the needs of senior management. The analysts were consequently spending more time than forecast designing new report formats, thus reducing the saving in forecast time.

- Senior managers were not personally accessing the system but were asking their analysts to run off reports on their behalf, thereby further eroding the expected time saving.

- Senior managers were occupying a further significant proportion of analysts' time in asking them to investigate further where they had seen points of interest in the reports presented to them. Again, this drilling down into the data warehouse was something that senior managers were expected to do themselves.

The first point was not considered to be serious, as it was a transitory blockage and the new reports designed by the analysts were ported to subsequent country implementations. The second two points were considered to be more serious as they could have become permanent issues and, interestingly, had been identified as potential risks in the benefit risk register. The problem was overcome with further application training for senior country managers and mentoring from their regional functional directors. In this example, the change measurements provided an early indication of what turned out to be a blockage to a correctly targeted benefit and led to successful remedial action to remove the blockage to benefits release.

CHAPTER TEN

Overview and initial work

Introduction

In Part 1 of the book we discussed the advantages of a rigorous benefits management environment and the principles and techniques employed when developing the benefits case and the benefits tracking plan, and using the latter to steer full release of project benefits and consequential financial contributions to the business.

Now, in Part 2, I will take you on a step-by-step journey along the end-to-end benefits management process; planning and applying the method in a way that has been found to be most effective in practice. In doing so, I shall introduce the various formats and templates used to develop and present the method's deliverables and will suggest some strategies for negotiating the trickier aspects of benefits workshop facilitation. Supporting all of this, I shall use examples adapted from the benefits management workings of two real global projects.

In short, Part 1 was mainly about the 'what' and 'why' of benefits management; this part is all about the 'how' and 'when'.

Overview

Before I can give you a feel for how the end-to-end benefits management process is executed in practice, you need to be clear about how the process is keyed to the life cycle of the project it is supporting.

Project life cycles vary from business to business and, within a single business, from project to project. Variations occur because businesses have different project governance practices and because life cycles need to be tailored to a certain extent to the type of project; for instance, the life cycle for introducing a bespoke IT system may not be appropriate for an IT package implementation.

For the purposes of this book I will adopt the project life cycle shown below.

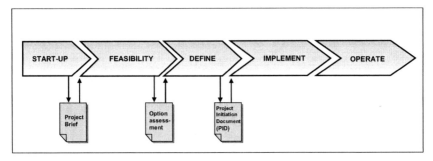

Figure 10.1 – Generic project life cycle

The main project activities within each the stages of this generic life cycle are:

Start-up

A short, minimally resourced stage in which:

- The project objectives, high-level benefits and fit with the organisation's strategy are clarified and communicated.

- The outline approach that the project will take to deliver its objectives and benefits is decided

- The initial project team is selected and engaged.

- The Feasibility stage is planned.

Feasibility

- The approach, objectives and benefits of the project are defined to a point where a realistic assessment can be made of its viability in terms of meeting a real business need, soundness of approach and delivery of a positive ROI.

- The high-level OfLs – the near-certain potential blockages to benefit achievement – are identified and start to be managed.

- The different options for project implementation are assessed in terms of costs, benefits and risks and a preferred option is selected.

- Plans for the Define stage are completed and costed.

- An appraisal of the proposed investment is made.

Define

- The selected option is designed in outline and its implementation is planned and costed in detail.

- Any contentious elements of the technical implementation are resolved.

- Project benefits are defined and the forecast financial contribution of the project is derived to a high degree of accuracy.

- A final business case is developed and submitted for approval.

Implement

- The solution is designed in detail and third party components procured.

- Any system development, build or configuration is completed and tested.

- New processes are designed in full and tested in a laboratory environment.

- The project is installed in the business environment.

- Project deliverables are user tested and handed over to the business.

The benefits management method described in this book fits naturally into this project stage structure but can be flexed easily to accommodate variations in the project life cycle (changes in the number or composition of project stages).

▶ Principal activities

Let us look again at the main benefits management activities in each stage and draw some conclusions from these. These stage-related activities are shown in Figure 10.2

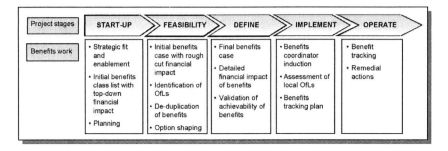

Figure 10.2 – Principal benefits management activities over time

Points to note from the diagram are:

- Prior to start-up, the programme and project are first shaped using benefit-led methods (Gerald Bradley [2]). Then there is some useful preparatory work to be done in Start-up; particularly identification of the strategic value drivers for the project and initial thoughts on benefits classes. It may even be possible to make an initial allocation of potential project financial impact by benefits class; albeit that the financial contribution of the project will have been derived by some top-down methodology.

- Until the Define stage gate has been passed, there is no guarantee that the project will be implemented. There is therefore a principle of the method, similar to one applied generally to project management, not to do any more work in each project stage than is necessary to achieve the immediate objectives of that stage, thus avoiding unnecessary expenditure. The benefits management activities of the Feasibility and Define stages are similar – particularly within the benefits workshops of both stages. However, to meet different stage objectives, the work is broader in scope during Feasibility and deeper in detail during Define.

- The financial contribution of the project to the business is definitively declared by the end of the Define stage and need not be revisited unless some event triggers the need for a review of the business case. Work from the Implement stage onwards focuses on ensuring that the forecast project benefits are achieved in practice.

▶ Resources

In Part 1 I described a possible organisational structure to manage project benefits and the people needed within that structure. Deployment of key resources to manage benefits across the project stages is shown in Figure 10.3:

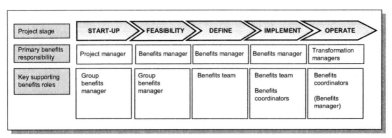

Project stage	START-UP	FEASIBILITY	DEFINE	IMPLEMENT	OPERATE
Primary benefits responsibility	Project manager	Benefits manager	Benefits manager	Benefits manager	Transformation managers
Key supporting benefits roles	Group benefits manager	Group benefits manager	Benefits team	Benefits team Benefits coordinators	Benefits coordinators (Benefits manager)

Figure 10.3 – Deployment of key benefits management resources over time

Points to note are:

- It is quite likely that resourcing limitations for the Start-up stage will not allow for the appointment of a benefits manager (remember, 'Benefits Manager' is my shorthand for the project business change manor in his or her benefits management role), in which case the project manager will probably take on initial responsibility for benefits management. If the project is initiated within an ongoing programme, and a Group Benefits Manager has been appointed, then this latter will need to provide the project manager with advice and support on the benefits management method and its application.

- It is essential that a benefits manager be appointed by the beginning of the Feasibility stage. Unless the project is very large, the benefits manager may well have to conduct benefits management activities without a supporting team. Again, if the project benefits manager is new to the role he or she may need a significant amount of mentoring from the Group Benefits Manager, where one exists.

- If the project is large enough to warrant a team to support the benefits manager (the 'team' might be just one extra person) it would be useful to have during Feasibility but it will be needed most during the Implement stage of the project. The team should be recruited in the Define stage to allow it to be trained in time to contribute fully to the various benefits workshops.

- The benefits coordinators must be recruited during the Implement stage so that they can participate in the workshops run to develop benefits risk registers and benefits tracking plans (indeed, there may well be an advantage in having regional benefits coordinators in place during the Define stage).

- I have suggested that the transformation manager in each region should take the lead in benefits management during Operate, when the primary activities are benefits risk management, benefits tracking and consequent remedial action. If such a role does not exist then someone else from the business should be appointed by the appropriate leadership team. This having been said, benefits coordinators are the primary focus for conducting benefits management activities and executing benefits tracking plans during the Operate stage.

▶ Examples used in Part 2

I want to reintroduce the two example projects that I will use from now until the end of the book. The first is the supply chain project, which included implementation of an advanced planning system (APS); this project will provide the examples in the chapters of Part 2 on the Start-up and Feasibility stages benefits work. The second example is the global MIS implementation project, which I shall use for the chapters covering the Define, Implement and Operate stages. Please remember that these were complex, global projects in a complex organisation; for this reason the benefits management organisation and processes were heavier than they would be for more straightforward projects.

Here is a summary of the first of these examples that I shall be using over the next few chapters. The company that wanted to introduce an APS system had previously grown through acquisitions and had, more recently, extracted supply chain installations and processes from the regional business units, which were primarily focused on marketing and sales, and created a separate global supply chain business unit. The final phase of these changes was to take the opportunities presented by the new global supply chain unit and transform it into a world-class part of the organisation. The supply chain transformation was a change programme with a number of elements; one of the most significant was the radical improvement of supply chain planning processes.

▶ Initial work

The rest of his chapter describes the initial benefits work within a project. This includes:

- Benefits work during Start-up
- Planning the Assess stage benefits activities

Start-up

The Start-up stage of the project is a metaphorical 'wet finger in the air' to establish whether or not an idea for business improvement is worth developing into a formal project. It will most likely have the following characteristics:

- **Short duration**. Three months is typical for this stage of even potentially large, global projects.

- **Minimal resourcing**. It is unusual for there to be more than three full-time project team members and very rare for one of them to be a benefits management specialist.

- **Self contained**. It is unlikely that the business community will become involved in the project at this stage to any significant extent.

These characteristics preclude any thoughts of attempting to derive initial project benefits using bottom-up methods. The forecast project financial contribution presented at the end of the stage will almost certainly come from vendor assessments or some form of industry benchmarking and may have a perceived accuracy no greater than plus or minus 50 per cent.

Despite these limitations there is some useful project benefits work that can be done which will enhance the stage deliverables and help the Feasibility stage benefits work get off to a good start. Of course, this presupposes that there is a member of the Start-up project team familiar with the benefits management method.

▶ Identifying strategic drivers

Up to now, when discussing the business value derived from project benefits, I have been talking exclusively about financial contribution; and of course, financial contribution is paramount when assessing the viability of a project in pure financial investment terms. However, a project may have value in a way that transcends direct financial payback if it is an enabler of the organisation's strategy. It may not be possible to attribute a financial value to strategic enablement; no matter – a strong contribution to an important business strategy can tip the balance in a project's favour when it is showing an indifferent ROI. Consider an example from another project in the panel below.

An international manufacturing company initiated a project to implement globally a customer relations management (CRM). The project had a payback only after five years of operation, which would normally not have been good enough to gain approval for implementation. However, the company saw its future development being largely dependent upon becoming world class in customer service. Introduction of a CRM system was considered an essential element of this strategy; the project went ahead.

The first thing needed in the process of establishing the project as a strategic enabler is a thorough understanding of that strategy. Not just the top-line strategic objectives but also an understanding of the capabilities needed to underpin the strategy.

Let us examine the CRM project further.

The company recognised that its position in the market was determined by its positioning, relative to the competition, on the offer triangle, shown in Figure 10.4:

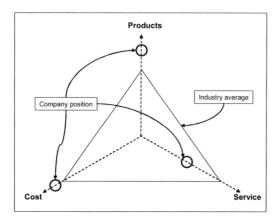

Figure 10.4 – A company's positioning on the offer triangle

The company had excellent products, sold at a premium price but with a worse than average track record for customer service. There was strong market pressure on the premium prices and the company decided that it needed to improve its customer service to a world-class standard to be able to preserve its pricing levels; thus the importance of the strategy.

The company's central strategy department had developed an understanding of the elements that were critical to the achievement of world-class customer service and illustrated this on a hierarchical capability diagram; part of which is shown in Figure 10.5 overleaf.

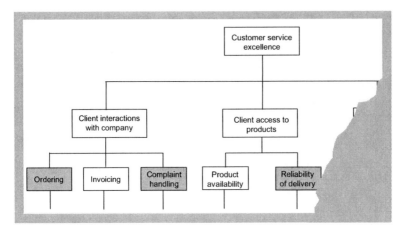

Figure 10.5 – Capability hierarchy diagram for customer service excellence

The point of the diagram is to illustrate all the capabilities that have to be in place to achieve excellence in customer service and to highlight those capability areas that need to be materially improved before the sought degree of excellence can be achieved.

The question then is:

To what extent would a CRM system contribute to one or more of the underperforming capabilities; as a supporting tool or as an essential enabler?

The answer to this question may not be immediately obvious. CRM as a supporting tool (which could be interpreted as merely 'nice to have') is not difficult to establish, but to claim that it is an essential enabler means that it is either the only solution to achieving the capability, or that it is the one of two or more options that is significantly more viable than the others.

In this example the hierarchical capability diagram has only been developed down to two levels of detail; typically, there may be four or five levels to a fully developed diagram. The CRM system was seen to be a significant contributor to many of the activities that fed into the second-level customer service capabilities shown on the diagram. In aggregate it was considered that a CRM system was an essential enabler to improving customers' experience in the ordering and complaint handling processes.

One of the Start-up stage activities will be to establish whether or not the project is a strategic enabler, as described above. This will require serious dialogue between whoever is conducting project benefits management at this stage and the company's strategy department.

▶ Identification of benefits classes

There is an element of 'chicken and egg' in defining benefits classes and their benefits. It can be argued that it is not possible to go firm on benefits classes until all the project benefits have been identified and classified by business process and financial category, which is unlikely to be achieved until well into the Feasibility stage. While this is true, there is still value in creating structure in the benefits work by establishing an initial benefits class list as early in the project as possible; with the proviso that this list is not considered fixed until much later in the project. Apart from providing structure, going through the process of defining benefit classes will help to provide some validation of the top-down benefits case and will begin to establish, at least at a high level, the essential link between project scope and contribution to the business strategy and financial improvement.

So how do you do this? To start with, it should not be difficult to block out the main business processes that will be affected and to identify the financial buckets into which the project will contribute value. In fact, the top-down benefits methodology, whether a vendor assessment or industry benchmarking exercise, should provide this level of detail.

Going back to our supply chain example, the company had engaged a subject matter expert and a pre-sales consultant from an APS vendor to assist in shaping the project in outline, based on a perceived need to improve all of its supply chain planning processes. The following factors helped to define the scope of the project and its likely sources of value:

- The company's supply chain strategy, which sought to improve responsiveness to customers while taking costs out of the supply chain.

- A comparison between the company's supply chain KPI figures and what was achievable within the industry (benchmarks provided by an industry association via the subject matter expert).

- An understanding of the extent to which the implementation of a global APS, coupled with revitalised planning processes, might be able to improve the company's current supply chain performance; again, information provided by the two external consultants.

A mapping between the aspirations of the supply chain strategy (which itself supported the company strategy), the weaker-performing supply chain KPIs and the opportunities that an APS implementation would provide indicated that the objectives of the project would be to:

- Improve customer satisfaction through faster and more accurate order promising and more reliable and responsive product delivery.

- Reduce the cost of goods sold through more efficient planning and scheduling of raw material purchasing, manufacturing and logistics.

- Reduce inventory levels.

Note that these primary project objectives were all described in high-level benefit terms. It therefore became a very simple exercise to translate these objectives into benefits classes. Similarly, the top-down forecast financial contributions were divided into the same categories. So, again, it was a simple exercise to provide an initial estimate of the financial contribution of each benefit class. The result of the exercise is shown in Table 10.1 opposite:

Benefit class	Asia Pacific	Americas	Europe	Rest of World	Total
Improve customer satisfaction	$1.3m	$1.8m	$1.7m	$0.8m	$5.6m
Improve procurement effectiveness	$9.0m	$9.0m	$12.0m	$7.0m	$37.0m
Improve manufacturing efficiency					
Improve logistics efficiency	$1.0m	$0.6m	$1.0m	$0.3m	$2.9m
Total annual value	$11.3m	$11.4m	$14.7m	$8.1m	$45.5m
Reduce inventory (one-off)	$8.0m	$1.9m	$6.0m	$6.1m	$22.0m

Table 10.1 – Example initial forecast financial contribution, by benefit class

I realise that the example I have used, and the way I have described it, may make it look like a trivial exercise to derive a Start-up benefit class list with associated financial contributions. Indeed, in this case it was not a difficult exercise, but only because:

- The strategy was defined and current weaknesses were understood.

- The art of the possible was sought from experienced external sources.

- The scope of the project was developed and described in high-level benefit terms.

These factors are by no means always in place, particularly the last bullet; but they should be.

▶ Planning for the next stage

Whether or not the activities to identify links to the company strategy and to define an initial list of benefit classes are undertaken in Start-up, one activity that must take place is to plan for benefits work to be done during the Feasibility stage. This planning is essential because project governance will require a good estimate of the time and resources needed to undertake Feasibility before it gives the go-ahead for the project to proceed to that stage. Planning for the benefits work is just part of the overall project planning needed for the next stage.

The planning needs to be about more than just time and money. The first, essential, element for ongoing benefits work will be to nominate, appoint and train the project benefits manager. Another important early planning activity will be to provide the business with advanced warning, at least in outline, of the need for its involvement in interviews and workshops.

As the newly appointed benefits manager, you will be in good shape for the Feasibility stage if you:

- Have had adequate induction into the responsibilities of the benefits manager role and into details of the method.

- Are aware of the strategic value of the project to the business.

- Understand the initial scope and objectives of the project and have a list of benefit classes, derived from the objectives, each with an initial estimate of financial impact.

- Have an outline plan for the benefits work to be undertaken during Feasibility, for which the need for benefits workshops has been notified to, and agreed in principle by, the business units that will be the project's clients.

Initial Feasibility planning considerations

The Feasibility stage encompasses the most complex part of the benefits management method – particularly for global projects within a programme of change and involving implementation of a modular system (as in the example we are using). For this reason, the activities to be completed have to be carefully planned. The Feasibility stage of the project may be fairly lengthy – six to nine months is typical – but this time will seem very cramping for all benefits management activities if planning is not completed very soon after the stage begins.

Before planning can get very far, there are some decisions that you have to make. These are:

- How much detail should be included in the benefits case?

- Should a strawman benefits case be drafted and, if so, should the business be involved in its creation?

- The extent of benefits workshops?

- Which supplementary activities need to be included?

▶ Detail in the benefits case

A fully completed benefits case will need to have been developed by the end of the Define stage of the project but for Feasibility you can, and perhaps should, take some short cuts. Let us look again at the elements contained in a regional business case, illustrated in Figure 10.6.

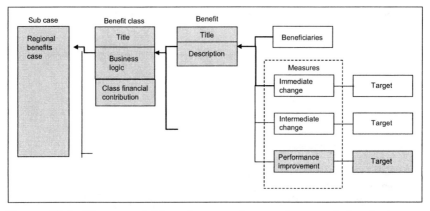

Figure 10.6 – The essential benefits case elements for completion during Feasibility

I have highlighted those elements that are essential to complete during Feasibility. This is the data that you need to allow you to de-duplicate benefits with other projects, support the option selection process and derive a project financial contribution to an accuracy of within plus or minus 30 per cent. This is not to say that the remaining elements should be totally ignored; indeed, as I have previously suggested, it may be necessary during benefits workshops to discuss targets for the project outcomes in order to get close enough to the performance improvement targets that you must set. However, you need not normally fret about, or allow specific time for, their completion during this stage.

▶ Strawman or not?

This is not such a simple question to answer; I have experienced projects that have and have not included a strawman benefits case and there are arguments for both approaches. What are the factors affecting the decision? I consider that there are four, although your circumstances may suggest others:

- **Time available.** There is more to the development of a strawman benefits case than mere drafting. It will usually require input from the business; possibly obtained through questionnaire-based correspondence. So the whole process might be to design, send out and receive back completed questionnaires and then analyse the responses and draft the strawman. This can take up to three months; perhaps half of the time available during Feasibility. There is an alternative approach, which is to draft the strawman document without business input – at least from the regional business units. Whether or not this is acceptable will depend on the use to which the strawman will be put.

- **Use of the strawman.** If the strawman is to be used merely as an input to the benefits workshops later in the stage, it may not be justifiable to involve the business in its creation. If, on the other hand, the strawman will be used as a tool for conducting benefit de-duplication with other projects (prior to the holding of workshops) then it will almost certainly require business input to give it the necessary authority.

- **Readiness of the business.** We must remember that people in the business are busy. You are already planning on keeping a dozen or so members of each region occupied attending interviews and workshops over a two-week period later in the stage. Completion of questionnaires will probably involve fewer people; nevertheless, a busy region may just not have the capacity or appetite to involve itself in both activities and running the workshops is unquestionably the more important activity of the two.

- **Character of the workshops**. I have already said that there are cases for and against using a strawman benefits case as an input to the benefits workshops. The most significant factor is the time that the business will make available. If two full-day workshops are scheduled, you can probably start the proceedings with a blank sheet but two half-day workshops would almost certainly not allow completion of all necessary work without the help of a strawman. There is also the nature of the delegates to consider. Will they prefer to develop something from scratch or review and revise something done earlier? And if the latter, would you uncover all the potential benefits and gain sufficient regional buy-in? This may be difficult to assess at the beginning of the stage, although an understanding of general company and regional cultures should help. Personally, I feel that the ideal situation is to start the workshop with an almost blank sheet but to have the strawman available in case the delegates run out of ideas.

Whatever the decision (no strawman, internal project strawman or strawman with business input) it needs to be made early as it will significantly impact detailed stage planning.

▶ Extent of workshops

You need to decide how extensive the regional workshops should be. I am assuming here the situation of our example; a global project involving four separate regional benefits cases. The same consideration would need to be given to any project that has to complete more than one benefits case. The possible options are to hold workshops in all four regions or hold them in one or two regions and extrapolate the results to the remaining regions. There is no doubt that, to capture regional differences accurately and to ensure regional business buy-in, the best solution is to hold workshops in all participating regions. It is likely to be considerations of time and cost that will restrict workshop coverage but the correct attitude is to do as many workshops as possible rather than to do as few as you can get away with.

▶ Need for supplementary activities

The activities concerned are benefit de-duplication and option modelling. I have called them 'supplementary' purely because not all projects will need them. Our example project does.

The decision on whether to include the activity of de-duplication of benefits with those of other projects will almost certainly not be in your hands but will be an activity directed by the programme office. Assuming that it has to be included, you will need to coordinate with the programme office to ensure that the activity is scheduled at a time that fits with the flow of other project benefits management activities. If we are talking about a programme-centric benefits management organisation, in which you are the benefits manager for all projects in a tranche, then de-duplication will be addressed routinely during the tranche (rather than project) benefits workshops and there will be no need for separately scheduled de-duplication activities before the workshops are held.

Option modelling is required when the options being considered include different partial system implementations; whether by geography, system module or both. If this is a requirement then time must be allowed, after the regional benefits workshops have been completed, to develop the additional granularity in the benefits financial model needed to support this type of option selection.

Planning the Feasibility stage

Having made the necessary preliminary decisions, you are now ready to plan Feasibility benefits management work in detail. To do this you need to:

- Identify all the activities needed to produce the stage benefits management deliverables, and the dependencies between them.

- Assess the time and resources needed to complete each activity.

- Schedule each activity on a timeline plan, allowing for some contingency.

- Check that the plan fits into the total time available and is acceptable to those outside the project who will be impacted by the plan. Adjust the plan if necessary.

▶ Identification of activities

The formal way of identifying activities and their interdependencies is to construct a work breakdown structure. While I would not suggest that this method should always be used, it can be very helpful if you do not have experience of practising the methodology. The work breakdown structure for the benefits management activities of our example is shown in Figure 10.8 overleaf.

I have not developed the work breakdown structure to the same level of detail for all major activities. This is partly a practical consideration of space available on the page but it also reflects real life, where some activity groups will be much more crowded than others. A full breakdown structure might go down other one or two levels. For example, the level four activity of distributing questionnaires could be further decomposed as shown in Figure 10.7:

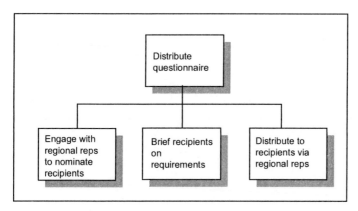

Figure 10.7 – Further decomposition of work breakdown structure

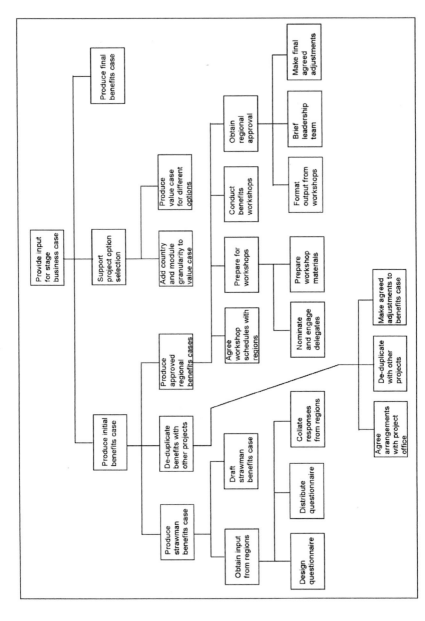

Figure 10.8 – Work breakdown structure for Feasibility stage benefits management activities

There is no hard and fast rule about how far to take decomposition. As a rule of thumb, if an activity box is sufficiently clear that time and resources can be allocated against it, and it can be executed without need for further explanation, then it needs no further decomposition.

Interdependency between activities can be read from the diagram by following these rules:

- An activity is not complete until all the sub-activities below it have been completed.

- Activities or sub-activities at the same level within the same parent activity group are completed sequentially from left to right.

▶ Allocation of time and resources

This is not a complicated task. The procedure is to take each of the lowest-level activity boxes from the work breakdown structure and assess:

- How long will it take to complete?

- Which roles, both within and outside the project team, will be needed to complete it?

- How much effort will each role need to put in to the activity?

Note that there is no need to complete this exercise for activities that have child sub-activities below them. However, it may be necessary or prudent to add contingency time at the aggregate activity level, such that the elapsed time for the activity will be greater than the sum of the time needed to complete each of the sub-activities.

Take the example activity 'Conduct benefits workshops'. This is an activity box that really does need to be decomposed further, as there is much detailed work that is not explained by the title of the activity itself; I have left this extra detail to the next chapter. However, if you are an experienced benefits manager who has run many previous such workshops, then the parameters of the activity shown in Figure 10.9 overleaf may be all you need to define its resource requirements.

```
Activity: Conduct benefits workshops

For each regional benefits workshop:

Elapsed time: 5 days

Resources:    Project benefits manager:    4 days
              Project subject expert:       2 days
              Additional facilitator:       3 days
              12 x delegates:               2.5 days each
```

Figure 10.9 – Time and resource allocation to a benefits management activity

► Scheduling the plan

This section of the book is in danger of becoming a manual on general project management planning techniques. I will therefore avoid describing how to do a timeline schedule – probably the most widely used tool within project management. It is likely anyway that the benefits management plan will need to be incorporated into the broader project schedule, using whatever software tool is standard within the company or change programme. Instead, I shall draw out some points from the specific Gantt chart schedule for our example, which is shown opposite at Figure 10.10:

- I have shown a plan that has an elapsed time of about 20 weeks, which includes some slack time to reflect reality, particularly in the lead-up to benefits workshops, when regions will need time to prepare themselves and clear diaries. This is still a tight plan for you personally because I have not included time to do the dozens of additional ad hoc tasks that will continually arise; such as producing presentations and briefs for the programme office, governance board and other sponsors.

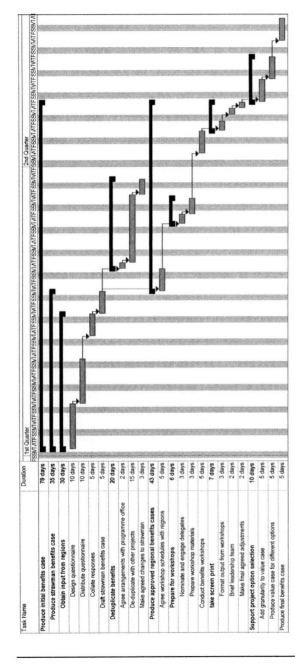

Figure 10.10 – Gantt chart for the Feasibility stage of benefits work

- For simplicity, the plan only shows benefits workshops in one region. Additional time will be needed to conduct workshops in the other three regions of the example, or to do the work necessary to extrapolate the approved benefits cases into regions where no workshops are held. Probably another month to six will be needed in either case.

- In summary, I have presented a plan that will take about six months to complete, using timings that I know from experience are realistic. For a project with as wide a scope as our example it will be difficult to complete the work in less time than this. In practice, I have known the benefits work during the Feasibility stage to take up to nine months for a similarly-scaled project.

- As a rule of thumb, the benefits work during Feasibility will take about as long to complete as the other aspects of the project. The benefits management plan is rarely on the critical path of the project but nor is it likely to finish much before other project work streams.

▶ Fitting the plan

The plan that you have produced has probably been created with no input other than from the project manager and other team members.

The final part of planning is to check with all those impacted by the plan that the activities can be resourced at the times specified. Again, this is standard project management procedure. The only difference, perhaps, is the need to give regions as much warning as possible of the workshops to be held there and the type of people needed as workshop delegates. So, the activity on the plan called 'Nominate and engage delegates' represents the conclusions of discussions with the regions that need to start at the beginning of this project stage.

Run-up to workshops

Introduction

Having completed the detailed stage plan for benefit work and lined up availability of the necessary resources, it is now time to start doing the work.

In this chapter I will take you through the initial Feasibility stage tasks: to produce a strawman benefits case (if one has been deemed necessary) and to undertake detailed planning for the stage benefits workshops.

So, where do you start? There are a number of inputs to get you going:

- The decisions made on which activities to include and which to leave out.

- The benefits workstream plan that you have already developed (see last chapter).

- Benefits-related deliverables from the Start-up stage (principally the initial top-down forecast of financial contribution by benefit class – see Table 10.1).

- A growing understanding, from the other project team members, of the capabilities of the project to be implemented and the opportunities it will offer the business.

Developing the strawman benefits case

You have decided that you will develop a strawman benefits case before holding the regional workshops and that you will involve the business in its creation. The first set of tasks is therefore to design a questionnaire, engage the business and receive back and analyse the completed questionnaires.

▶ Designing the questionnaire

Before you begin thinking about a design for the questionnaire you must be very clear about why you need it and what it is intended to achieve. The purpose of the questionnaire is to help you do a gap analysis on the processes that will be impacted by the project. Why do you need this? Gap analysis is a highly useful, if not essential, tool to help transform the generic top-down benefits case produced for the end of Start-up into a company-specific, region-specific or even country-specific top-down value case. Tailored top-down benefits cases can be used to:

- Indicate where the project should focus its efforts for the greatest benefit to the business.

- Provide a much better cross-check of the financial impact derived from the bottom-up benefits cases produced during benefits workshops.

How does the gap analysis help? An example will explain this. Industry and supplier benchmarks suggested that the implementation of an advanced planning system (APS) would allow stocks held to be reduced by 40 per cent to achieve an industry best practice level of 15 days of stock in the supply chain. But this benchmark percentage improvement pre-supposes a given pre-implementation stock level and that the conditions that allow a level of 15 days stock to be achieved also apply in our company.

Completed questionnaires will reveal the current state of the processes concerned and will also indicate what local factors would preclude the achievement of industry best practice and by how great a shortfall. In this case they showed that current stock levels stood on average at 21 days and could potentially be reduced by 20% to 17 days, as illustrated in Figure 11.1.

This is perhaps a slightly misleading example, chosen to illustrate the principle clearly, as the current stock levels are known quantities that do not need answers to a questionnaire to identify. However, the current states of many processes are more difficult to define and often need to be stated in subjective terms; the questionnaire then becomes invaluable.

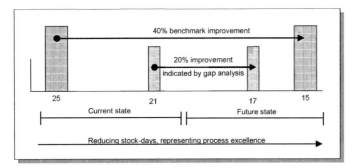

Figure 11.1 – Adding realism to an industry benchmark

The first task is to design the questionnaire. This will probably require input from the whole project team because it needs a thorough understanding of the various factors that characterise a process and its maturity. Knowing these factors helps frame the questions to ask.

For our example project – the global APS implementation – we needed to do gap analysis on 10 different processes or sub-processes that, at that stage in the project, were considered to be those that would be impacted. The 10 were:

List of processes needing gap analysis

Demand forecasting

Supply planning

Strategic sourcing

Supplier management

Procurement of raw materials

Site (manufacturing) operations

Primary scheduling

Primary management

Customer offer

Secondary transport

The questions needing answers were too numerous to be addressed with a single questionnaire and a separate question sheet was drafted for each of the 10 processes. The demand forecast questionnaire is shown at Figure 11.2 opposite.

Points to note from the example questionnaire sheet are:

- Those being asked to complete the questionnaire may at this stage know very little about the project. The questions being asked therefore need to be put into context; this is what the information boxes under the heading 'Future view of process' are for.

- The information box entitled 'Characteristics of the "To be" process' is split into two parts: the top part indicating future process characteristics and the bottom part new capabilities that will be provided to the process by implementing the APS.

- The challenges requiring a response are not worded in a way that directly asks 'How good is your process?', as this would almost certainly result in a biased response. Instead, the questions asked should provide responses from which the benefits manager and other members of the project team can deduce the local process maturity in a more objective way.

- The questionnaire gives respondents the opportunity to provide information in a variety of different ways, including the catch-all box at the bottom. As this is going to be a once-only exercise it is important to spread the net for information capture as widely as possible.

- It was felt psychologically important that each questionnaire sheet be limited to one page in the event that it was printed out.

Improve demand planning [1.4.1]

Benefit class:
Supply Chain Management - Tactical [1.4]

Country/cluster

Regional and country views of gap between 'As is' and 'To be' processes

Future views of process

Process vision:

A collaborative process of forecasting future market demand that will consolidate all functional areas such as sales, finance and customer service into a single integrated process, including collaboration with key customers and suppliers

Characteristics of the 'To be' process:

? Monthly regional-level forecasting cycle, including amalgamation of:
  - steady-state forecast based on budgets and historic trends
  - one-off variations based on marketing campaigns etc
? Single forecast signed off by all impacted parties - re

? Supported by a regional-level forecasting tool producing a multi-level single forecast model
? Internet interface allowing access to sales forecast data to LSC and Sales & Marketing staff region-wide

Potential problems/business challenge:

Significant percentage of orders need to be made specifically because they have not been planned in advance. A special order costs significantly more than a planned order (admin, planning, etc costs)

A significant number of stockouts per year occur as a result of high peaks of unanticipated demand. Upcoming events such as promotions are invisible to production, who are then caught unprepared

Do you have any other points, not covered above, concerning this process, its current issues and potential improvements?

Challenges	Response
? Are you following the SOIP process rolled out by LSC in 2003? Has it improved sales forecast accuracy? How accurate, on average, is the current sales forecast? How often recast?	
? How does sales forecasting take new products, campaigns, promotions and product withdrawal plans into account? Could this be improved (if so how?) and which of LSC, sales, marketing, key customers & suppliers are not involved?	
? Are SKUs A:B:C classified by BU/OU?	
? Is sales forecast accuracy on the performance contract of all contributors? Is the current level of sales forecasting skill OK?	
? Do key/senior sales managers and FLSKA managers have full involvement in creation and sign-off of the forecast?	
? What sales forecasting tools are currently in place? Can they continuously map actual sales to system-generated forecasts to track demand variations? Are they accessable on-line to key customers/suppliers?	
? Do you have an audit trail of contribution to the sales forecast, by sales manager/exocutive? Is this maintained automatically by your forecasting tool, or manually?	
Are there any current or planned initiatives in the country/cluster that will address the shortfalls in this process?	

	Do you agree?				Comments?	Who should we talk to for information?
	VH	H	L	VL		

Figure 11.2 – Example questionnaire for process gap analysis

▶ Distributing the questionnaire

So, you want the completed questionnaires to allow you to do gap analysis on all the impacted processes in each area where the processes are independently operated. In our example this implied, in one region (admittedly the most complex one) a separate questionnaire for each of 10 processes or sub-processes in each of 12 countries; a major task for the region to complete and for the benefits manager to analyse. To get over this problem, we identified which countries within the region had processes operated in a similar manner at a similar stage of maturity and got one country to answer for all countries in this group. The grouping of countries with similar operations is not necessarily the same for each process, so this grouping exercise can itself be complicated.

I now need to introduce two specific regional roles used in the example we are using. These were, in each region:

- **Transformation delivery manager (TDM).** This was a semi-permanent role within the supply chain organisation. Responsibilities were similar to those of the regional transformation manager, or RTM, but with a narrower regional programme-level responsibility for all the projects within the supply chain transformation programme (of which our example project was one).

- **Lead subject matter expert (Lead SME).** This was a project-specific role to act as the link between the central project team and the region on specific project matters. Responsibilities included local organisation of all regional activities for this project. The role would grow into a regional project manager role before the start of the Implement stage.

Back to the example questionnaire design exercise. Not only the questionnaires but also the instructions for their completion need to be carefully thought through. For the example project, we first sent the regions guidance on how to distribute the questionnaire, as shown opposite:

Introduction

This guidance sheet is to assist TDMs/Lead SMEs to decide how to distribute the gap analysis questionnaires.

Scope

The questionnaire has been designed to help the project team understand:

- the degree of process maturity currently experienced by individual countries for each of the processes to be addressed by the project
- the level of opportunity in each country to improve the business by improving Supply Chain processes
- any particular issue or 'hot button' that the country would like the project to address.

To this end, there is a comprehensive question sheet for each of the 10 processes potentially impacted by the project (excluding the strategic network optimisation process, which is being addressed elsewhere).

We are not attempting to extract baseline performance figures through this questionnaire (e.g. volumes moved, stock levels etc). This information will be gathered elsewhere, through the Finance community.

The requirement is to clarify the process maturity level and improvement opportunity for each country in the region. However, there may not be a need to ask every country to complete each process question sheet; indeed, we would advise keeping distribution to a minimum that will achieve the requirement.

Procedure

We recommend that the TDM/Lead SME/RTM take a view on what groupings of countries are characterised by very similar process maturity and improvement opportunity and nominate an individual from one of these countries to respond on behalf of the entire group of countries. Some countries may not form part of a group and the country groupings may be different for different processes. Where an individual is responding for a group of countries, please enter his or her name against each country in the group and indicate which country the individual comes from.

The decision on questionnaire distribution will need to be approved by the Regional Transformation Manager in consultation with the Project Manager. A matrix is included on the next sheet and TDMs/Lead SMEs are asked to complete this within two weeks of receipt of this guidance sheet and return it to the Project Manager.

Any points of clarification should be addressed to:

Mike Payne,
Benefits Manager, etc

Once the distribution of questionnaires has been agreed with the regional TDM and Lead SME, they can be distributed.

It is vital that respondents understand what is required of them. So, when sending out the questionnaire it is sensible to provide guidance on how to complete them and an example of a completed sheet. Even if questionnaires are distributed locally by the Lead SME, which is a sensitive way of doing it, the guidance documentation will need to be designed centrally. Examples of a guidance sheet and completed questionnaire are shown at Figures 11.3 and 11.4 respectively.

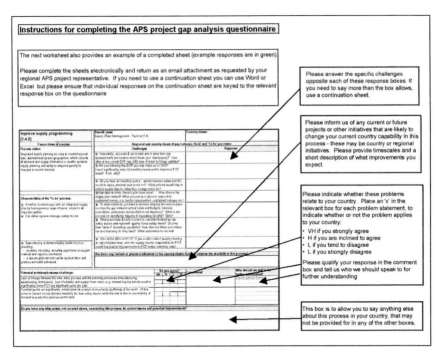

Figure 11.3 – Instructions for completion of gap analysis questionnaire

Improve supply programming [1.4.2]	Benefit class: Supply Chain Management - Tactical [1.4]	Country/cluster xxxxxxxxxxxxxxxx
	Regional and country views of gap between 'As is' and 'To be' processes	
Future views of process	**Challenges**	**Response**
Process vision: Integrated supply planning process at cluster/regional level, standardised across geographies, which collects all demand and supply information to enable dynamic supply planning and ability to respond quickly to changes in market demand	- How visible, accurate & up-to-date and in what form (eg spreadsheet? Stock levels not very accurate, extracted from ERP onto spreadsheets are location stock levels (incl distributors)? How often is the current ERP weekly for 15 locations. Have no view of distributors stock holdings. JDE (eg JDE) view of stock holdings updated?	stock holdings updated twice a week.
	- Are you following the SOIP process rolled out by LSC in 2003? Has it significantly reduced inventory levels and/or improved IFOT levels? If not why?	Yes we do, but key people don't attend. It hasn't had significant impact on inventory levels or IFOT because current sales processes are more push-orientated, so don't reflect true market demand; also business processes, e.g. promotions, not followed.
	- Do you have an inventory policy - agreed between sales and SC - on stock levels, promise lead times etc? What policies would help to reduce supply issues, shop floor change-overs etc?	We have an inventory policy but not strictly adhered to yet. Promise lead times are 3 days for all products. We need longer lead times for some SKUs.
Characteristics of the 'To be' process:	- How often is stock check/cycle count done? How often is the supply plan revised? What process is in place to respond to unplanned events; e.g. tender opportunities, unplanned outages etc?	Stock take and update of ERPs once a year. Supply plan revised once a month. No documented process for unplanned changes - dealt with on a case-by-case basis. Not involved in tendering.
- Provides clusters/region with an integrated supply plan by homogeneous range of items, visible to all impacted parties	- To what extent do you have a 'demand shaping' process in place to close the gap between actual sales and GFOs, address promotions, unforeseen demand/stock-out situations? What is the process for identifying, flagging & liquidating SLOBS? Who?	No current demand shaping process, but would be a good idea to review stocks regularly and offer discounts to clear excess stock. This would address the SLOBS issue (no-one currently responsible).
- Calculates dynamic strategic safety stocks	- What processes & tools in place to calculate finished goods safety stocks and replenish against these safety levels? Do they have 'what if' modelling capability? How often are these processes run and how long do they take? What automation to run and	Use spreadsheets to calculate safety stocks once a quarter for A class SKUs, but these don't take into account revised service levels fro S & M. Replenishment plan done manually on monthly basis with mid-month check. Don't have 'what if' modelling capab
- Supported by a demand/supply balancing tool, providing: - complex modelling, including algorithms to support material and capacity constraints - a speedy process that can be applied often and produce accurate schedules	- Who is the SPA for IFOT? If you could conduct supply planning at region/cluster level, with the supply planner responsible for IFOT, would this lead to improvements in IFOT and/or inventory cost?	SC is responsible for IFOT but no individual nominated. Yes, would be beneficial but would need product harmonisation and full stock visibility, agreed process and appropriate tools.
	Are there any current or planned initiatives in the country/cluster that will address the shortfalls in this process?	
	Don't know of any other initiatives targetted at improving this process in this country	

Potential problems/business challenge:	Do you agree?				Comments?	Who should we talk to for further information?
	VH	H	L	VL		
Lack of linkage between the order entry process and the planning processes (manufacturing, warehousing, distribution), loss of visibility and supply chain errors (eg manual keying errors) result in significantly lower IFOT and significant costs per year	Y				IFOT is impacted by about 3% and additional annual cost is estimated at $US350k	Supply planner [name]
Finished goods are significantly overstocked as a result of uncertainty (buffering) of demand? Of this some is caused by true demand variability (ie. true safety stock), while the rest is due to non-visibility of demand to production planners and/or lack			Y		There is certainly overstocking as a result of this problem (perhaps 1 to 2 days). Don't know the breakdown but both problems contribute	Supply planner [name] Demand planner [name]

Do you have any other points, not covered above, concerning this process, its current issues and potential improvements?
We have a real problem getting visibility of Marine forecast and order visibility, including location of servicing.

Figure 11.4 – Example of a completed gap analysis questionnaire

▶ Analysing completed questionnaires

Analysis of returned completed questionnaires is not a trivial exercise. An approach I would recommend is to take each region in turn and, within each region, do the analysis process by process. For each process, look for regional trends and country or cluster level variations from the regional trend.

I also recommend that the analysis be brought together in a summary document for each process, rather than using it as direct input into the strawman benefits case. An example of part of such a process analysis is shown in the text box below.

Supply Planning [Inventory Planning]

- Importing countries need to plan FG imports well in advance – typically 60 days

- Singapore is a major marine hub, but imports half of its domestic demand from Malaysia (probably 60 day lead time) and derives the rest from toll blenders

- Indonesia, Philippines, Taiwan all import from Malaysia

  o Taiwan – imports from some countries are not supplied on time [imports from Malaysia and Singapore]

  o Philippines – inventory reduction restricted because importing from Malaysia

- Generally VH/H response to FG buffering:

  o Malaysia – buffering is due to uncertainty of demand, not lack of stock visibility

  o Philippines – over/under stocking is mainly caused by a misreading of demand by the Sales Execs who are supposed to sell what they have forecasted. Sales people are trained to sell what they forecast ±25%

  o Philippines places a monthly order of 130% of forecast to Malaysia

  o Singapore – inventory reduced through right stock keeping

Drafting the strawman benefits case

► Rethinking the purpose

We have previously discussed why you might want to produce a strawman benefits case. Now that you have all the input material that you need (or, at least, all that you can reasonably expect to obtain at this stage of the project) you are in a position to start drafting. There is, however, the problem of deciding the format to adopt and level of detail to include. It is therefore worth revisiting the purpose of the document to help guide decisions here.

The strawman will serve three useful purposes. It will:

- Provide an initial basis on which to conduct benefits de-duplication with other projects.

- Help to guide the project team in its initial work to develop a list of implementation options.

- Provide input to the regional benefits workshops; either as a starting point for the workshops or as material to support discussions during the workshops.

I suggest that two conclusions can be drawn from this understanding:

- It may be difficult to devise a single document to satisfy all its purposes.

- The strawman will almost certainly not survive the benefits workshops unscathed in whatever format it is written. In which case, the detail included should be just enough for its purpose.

Having said this, there is no single right way of formatting the information you have into a current picture of the project's benefits aspirations. The suggestion I make here involves producing two documents which have certainly shown to work in practice. These are:

- A confirmatory mapping of the relationship between business processes impacted by the project and its forecast financial contributions.

- A cut-down version of the final benefits case format, with a sheet for each benefit class, summarising the trends and variations identified from analysis of the questionnaire responses.

▶ Process to value mapping

The main point of this exercise is to review and revise the relationships, triggered by implementing the project, between improvement in business processes and additional financial value generated for the business. These relationships were tentatively stated at the end of the Start-up stage but questionnaire responses will have provided the evidence, or at least local perceptions, of where potential financial contribution is there to be made. The mapping is an essential input to the initial de-duplication exercise that is covered in Chapter 14. It is also a good tool to help firm up the project list of benefits classes. The mapping for the Asia Pacific region of our example project is shown below.

Benefit class	Revenue	COGS (RM)	COGS (Conversion)	NCC (Shared services)	Cost to deliver	Inventory
Improve customer satisfaction	$3.0m					
Improve procurement		$1.5m				
Improve manufacturing			$1.0m			
Reduce overheads				$0.5m		
Improve logistics					$3.5m	
Reduce inventory						$7.5m

Figure 11.5 – Process to value mapping from questionnaire analysis

▶ Strawman business case

When deciding what to put into the strawman benefits case it is worth asking yourself the question 'If the benefits workshops are a complete disaster, what benefits information do we need to get successfully through stage approval processes?' I am not suggesting here that you should plan for failure but rather that the facilitators should at least have their own ideas on the answers expected from the workshops; it is one thing to start the workshops with a blank piece of paper but, as the benefits manager, you at least must not start with a blank picture in your mind.

We have already discussed the essential benefits-related information to be defined by the end of this project stage, which was shown graphically in the last chapter at Figure 8.6. To this list you should add something that captures the country-level variations that were identified from questionnaire responses. An example of the strawman case for one benefits class is shown at Figure 11.6 overleaf.

By now you should be familiar enough with the elements of a benefits case for this diagram to be self-explanatory. There are just a few points to say about this spreadsheet:

- The benefit class of the example is a hybrid between the classes listed in Table 10.1 and the structure of questionnaire responses. This 'half-way house' format will help workshop discussions.

- The 'Measure' column refers to an improvement in operational performance, rather than measures for the outcomes leading to this improvement. In most cases, the benefits description provides enough information, in the absence of specific outcome measures, to identify and justify the performance improvement measure.

- Where the performance improvement targets are stated in percentage terms there is no need, in most cases, to define corresponding baseline measurements. However, they should be included where it is necessary to highlight the need for a measurement to be made before a financial impact can be derived (this mainly applies when the measure is not an existing company KPI and the baseline measurement cannot be assumed).

- We have said that the beneficiary role is not needed at this stage of the project. The column is included as much as anything as an aide-mémoire on the best sources of information, which should probably be included in the list of workshop delegates.

- The value split between 'BPI' and 'BPR' should be explained. For this company, there was a need to know how much value could be generated by process improvements alone (business process improvements (BPI)) and how much was dependent upon system implementation (business process re-engineering (BPR)).

Benefit Class - Supply Chain Management (Tactical)

Benefit	Benefit description	Measure	Beneficiary	Baseline	Target
Improve demand planning	Provide a collaborative process of forecasting future market demand, supported by a comprehensive modelling tool, resulting in an up-to-date, fast forecast bought into by all parties. This will provide a firm and more accurate basis for supply programmin	Sales forecast accuracy	Demand planner	Average sales forecast of x% accuracy	Improve average sales forecast accuracy to y%
Improve supply programming	Build an integrated supply planning process at cluster/regional level, standardised across geographies, which collects all demand and supply information to enable dynamic supply planning and ability to respond quickly to changes in market demand	Actual stock levels per installation compared with planned stock levels	Supply programmer		Reduce overstocking at plant/warehouse level by 50%
Improve primary scheduling	Transportation management processes and tools, integrated with other key supply chain management processes ; that support the full transportation lifecycle (eg. outhauls/backhauls or milkruns) and enable benefits for both the company and its transportatio	Cost of primary transport per litre sold	Country logistics manager		Reduce transportation costs per litre by 10%
Improve primary management	Improve the efficiency of assigning loads to contracted and spot carriers and will support procedures for block payment of consolidated carrier invoices	Average percentage truck utilization (actual load cw capacity)	Country logistics manager		Increase capacity utilisation by 5%

Business logic

Improvements in all stages of forecasting - from sales forecast to demand forecast for raw materials - will allow the supply chain process to approach nearer to a buy-build-distribute-to-order model than is currently possible This will allow reductions

Financial category	Snapshot Value ($k)		
	BPI	BPR	TOT
Sales volume	100	350	450
COGS	50	200	250
Cost to deliver	25	75	100
TOTAL Annual	175	625	800
Working Capital (WC)	250	650	900

Country variations:

	Annual	WC
Malaysia, Singapore	As targets above	As targets above
Vietnam, Thailand, Korea	COGS -15%, CTD -10%	As targets above
Japan	COGS, CTD +10%	WC +5%
Australia, New Zealand	As targets above	As targets above
Indonesia, Philippines	COGS, CTD -15%	WC - 5%
China, Hong Kong	COGS +15%	WC +5%
Taiwan	CTD -5%	As targets above

Figure 11.6 – Example of the strawman benefits case for one benefit class

Preparing for benefits workshops

The benefits workshop is the pivotal point of benefits management; many of the fundamental principles of the method are brought to life in the workshop environment. While it is conceivable that a benefits case could recover from a poor series of workshops, your work as benefits manager would be immeasurably more difficult if this happened. It is therefore essential that you take the greatest care both in the preparations for the workshops and in their conduct.

In this section I describe the preparation for workshops in some detail. Remember that we are using the example of a complex global project in order to bring out all aspects of the end-to-end process. I will offer a particular way of doing things but will indicate where a simpler treatment may apply. As far as workshops are concerned, the same degree of care is needed for all projects, big or small; the main difference with a smaller project would be the number and geographical spread of workshops held.

There are three main aspects to preparations for benefits workshops:

- Scheduling the event
- Selecting and engaging delegates
- Preparing workshop materials

The first two of these are interdependent and require close cooperation with the regions concerned; so a fourth implicit aspect of preparation is engagement with the local business unit.

▶ Scheduling workshops

I will go through the process of scheduling workshops for the relatively simple case of the single-function project of our example and then show the more complex variant of a multi-function project.

What factors do you need to take into account? There are a few:

- The two workshops (benefits and financial impact) need breathing space between them. You will want to develop the details of individual benefits before starting to think about financial impact. The breathing space is both to formalise this deliberate split and to allow facilitators and delegates alike to do some preparatory work for the second part based on output from the first. The gap between the two parts should be at least half a day; ideally a full day.

- Additional time may need to be scheduled to bring delegates up to speed with the details of the project and its capabilities. The amount of time needed will depend on the level of previous exposure to the project and its complexity. It may be necessary to allow a full day for this activity to give delegates sufficient information that they can make sensible judgement calls in sessions such as target setting.

- It is better to schedule more time than you think will be needed, rather than less. It is sometimes possible to cram one of the workshops into half a day – particularly the financial impact workshop, which can sometimes be completed quite quickly – but it is as often necessary to take six hours or more to cover all the ground fully. Workshops should be conducted with pace but with reasonable breaks and without the need to rush to complete things towards the end of the time allotted. When workshops are rushed, output quality can be poor and delegates can feel cheated of the opportunity fully to have their say, whereas an early finish after successful completion of the work is normally well received by delegates.

- Depending upon whether or not a strawman benefits case has been developed with local business input, there will be a need to spend a small or larger amount of time interviewing delegates before the workshops are held. If there has been such involvement, there may be a need for clarification of some of the responses; you will recall that there is provision on the questionnaire for nominations to provide such additional clarity. If a strawman benefits case has not been drafted, or there has been no local input to one that has, then more interview time will be needed to gain a feel for the local business processes whose improvement will be the source of project benefits. It is not sensible to use workshop time to expose the project team's lack of knowledge of local process capabilities and issues.

▪ Availability of the delegates we need is paramount; local as well as individual circumstances need to be taken into account. Early engagement with the local business can avert potential disasters. For example, I was involved in a series of workshops in the Asia Pacific region where the two parts (each part comprised three function-based workshops) had to be separated by a fortnight because of the impact of Chinese New Year on delegate availability. Similarly, the non-availability of a single critical delegate may force workshop timings to be adjusted.

Now let us look at what a regional schedule might look like. Firstly, Figure 11.7 provides a reminder of the activities to be completed:

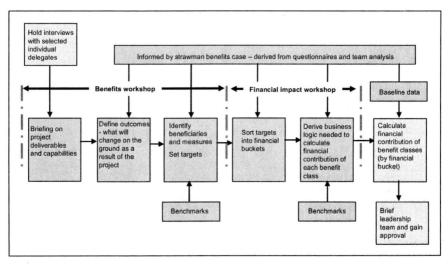

Figure 11.7 – Activities within a regional benefits workshop visit

So, how might we schedule these activities? One option is shown at Figure 11.8:

Sunday	Monday	Tuesday	Wednesday	Thursday	Friday	Saturday
Team travel	Arrival, admin and interviews / Project briefing	Benefit workshop	Preparation for financial impact workshop	Financial impact workshop	Prepare briefing / Brief leadership team	Team travel

Figure 11.8 – Typical schedule for a single-function benefits workshop

I am suggesting this very crowded schedule for one reason only; it allows workshop delegates who are travelling a fair distance (think of the Asia Pacific region that stretches from China to Malaysia to Australia) to come, attend and return home within a working week. This may be an important consideration but could result in an unworkable schedule because more time is needed for:

- The project team to conduct individual interviews before workshops start

- Bringing delegates up to speed with project capabilities, which may need a whole day

- Preparing for and briefing the leadership team (who may, anyway, be less than impressed with a Friday afternoon briefing and decision-making session)

The obvious way around this dilemma is to extend the visit until the beginning of the following week, briefing the leadership team on the second Monday. This may spoil the project team's weekend but should not be any more inconvenient for delegates. If the team is concerned that it is being asked to hit the ground running too fast, the visit can be extended further in one of two ways:

- Extend into the middle of the second week and hold the second workshop on the second Monday. This allows week-one activities to have a slower start but does begin to significantly disrupt delegates' work and leisure time.

- The project team arrives in the region the previous Thursday evening; doing administration and interviews of those locally based on Friday. In this case it is mainly the project team that is disrupted, which is perhaps how it should be.

Now look at the schedule below for the benefits workshops of a multi-function project. I have used this schedule on two such projects and it works.

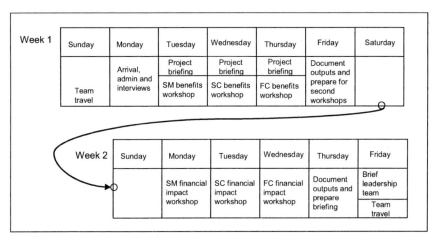

Figure 11.9 – Schedule for multi-function benefits workshops

In this case, separate workshops were held for the functional groupings of sales and marketing (SM), supply chain (SC) and finance and control (FC). We got away with a shorter time for project briefings before each of the first workshops because, in both of the multi-function project examples (the MI system implementation and an ERP consolidation) the project capabilities were quicker to put across to, and be absorbed by, delegates than those for an APS implementation.

The schedule here is slightly more relaxed than in the previous single-function project example and there is a weekend when some sight-seeing time can be given up if necessary to complete any outstanding work resulting from the first set of workshops.

▶ Selecting and engaging beneficiaries

We discussed the selection of beneficiaries in some detail in Part 1; particularly, numbers of delegates needed for a workshop and the roles and personal characteristics to look for. So, as far as selection is concerned, we need here only to talk about how to achieve the ideal delegate list and provide an example.

The project we are following provides a convenient start point for the delegate selection process. We started to engage seriously with the regions when they were asked for help in selecting recipients for gap analysis questionnaires. This was over 10 weeks before workshops were due to start. At that time the project had a firm idea of which business processes would be impacted and the names of those selected to answer the questionnaire – all people associated with the impacted processes – provided a good long list from which to select workshop delegates. The return of completed questionnaires gave the project team a good feel for the knowledge and experience of respondents and the answers also provided additional names to add to the long list (names offered to provide further clarity to questionnaire responses). The list now contained many more names than needed for the workshops; even if answers were by clustered countries there will have been at least three or four names for each process covered.

The list now needs to be whittled down to eight to 12 names. As well as the considerations of spread of functional knowledge and seniority and personal characteristics discussed in Chapter 6, other factors need to be taken into account:

- **Geographic spread.** Ideally, delegates should be representative of all parts of the region. This does not mean a delegate from each country but certainly at least one from each country cluster. On the other hand, there may be company travel restrictions in place which would lead to delegates being limited to those based in the country where the workshop is taking place or from nearby countries. There needs to be good cross-region representation whatever the travel restrictions.

- **Availability**. Of course, the availability of individuals must be taken into account. The region and project team between them will have a view on which individuals are essential to the success of the workshops; for these individuals, workshop dates may have to be adjusted to ensure their availability. For the rest it is a question of making a selection from those that that will be available on the dates fixed for the workshops; incidentally, availability here means for both workshops. This suggests that availability of key delegates needs to be confirmed before the selection process for other delegates is completed.

The delegate list should be firm about a month before the workshops are due to be held. This means that there are about four weeks available to complete the selection process from the time that questionnaires are returned. This may seem like a long time but, with all the other things going on, it will pass fast enough. I strongly recommend that during this time a weekly audio conference should be held between the project team and the RTM and Lead SME of each region affected, during which, among other matters to be discussed, the workshop delegate lists can be refined.

For the APS implementation project the delegate list was, naturally, heavily biased towards supply chain roles. However, customer satisfaction was an important objective of the project and one or two key customer-facing roles were also included. The roles selected as delegates to the benefits workshops of this project are listed in the text box below.

Delegate list for APS project benefits workshops

Regional supply chain performance manager	Regional sales director
Regional supply chain network manager	Marketing manager
Demand planner	Country sales manager
Supply planner	
Purchasing manager	
Country supply chain manager	
Plant manager	
Country logistics manager	

It is worth noting that:

- All the roles in this list are either from the regional headquarters or are relatively senior; perhaps belying my previous remarks about needing a spread of seniority among delegates. This is normal for the workshops held during the Feasibility stage; I would expect to see more junior roles attending the Define stage benefits workshops.

- A number of delegates were invited from the Sales and Marketing functions, even though this was a Supply Chain project.

Engagement with most delegates started with their involvement in answering gap analysis questionnaires. The next step, for all delegates, was a discussion between them and the lead SME over their attendance at the benefits workshops. The final step in the engagement process was to send each delegate a briefing pack, about a fortnight before the workshops started, containing:

- A detailed schedule for the workshops they are attending

- A brief explanation of the benefits management method

- An outline of the input expected of delegates, including workshop rules of engagement

- Administrative details

▶ Preparing workshop materials

Materials needed for the workshops include:

- Slides for an introduction to the workshop

- A presentation pack to support the briefing on project capabilities

- A presentation pack to support a briefing on the methodology

- Slides to introduce and explain each workshop session

- Materials for the interactive workshop sessions

- Formatted spreadsheets to receive workshop output

- Hard copies of the strawman benefits case

I will not cover the details of these materials here. The presentation on project capabilities will be the responsibility of one of the subject experts on the project team, a suggested presentation for the methodology briefing is at the Appendix and material used for each workshop session following the initial methodology briefing is discussed when we cover these sessions in detail in the next two chapters.

Instead, I end the chapter with a word about media. I have found that what works best is a combination of electronic presentations (using presentation software such as MS PowerPoint delivered from a PC via a digital projector) and brown paper for interactive sessions. If a digital projector is not available then slides will need to be converted to vufoils for overhead projection.

CHAPTER TWELVE

Conducting benefits workshops

Introduction

The moment has arrived to start the benefits workshops. The right delegates have been engaged and have arrived and the team is well prepared for the event. All you need to do now is ensure that the workshops go well to get an outcome that satisfies both the project team and the region.

In this chapter I will take you through all aspects of running the first of the two workshops, session by session. The chapter is divided into the following sections:

- Introductory sessions
- Developing benefit definitions

In the following chapter we will cover the second workshop, to derive the financial impact of benefits, in a similar fashion.

Introductory sessions

The first few hours of the workshop (in our example, Monday afternoon plus the first hour of Tuesday morning – see Figure 11.8) are spent on introductory matters. These include:

- Welcome and introductions
- Project briefing
- Briefing on the benefits management methodology

▶ Welcome and introductions

It is important to get the workshop off to a good start by setting the right pace, energy level and expectations. A plan that works includes:

- Opening statement by an appropriate senior executive

- A briefing on the overall schedule and administrative matters

- Introductions and an ice breaker

I am assuming here that these workshops are being attended by a strong project team. In our example, the 'home' team included the project manager, two subject matter consultants and the benefits manager. They were supported by the local TDM and Lead SME. This is not always the case; sometimes the visiting team is limited to the benefits manager, supported by a member of the local project team. It largely depends on what the workshop is intended to achieve. In our example the required outputs included obtaining strong regional buy-in and local opinions on possible regional implementation options as well as the benefits case itself; thus the strong team.

The size of the team and overall nature of the workshops will influence the decision on who should make the opening statement. In this case it was made by the regional supply chain director. The statement should be upbeat and strongly supportive of the project (if the speaker cannot commit to this then the project is probably in big trouble already). In our example, the supply chain director's very supportive statement was reinforced by short and equally supportive video statements by the Group Supply Chain Director and the Group Strategy and Transformation Director. These opening statements should be short and punchy, emphasising the strategic importance of the project to the region.

Having been inspired, the delegates now need to be made to feel comfortable. You do this by carefully explaining the schedule for the rest of the week, clearing up any administrative issues and explaining what to do in the case of fire. It is a good idea to get one of the local team (Lead SME, for instance) to deliver this.

Finally, you get the team and delegates to introduce themselves to each other. You can introduce a simple ice-breaker by asking everyone to state their name, role, expectations from the workshop and one unknown interesting fact about themselves. While this is going on, a member of the team should record the answers on a flip chart.

▶ Project briefing

If the full team is present, the project briefing should be given by the project manager and one or both of the subject matter experts. What is covered depends on the objectives of the workshop but could include:

- Outline details of the project; how it supports the organisation's strategy, how it fits into the overall change programme and when it is scheduled to complete its various project stages.

- Details of project capabilities, business process by business process. This part can be powerfully brought to life through the use of video clips or an animated slide presentation and be made as specific to the region as possible.

- An introduction to possible implementation options within the region (if this is one of the objectives, as in our example project).

▶ Briefing on benefits management

The benefits management briefing should be given just before the benefits sessions start; in our example, it starts proceedings on the second day (Tuesday). Apart from getting the necessary information across, it is your opportunity to impress upon delegates the importance of making serious and considered contributions to the benefits sessions.

The briefing should not last too long; it needs to continue the pace set during the first day and should not include details that will be covered in the introductions to the various benefits sessions to follow. I suggest the following agenda for the briefing:

- Importance of benefits management in releasing full project benefits.

- Principles of the benefits management method.

- The three steps to developing a benefits case.

- Broad outline of benefits work over the project stages.

- Introduction to the benefits schema.

- Schedule for the benefits workshop sessions.

I have included a generic slide pack to support this briefing at the Appendix and with it some explanatory notes. We have already covered much of this detail in discussions earlier in the book. I want to cover just two points here: the three steps to a benefits case and the session schedule.

Three steps to a benefits case

In view of the previous discussions on developing a benefits case, it may seem strange that I am now suggesting a process of merely three steps. This is, I have to admit, pure artifice. It is a way of introducing the process of benefit development in an easily digestible form and then providing some navigational structure when we break down to the detail. The three steps are illustrated at Figure 12.1 below.

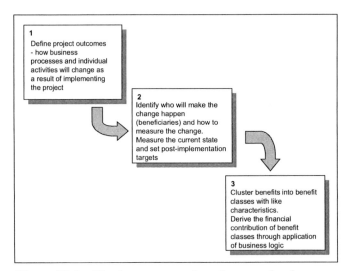

Figure 12.1 – The three steps to benefits case development

We will see that the detailed process steps and the benefits workshop sessions all roll up neatly into this three-part summary. Perhaps the most valuable contribution of this view of applying the method is that it gives due weight to the definition of benefits and their associated outcomes; elements of the benefits case that can be underestimated and therefore skimped during workshops.

Session scheduling

Having already split the delegate work into two workshops – benefits and financial – how should these be further broken down into separate sessions? To a certain extent the splits are pragmatic; allowing for necessary refreshment and lunch breaks at appropriate times during the day. The split into sessions also emphasises the stepped approach to developing benefit definitions and financial impacts of benefits and each session ends with the production of an intermediate or final deliverable. The sessions and schedule I recommend are shown in Table 12.1 below:

Benefits workshop	Benefits management briefing
	Session 1 - Identifying benefits
	Refreshment break
	Session 2 - Defining benefits
	Lunch
	Session 3 - Identifying measures
	Tea
	Session 4 - Setting targets
	[Extra session - Identifying beneficiaries]
Financial impact workshop	Benefits workshop wash-up
	Refreshment break
	Session 5 - Allocating financial buckets
	Lunch
	Session 6 - Building business logic

Table 12.1 – Example schedule for benefits workshops

I have added the additional session on identifying beneficiaries as a gap filler for either day, even though it is not an essential deliverable for the Feasibility stage benefits case, should sessions go a lot quicker than estimated.

Developing benefit definitions

▶ Introduction

The rest of the day, and the balance of the first workshop, is spent defining those parts of the benefits definitions needed for the Feasibility stage. Let us remind ourselves once again what these are. They are illustrated below in Figure 12.2:

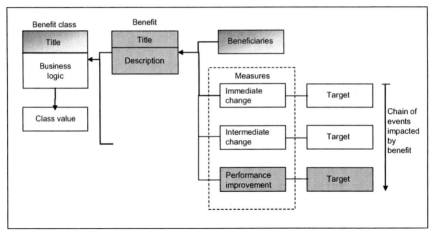

Figure 12.2 – Benefits case elements to be defined in benefits workshop

I have shown some ambivalence in partly shading two of the elements – the benefit class title and beneficiaries:

* We do not need to go firm on benefit class titles, or the grouping of benefits within classes, until the financial impact workshop. However, having a feel for these groupings can help structure the benefits definition work and is addressed in the first session of the day.

- I have already mentioned that beneficiaries need not be defined in this project stage and, indeed, unless we stray into the area of the changed chain of events (which we might have to in some cases) we are unlikely to do so. This should not be confused with identification of those responsible for achieving performance improvements; something we must do if the targets we set for performance improvements are to stick. These people are not necessarily beneficiaries in the true sense, in that their own direct actions may not cause the changes on the ground that lead to performance improvements.

▶ Session 1 – Identifying benefits

This session is best done as a brainstorming exercise, with all delegates facing the principle facilitator, preferably yourself, standing at a white board or flip chart. Ideally a second facilitator, any other member of the team, will be poised over a PC ready to enter output from the session into a pre-prepared spreadsheet template.

This session is fairly unstructured – not a bad thing to get people going – so there is no need for a formal introduction supported by slides. However, as this is the first session proper of the benefits workshop, it would be worth reminding delegates where the session sits in the context of what needs to be achieved by the end of the day. I suggest showing two slides at the beginning of the session: one based on Figure 12.2 and the second a simple list of tasks as in Figure 12.3 below:

What we need to achieve in this workshop
• Identify the list of benefits (this session)
• Define the benefits
• Identify performance improvement measures
• Identify roles responsible for achieving performance improvements
• Set targets for each performance improvement

Figure 12.3 – Slide to introduce benefits workshop

So, here we are starting with a blank canvas. Despite this, it really should not be difficult to extract ideas from delegates as the demonstrations within the previous day's project briefing will have given a strong indication of where benefits can be found. Rather than allowing a complete free-for-all, I suggest that benefits be considered in chunks, by benefit class. This will help control the session and starts delegates thinking about grouping benefits into classes. As we have discussed, you should already have an initial list of benefits classes; if not, Chapter 6 gives some tips on how to select them.

You might therefore start the session by asking 'What benefits do you think the project will provide to improve customer satisfaction?' and then allow delegates to call out their ideas while capturing them on the flip chart. Carry on doing this for about 10 minutes, or until ideas dry up, then do a quick tidying up; deleting duplicates, consolidating near duplicates and checking the list against your 'back pocket' strawman list. In all likelihood you will at this stage have a list of benefits that almost mirrors the strawman list; probably with one or two strawman benefits missing and, with luck, one or two new ones. Propose to the delegates that the 'missing' benefits be added to their list; in most cases they will agree. Then move on to the next benefit class and repeat the exercise.

Despite this being, probably, the simplest exercise within the workshop, there is a lot to get through in about an hour and change-overs from one benefit class to the next should be as slick as possible. I suggest that two flip charts be used. While one is in use to record delegates' ideas for benefits within a class, the assistant facilitator should be transposing benefits from the other flipchart into the PC. In this way, there need be no delay between addressing successive benefits classes.

The session is ended by projecting a consolidated list of the identified benefits, by class, and checking with delegates that they agree that the list is complete and correct. This is something that delegates can continue to think about while they drink coffee and munch doughnuts during the refreshment break. In our example, output from the session looks like Table 12.2 opposite:

Benefit class	Benefits
Improve customer satisfaction	Improve customer intimacy
	Enable better customer offers
	Improve deliveries
	Inform customers of delivery delays
Improve procurement	Improve RM demand forecasting
	Improve accuracy of RM orders
Improve manufacturing	Improve efficiency of plant scheduling
Reduce overheads	Reduce the need for country-based managers
Improve logistics	Improve transportation scheduling
	Reduce cost of invoice processing
Reduce inventory	Improve inventory planning and optimisation

Table 12.2 – The benefits list from Session 1

Interestingly, this list was somewhat different from that of the strawman benefits case. Two benefits were rejected, on reflection, as being inapplicable to this region but delegates came up not only with two new benefits but with a whole new benefit class; the ability to reorganise the supply chain planning function along regional lines and thus release a number of country-based supply chain managers had not been foreseen as a benefit of this project.

► Session 2 – Describing benefits

You need a different approach from the first session to come up with benefit descriptions. The approach I suggest is briefly to explain the exercise and then split the delegates into groups. Three or four groups work well. The benefits list is divided up and allocated to the groups (in the example we had four groups of three people, each allocated up to three benefits to describe).

The exercise is a bit more difficult to get right and needs careful positioning. You should introduce the session with an explanatory slide similar to that at Figure 12.4 overleaf:

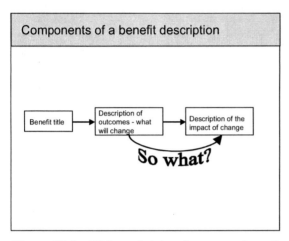

Figure 12.4 – Slide explaining the way to describe benefits

This diagram, on its own, is a bit cryptic. I would therefore recommend that you follow it with an example; even if this means making the work of one group easier. An example used for this project is shown in Figure 12.5:

Example benefit description

Benefit	Outcome	Impact of change
Improve accuracy of raw material (RM) orders	Improved forecasting and demand/supply balancing will allow RM orders to match actual foreward need more closely	A reduced level of expiditing activity needed (eg demurrage or emergency movement of RM stocks between plants) to offset short-term over and under ordering of RM

Figure 12.5 – Slide of a benefit description

This exercise needs to be conducted carefully. This means giving the delegates time to work out their descriptions while still allowing time for all benefit descriptions to be reviewed by the whole workshop. In our example the workshop is lucky enough to be facing only 11 benefits – three per group; it could have been more. Under these circumstances I would allow ten minutes for the introduction and organisation into groups, 45 minutes for the groups to produce their descriptions and about 35 minutes to review the work; one and a half hours in total. This will allow the group to break for lunch at 12.30 (assuming an 8.30 start and no undue delay in the previous sessions).

Stage managing this session can be tricky. First of all, there is every chance that one or more of the groups will not have got the hang of the exercise, despite having seen the example. A good way round this is for you and other members of the team (particularly those who gave the project briefing the day before) to circulate among the groups to make sure that their work remains on track.

A more difficult part to organise is the review at the end of the session. The best way of conducting this is to display each benefit description on the screen in turn, via the second facilitator's PC projector, and get him or her to make amendments to the wording as they are agreed by the workshop. The problem is how to get the groups' words into the PC without a significant delay. Two ways round the problem can work:

- Ensure that each group has a PC with a pre-loaded copy of a benefit description template (such as that shown in Figure 10.5). Get them to enter their descriptions directly into the PC (they do not need projectors; there is no problem in having three delegates huddled around a PC screen) and then transfer the completed templates to the facilitator's PC using memory sticks.

- If it is not possible to equip the delegate groups in this way (this becomes less likely as business laptops become more of an essential personal accessory) and they produce their benefit descriptions on paper, a less technologically advanced solution is to enter the first group's work into the facilitator's PC and review these benefits while the remaining groups' work is entered by a third member of the team on another PC. Once the first group's work has been reviewed then the projector cable is switched to the second PC to complete the exercise.

In Chapter 6 we covered in some detail what to look out for to ensure that the two elements of the benefits description are correctly drafted. You need to keep these points clearly in mind while conducting the review of benefits description. However, the point of this real-time review is not to polish the syntax and grammar but merely to ensure that the essence of the cause and impact of change has been correctly captured. No one will object if some further tidying up of the wording is done by you after the workshop is over, as long as the meaning of the words remains intact.

▶ Session 3 – Identifying measures

This is an important session, not just for the development of a good benefits case but also because selecting the wrong performance improvement metric could skew the project's financial contributions derived during the subsequent financial impact workshop. You face a dilemma in deciding how to approach this session; whether or not to consider in any detail the changes along the chain of events that lead to the performance improvement. The pros and cons are:

- Addressing the measures and targets for outcomes and knock-on changes that lead to performance improvement can help ensure that the right performance improvement measure is selected.

- Spending undue time on these changes on the ground will jeopardise the chance of completing, within the time scheduled for the workshop, those elements of the benefits case that are essential for this stage of the project.

There is a third way; a compromise approach that will work for most benefits, leaving just a few where it may be necessary to delve into the details of measures for outcomes. I suggest you construct a simple chain of events diagram for each benefit, without worrying about the measures and targets associated with each change in the chain; apart, of course, from the final change in performance improvement. Look at the example at Figure 12.6:

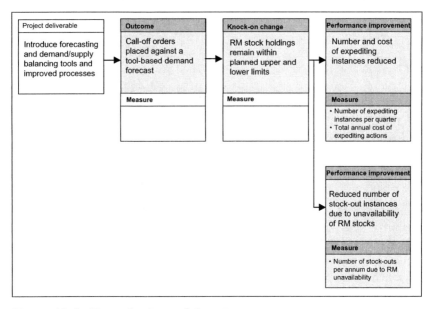

Figure 12.6 – Example chain of changing events

Here, the benefit description example used in the previous session (Figure 12.5) has been formatted in a more explicit cause-and-effect way to produce the chain events for this benefit. Understanding of the intermediate changes on the ground will help to identify the performance improvements and their measures (and, in the next session, the associated targets) without necessarily needing, themselves, to have their measures defined.

Another consideration is how to conduct the session. Although important, it has been assigned the graveyard slot, with delegates perhaps concentrating more (if they are concentrating at all) on digesting their lunch. So, while there are several ways of running the session, it would be wise to choose an approach that keeps delegates on their feet as much as possible. Enter, then, our secret weapon – the sheet of brown paper. Actually, not just a sheet of brown paper but a large one that has been previously marked up and stuck onto a free workshop wall at a height such that the top and bottom are easily reached by delegates without stretching or crouching. Typically these sheets are four feet by five feet in size and one is usually needed for each benefit class. In our example, because some of the classes have few benefits in them (see Table 12.2) you can get away with three or, at most, four sheets. Ideally, these should all be mounted on the wall simultaneously, requiring a length of up to 20 feet of free wall space; a consideration when choosing the venue for the workshop. The first sheet, devoted to the benefits within the 'Customer satisfaction' benefits class, will look like the illustration at Figure 12.7:

Benefit class	Improve customer satisfaction	
Benefit	Impacted chain of events	Performance metric
Support customer collaboration		
Enable better offer promise		
Improve deliveries (IFOT)		
Warn customers of delays		

Figure 12.7 – Example of a brown paper sheet for the measure identification session

The handwritten pieces of paper are those that will have been prepared over lunch, from the output of Session 1; the titles were printed before the workshops started.

I am in danger of getting ahead of myself. Please bear my introductory remarks in mind as we now walk through the session.

You cannot avoid an initial introduction to the session, despite possible torpor within the delegate community. The presentation should follow the story line suggested by the supporting slides shown in Figure 12.8 opposite:

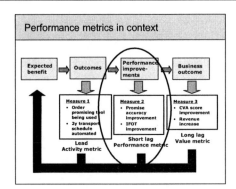

This diagram reminds delegates of the three different types of measure: for outcomes, performance improvement and financial impact and the fact that, at this stage, we are focusing on measures for performance improvement

Agenda for Session 3

- Discuss example (5 minutes)
- Workshop split into 3 groups
- Groups define chains of linked effects of change (30 minutes)
- Review chains (10 minutes)
- Groups select performance improvement measures (30 minutes)
- Review performance improvement measures (15 minutes)

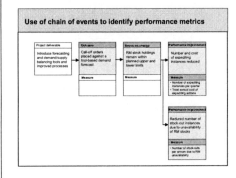

The example of Figure 12.6 used to demonstrate how the chain of events impacted by change is used to help identify relevant performance improvement and thus select performance improvement measures

Figure 12.8 – Introductory slides for the measure identification session

The workshop now needs to be split into groups again. In this example I would make three groups of about four delegates each and allocated benefits as in Table 12.3 below:

Group 1	Improve customer intimace
	Enable better customer offers
	Improve deliveries (IFOT)
	Inform customers of delivery delays
Group 2	Improve RM demand forecasting
	Improve accuracy of RM orders
	Improve efficiency of plant scheduling
	Improve inventory planning and optimization
Group 3	Reduce the need for country-based managers
	Improve transportation scheduling
	Reduce cost of invoice processing

Table 12.3 – Allocation of benefits to groups for measure identification

This allocation may need some care. For instance, in our example:

- Given that we have used the benefit of improving accuracy of RM orders to provide a worked example during the session's introduction, the workload on Group 1 will be greater than for the other two groups and the group should be given a commensurate proportion of resources (number of delegates and proportion of facilitators' time).

- There is some sensitivity in the benefit to reduce the number of country-based managers. Group 3 should mainly comprise delegates from the regional headquarters plus a transportation manager (this role is not one of those at risk because of this benefit).

Each group will need a printed copy of the benefit descriptions for each of the benefits that they will be working on. Given the work to prepare these and the brown paper sheets, one or two members of the team will have to take a very hasty lunch.

Armed with the benefit descriptions, groups should not have much difficulty in constructing the chains of events impacted by the relevant outcomes. They should be given strips of paper that will fit the space allotted on the brown paper and asked to draw their completed chains on these. Again, members of the team circulate among the groups to provide guidance where necessary. When the half hour is up, the groups reassemble in the workshop room and post their solutions in the appropriate place on the brown paper sheets.

In reviewing group solutions, you will go through each benefit with the delegates clustered around the brown paper sheets. Those that look right should be agreed quickly, leaving more time to discuss possible amendments for those that look incomplete or wrong. To be able to do this reasonably slickly, you need to be familiar with your version of each chain of events; most of these worked out before the workshops started.

Now it just remains in this session for the measures for each of the performance improvements to be identified. For this, it is as well to keep the same delegate groupings and benefit allocations as for the previous task. It may be tempting to rotate group allocations but the same sensitivities that applied previously still exist. If such sensitivities do not apply then there is merit in swapping the groups around to get a fresh approach. The groups can stay standing around the brown paper sheets and stick up their suggestions as they complete them. The session is completed with a review of the performance measures, in a similar fashion to the first review. When reviewing the measures, remember the pointers to their selection we discussed at the beginning of Chapter 7. The brown paper sheets should now look something like the illustration at Figure 12.9 overleaf.

The delegates now retire for half an hour for tea and you have some more stage management to do on the brown paper. The sketches of chains of events are not needed for the next session and can be removed and put to one side for post-workshop documentation. In their place, other columns are drawn and new column titles added.

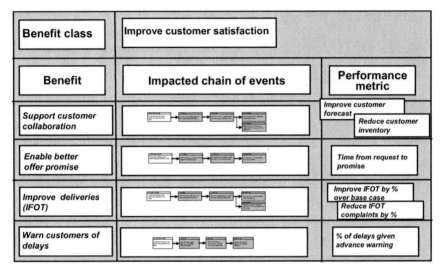

Figure 12.9 – Example of a completed measure identification sheet

▶ Session 4 – Setting performance targets

The final session of the day is also the most difficult. We discussed at length, in Chapter 7, the probable blockages to achieving realistic targets for performance improvement and a variety of techniques for overcoming these obstacles. The suggestions made then were not specific to workshops of a particular project stage and, in the Feasibility stage workshops, two factors work in your favour:

- Project implementation and operation are still a long way off and those delegates responsible for operational performance will be more relaxed at this stage about agreeing significant performance improvement.

- At this stage the project is looking for a quantified benefits accuracy of plus or minus 30 per cent, so pinpoint precision in target setting is not necessary. This is just as well, as much finer value accuracy will need a closer examination of the degree to which the project can cause the changes on the ground that lead to performance improvement than is possible or desirable during the Assess stage.

I suggest that a good way of conducting this session is, taking each benefit in turn, to agree around the table who is responsible for the performance improvement in question and get that person to stand and present his or her view of what the performance target should be. Of course, the responsible person may not be at the workshop but, if we have got the delegate list right, there should be someone present with the role and experience, if not the authority, to speak for the accountable person (at least provisionally). If you are going to adopt this approach, which has some advantages, it is only fair to have warned the delegates before they went off to tea.

The brown paper sheets now look like Figure 12.10

Benefit class	Improve customer satisfaction				
Benefit	**Performance measure**	**Responsible role**	**Target range**	**Performance target**	
Support customer collaboration	Improve customer forecast / Reduce customer inventory				
Enable better offer promise	Time from request to promise				
Improve deliveries (IFOT)	Improve IFOT by % over base case / Reduce IFOT complaints by %				
Warn customers of delays	% of delays given advance warning				

Figure 12.10 – Brown paper sheet for performance target setting

You might ask why we are letting delegates off the hook by getting them to quote a target range rather than insisting on a spot figure. We discussed the bracketing technique in Chapter 7, where I implied that it was a near-final resort. In fact, I think we should be pragmatic and include range-quoting as a deliberate step towards achieving a single target figure; the delegates will be more comfortable with this approach and it could be useful for future reference to document the workshop's consensus opinion of what the minimum and maximum improvement levels could be.

The main advantage of getting the appropriate delegate to run the mini-session concerning his or her business process is that it then becomes a local debate between that person and the other workshop delegates. There will be an internal tension between the responsible delegate, who will have some reluctance to be bold in proposing stretched targets, and the others who will be keen to talk up the value of the project to the region. You are out of the firing line for the moment and can focus on bringing forward balancing arguments (such as introducing tailored benchmark figures) at the right moment in the debate.

The responsible delegate will no doubt express reasons and justifications for the upper and lower limits when giving an opinion on the achievable performance improvement targets. One of the visiting team should be detailed to take notes of what the delegate says by way of justification and also note any subsequent material changes in the consensus view of achievable targets. A summary of these notes will be included in the workshop output which, again, may be very useful in the future.

You need to be sensitive to a few factors during, and particularly towards the end of, this session. Of course, the primary objective will be to set reasonably stretched but achievable targets and there may be a temptation to push and push, using all the techniques discussed in Chapter 5, until this happens. However, it would be quite wrong to get bogged down in arguments over one target and you would be advised to set a mental limit of, say, 15 minutes to discuss any one target. If the time limit is reached you should take whatever is on the table and move on. It is likely that such an impasse will only happen in a few cases; the majority of targets being agreed well within the time limit. Another factor to take into account is that this is happening at the end of a long day and you will want workshop delegates to be in a friendly and cooperative mood for the next workshop.

The brown paper should look like Figure 12.11 at the end of this last session.

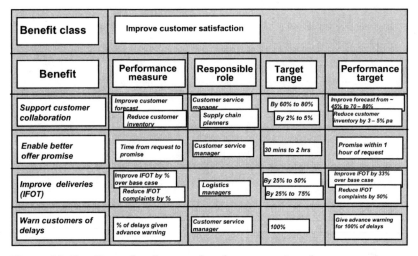

Benefit class	Improve customer satisfaction			

Benefit	Performance measure	Responsible role	Target range	Performance target
Support customer collaboration	Improve customer forecast / Reduce customer inventory	Customer service manager / Supply chain planners	By 60% to 80% / By 2% to 5%	Improve forecast from ~ 45% to 70 – 80% / Reduce customer inventory by 3 – 5% pa
Enable better offer promise	Time from request to promise	Customer service manager	30 mins to 2 hrs	Promise within 1 hour of request
Improve deliveries (IFOT)	Improve IFOT by % over base case / Reduce IFOT complaints by %	Logistics managers	By 25% to 50% / By 25% to 75%	Improve IFOT by 33% over base case / Reduce IFOT complaints by 50%
Warn customers of delays	% of delays given advance warning	Customer service manager	100%	Give advance warning for 100% of delays

Figure 12.11 – Example of a completed target setting sheet

► Ending the workshop

The only thing that remains before the workshop breaks for the day is to set the delegates their homework, for completion before the beginning of the next workshop (with the example schedule illustrated at Figure 11.8, delegates will have a full working day to complete this). The work concerned is to fill any gaps in the benefit definition information that should have been completed during the workshop, by discussing the matter with colleagues who may have specialist knowledge of the area of information concerned. For the detail needed in the Feasibility stage there are likely to be few gaps, so little work for delegates to do. There may well be a need for consultation with accountable directors or managers who were not present at the workshop to confirm targets that were provisionally set during the workshop. The tasks should be agreed specifically with the appropriate delegates.

▶ After the workshop

Delegates are not the only people with work to do before the financial impact workshop. You will need to take the brown paper output and convert it into a revised benefits case (without the financial element at this stage) for the region. Part of the benefits case produced at the end of the first region's benefits workshop in our example project is shown at Figure 12.12 opposite.

You also need to review the financial part of the strawman benefits case to see whether any of the output from the benefits workshop would impact the business logic or financial calculations, or both, of the case. The most likely causes of such changes would be:

- New benefits or benefit classes

- Deleted benefits

- Significant differences between strawman and workshop performance target levels

- Indication of an incorrect assumption in the strawman case about one or more financial baseline figures used to calculate financial contribution

You and other team members also need to make yourselves available to delegates during the period between the two workshops in case any further clarification is needed for the tasks that they have been asked to complete.

Financial bucket	Benefit	Outcome	Responsible role	Performance measures and targets
Revenue	Support customer intimacy: - collaborative forecasting - VMI implementation	Introduce collaborative forecasting and/or vendor managed inventory (VMI) for our key customers, linking to the internal APS demand forecasting, supply programming and inventory management systems		For those customers who accept collaboration offer: - Improve customer forecast accuracy from – 45% to 75% - Reduce customer inventory by 3% to 5% p.a
	Enable better offer to the customer	Provide a clear picture to sales teams inventory, incorporating stock held, stock already promised, stock re-supply details and customer priority algorithms; taking into account stocks at all potential re-supply points for each order. Achieved by supporting sales teams with APS demand forecasting and assignment tools	Customer service manager	Provide promise within 1 hour of customer request
	Deliver in full, on time, every time	Improve our ability to deliver in full, on time, through improved visibility of forthcoming promotions and their impact on demand, stock level planning, plant scheduling and control of secondary transportation (optimised and integrated secondary transport)		- 33% improvement over base case - Reduce number of IFOT-related complaints by 50%
	Inform customers of delivery delays	Use associated APS functionality to improve tracking of transport and provide alerts and visibility to customer service teams		100%
COGS (RM)	Improve accuracy of RM call-off orders	Provide a more accurate and agile RM call-off process, enabled by more accurate short-term RM forecasting, thus minimising demurrage and associated expediting RM reception costs	Regional master supply planner	Reduce RM demurrage and expediting transfer costs by 50%
	Improve medium and long term RM forecast	Provide a more accurate view of needs, by RM, over the next 3 and 12 months by improving direct procurement demand planning and also the ability to predict RM requirements to meet FG demand. Achieved by improving procurement demand processes and providing APS forecasting tool		Reduce RM purchase costs per volume by 0.5% to 1%
COGS (Conversion)	Improve efficiency of plant scheduling	Achieved through process improvements external and internal to plants: Better forward demand visibility (including promotion blips) and more agile supply programming (including better inter-plant production balancing) and RM demand	Plant managers	Increase blending/filling efficiency by 5% to 10%; Reduce plant labour costs by 2% to 5%
COGS (Regionalisation)	Reduce the need for country-based SC managers	Revise operating procedures and provide APS tools to enable cross-region forecasting and supply programming to be done in one (or 2) locations for the whole region. Rationalise transportation management through improved processes driven by APS transport	Regional SC network manager	Free up 10 to 20 country-based SC managers
Cost to deliver	Improve primary and secondary transportation scheduling	Optimise the scheduling of primary and secondary transport, including maximising opportunities for load sharing, back-hauling and multi-dropping, by improving processes leveraged by APS transport scheduling and management tool	Country logistics managers	Reduce primary and secondary transport costs per litre-mile moved by 5% to 10%
	Reduce administrative cost of invoice processing	Use associated APS functionality to improve and consolidate transportation billing by 3rd party hauliers		Reduce cost of invoicing (per 1000 invoices) by 40%
Inventory	Reduce inventory through better forecasting and planning	Improve inventory planning and optimisation (including management of distributor and key customer stocks) Achieved through improved stock visibility, better 30-day forward demand forecasting (60-day forward for importing countries) and more agile and accurate ordering; all enabled by APS stock planning tools	Cluster supply planners	Reduce FG stocks held by 3 to 5 stock days

Figure 12.12 – Example of a benefits case at the end of the benefits workshop

CHAPTER THIRTEEN

Conducting financial impact workshops

Introduction

After a day of comparative rest, you, the other facilitators and the delegates are ready to undertake the financial impact workshop.

The atmosphere should be different from that of the first two days of workshops. Delegates know each other and the members of the project team, are comfortable with workshop procedures and rules of engagement and are familiar with the benefits management method and shape of the region's benefits case. Hopefully, they are also feeling engaged in, and empowered by, the benefits case development process. Because of this, and the nature of the sessions in the financial impact workshop, you can be less rigid over workshop structure and timekeeping.

The workshop has three elements:

- Review of benefits workshop findings
- Briefing on derivation financial contribution and financial buckets
- Development of business logic

Although you can be less structured you still need to follow an agenda. I suggest that an hour and a half be allowed to cover the first two sessions, followed by refreshments. This means that the final session will be split, part before and part after lunch. This is no bad thing, as the session can be quite dry and a little tedious to complete.

The workshop sessions

▶ Review of benefits workshop

The main purposes of this session are to:

- Remind delegates of the position reached at the end of the benefits workshop.

- Add in the results of work undertaken by delegates during the break between workshops to fill gaps in the benefits case and confirm provisional performance improvement targets.

No props are needed for this session, other than a projection of the benefits case developed so far (and written up by you in the break between workshops). I suggest that the format for the session should be:

- Receive all input, other than performance targets, from each delegate tasked in turn and add it to the projected benefits case; any issues can be debated around the table as the detail is added.

- Any outstanding performance targets be presented by the responsible delegate and discussed around the table, in the same way as in the benefits workshop. Again, changes can be incorporated on the fly as they are agreed.

- Finally, quickly go through each benefit class, checking that the delegates are still happy with the content.

Once this exercise has been completed, one of the team members needs to extract the completed benefits case on a memory stick and arrange for a copy to be printed for each delegate before the start of the third session of the day later in the morning.

▶ Session 5 – Allocation of financial contribution

Up to this point in the series of two workshops, the subject of financial contribution has been covered only fleetingly in passing. Now that we have finalised the benefits definitions it is time to address the subject full on.

Having said that, you are unlikely to get as far as calculating the regional contribution to the dollar value of the project but will define everything that is needed to be able to derive that figure (other than the financial baseline figures, which are not a matter of debate and which you get from elsewhere).

Before you go through the exercise to define the financial impact of benefits classes, the delegates are briefed on the way that improvements to business processes lead through eventually to improvements in the organisation's financial position. Such an understanding is arguably not essential for delegates to be able to contribute fully to the business logic building exercise; so why provide it and, more pertinently, why now? Answering these questions in the order they are asked:

- Delegates will almost certainly be asked for their opinions by members of the leadership team when the latter are invited to agree the stated financial contribution of the project and the regional budget changes that will follow its approval. The financial value summary will be presented in financial bucket terms and it is important that delegates can follow how this financial model has come about.

- An understanding of the mapping from business process to benefit to financial bucket can help in framing the wording for the business logic of each benefit class.

I must emphasise that the briefing is not about the organisation's financial structures themselves; delegates to these workshops will be very familiar with them already. Equally, delegates will fully understand the concepts and specifics of its business processes. What will probably be new to them is the concept of benefits mapping.

There are two ways of conducting this exercise; with or without brown paper. I think that it would be a good idea to provide a bit of contrast from other interactive sessions by not using brown paper in this one, in which case the only prop for the session is the single projected slide shown at Figure 13.1 overleaf.

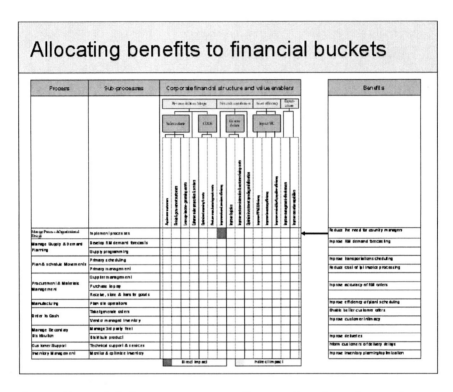

Figure 13.1 – Slide for presentation on allocating benefits to financial buckets

This slide is actually a living spreadsheet, either standing alone or embedded in the usual presentation software, for reasons that will become clear in a minute. The briefing then need only familiarise delegates with this format for the organisation's financial breakdown structure and explain, by going through one example, how to map benefits against financial category.

Points to put across in the briefing are:

- The rows and columns in the top half of the spreadsheet, under the heading 'Corporate financial structure and value enablers' represent the part of the organisation's hierarchy of financial categories that will be impacted by the project. You may have to spend some time ensuring that delegates recognise this and it would be prudent to have a slide, or printed copies, of the financial structure in its normal format so that delegates can see that the format in the spreadsheet is valid.

- Similarly, in the bottom half of the spreadsheet, the rows in the first two columns represent the defined company business processes, and sub-processes, that will be impacted by the project.

- The benefits column to the right of the spreadsheet aligns benefits opposite the business processes that they primarily affect. However, it may not be possible to achieve level alignment in all cases, particularly where a benefit impacts more than one business process.

Having made these points, you should go through one example of this mapping exercise. Taking the first benefit, 'Reduce the need for country managers', first explain that this benefit affects the business process 'Managing Process & Organisational Design' and indicate this by drawing an arrow as shown at Figure 13.1. The second part of the exercise is to decide which financial bucket this benefit will favour; in the example it is to 'Improve shared services efficiency' within the top-level financial category of 'Net cash contribution'. This mapping is indicated by selecting the cell where the selected business process and financial category intersect, and changing its colour to red.

The workshop then goes through the same procedure with the remaining ten benefits (as I have mentioned before, other projects could have many more than this number of benefits; we will see an example of such a project in the chapters on benefit tracking). This exercise should not take long and I suggest that you facilitate it, with another team member operating the PC and the delegates seated together round the table. Each benefit is taken in turn and the group asked for suggestions as to which process will be impacted and which financial categories affected. Once a consensus is agreed on each of the two parts, the team member at the PC draws in the arrow or arrows and changes cell colours as appropriate; we use red for directly impacted categories and yellow for those indirectly affected. When the exercise has been completed the spreadsheet will look like the one in Figure 13.2 overleaf.

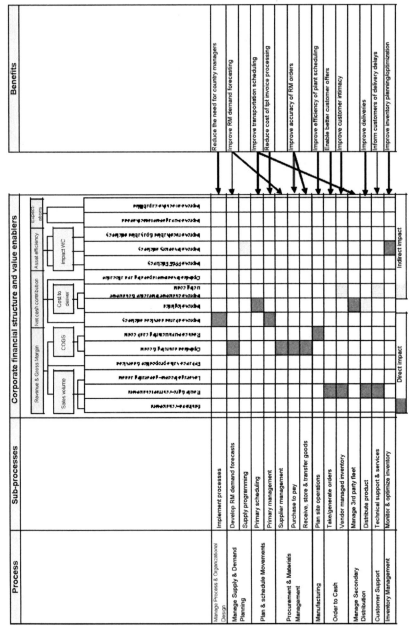

Figure 13.2 – Completed allocation of benefits to financial buckets

At this stage you need another piece of slick stage management. The spreadsheet is downloaded onto a memory stick and a third member of the team rushes off to print copies of it for the delegates; ideally the operation should be completed in less than five minutes.

In the meantime, the second slide, shown at Figure 13.3, is projected onto the screen.

Benefit class	Revenue	COGS (RM)	COGS (Conversion)	NCC (Shared services)	Cost to deliver	Inventory
Improve customer satisfaction						
Improve procurement						
Improve manufacturing						
Reduce overheads						
Improve logistics						
Reduce inventory						

Figure 13.3 – Format for mapping benefit class value to financial category

The final exercise in the session is simple almost to the level of triviality. However, we do it anyway to ensure that delegates will be able to follow the complete process of distilling the project financial value from the benefits case to a format that will be used for higher-level presentations and project documentation. The exercise is merely to take each benefit class in turn and, using the output of the previous task (Figure 13.2) and the list showing the benefits within each benefit classes (Table 12.2), assigning a placemarker for its financial contribution to a financial category. You may as well continue using the same workshop format to complete the exercise, calling out for suggestions, one benefit class at a time, and discussing any differences of opinion (I would not be surprised if there were none) before entering the consensus answer onto the spreadsheet; again by colouring in the appropriate cell. The completed spreadsheet will look like Figure 13.4 overleaf.

Benefit class	Revenue	COGS (RM)	COGS (Conversion)	NCC (Shared services)	Cost to deliver	Inventory
Improve customer satisfaction	■					
Improve procurement		■				
Improve manufacturing			■			
Reduce overheads				■		
Improve logistics					■	
Reduce inventory						■

Figure 13.4 – Completed mapping of benefit class value to financial category

Apart from the spreadsheet's simplicity, its immediately obvious characteristic is its symmetry. The reason for this is that, when we selected the benefit classes, we had the company's financial structure in mind; thus there is a very straightforward mapping between the two. This completes the session. It has been a short one but you need the delegates to leave the room while it is prepared for the final session. So the mid-morning refreshments are scheduled somewhat early.

▶ Session 6 – Deriving business logic

The purpose of business logic is to transform the forecast performance improvement targets into a financial contribution for each benefit class. The elements of this transformation are shown at Figure 13.5 below:

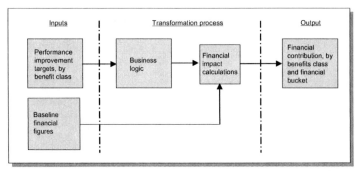

Figure 13.5 – Schematic of the elements needed to derive financial value

You have the inputs; performance improvement targets agreed during the benefits workshop and baseline financial figures for the region collected from the finance department before the workshops started. Only part of the transformation process will be undertaken during the workshop. You will make final calculations before the last activity of the team's visit to the region – briefing the leadership team. Developing business logic is the equivalent of deriving an algebraic equation, while the calculations equate to plugging specific values into the equation variables to produce a numeric solution.

I suggest that the brown paper sheets be reintroduced for this last session of the workshop. The delegates will return to see sheets like Figure 13.6 on the wall.

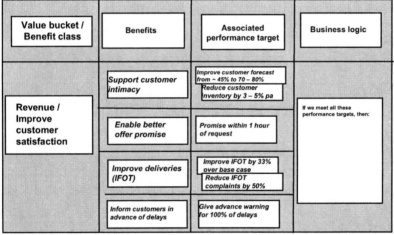

Value bucket / Benefit class	Benefits	Associated performance target	Business logic
Revenue / Improve customer satisfaction	Support customer intimacy	Improve customer forecast from ~ 45% to 70 – 80% Reduce customer inventory by 3 – 5% pa	If we meet all these performance targets, then:
	Enable better offer promise	Promise within 1 hour of request	
	Improve deliveries (IFOT)	Improve IFOT by 33% over base case Reduce IFOT complaints by 50%	
	Inform customers in advance of delays	Give advance warning for 100% of delays	

Figure 13.6 – Brown paper sheets for derivation of business logic

Normally you would use a separate sheet for each benefit class but in this example, where some of the benefit classes have few associated benefits and performance improvement targets, some sharing is acceptable; so, again, three or four sheets will suffice.

Start with a short discussion about how to derive business logic, using the pointers covered in Chapter 7. It is difficult to be prescriptive here as you will find that the approach needed will be quite different from business class to business class. I shall show two examples in a moment which will illustrate this quite vividly. Having discussed the process, a good way of carrying out the exercise is to divide the delegates into enough groups to give each the task of deriving business logic for all of the benefit classes on one of the sheets of brown paper – this means one to three benefit classes per group. Give the groups a reasonable length of time to carry out the tasks, I suggest 45 minutes to an hour, and make sure that each group is visited regularly by team members to make sure that they do not go off the track or (maintaining the metaphor) run out of steam.

After lunch, each group is asked, in turn, to post its solution on the brown paper and present it to the other groups. For each presentation, you and the other delegates need to be satisfied that:

- The business logic is sound and complete.

- All the information needed to be able to calculate a financial value, including specification of the financial baseline to use, is present.

Let us now look at two very different examples. The first is the business logic for the benefit class 'Improve customer satisfaction', whose performance improvement targets are illustrated in Figure 13.6. This is probably one of the most difficult instances of business logic to complete because of the dominance of the element of unguided business judgement needed; by unguided, I mean that someone has to make a judgement without any facts to help. The wording in the text box below shows this.

Our customers in this region generally perceive us as a company that provides expensive, high-quality products but that our level of service tends to let us down; we are difficult to do business with and our deliveries are not as reliable as those of our competitors. We know that, for a significant proportion of our customers, service levels are as important as product quality. There has been a constant loss of these customers to our competitors at a rate of about five per cent per annum by volume of product sold, which has eroded efforts to grow our customer base.

Cont.

If we improve the way we engage with customers to take orders, our delivery reliability and our ability to give prior warning of delivery issues, then we will improve the level of satisfaction held by most of our customers. On top of this, if we offer collaborative forecasting tools and vendor-managed inventory to those customers that would benefit from these facilities, we will provide an enhanced level of intimacy and satisfaction for these customers.

Meeting the targets of this benefit class will bring our service levels at least up to the level of the best of our competitors and will stem the loss. The loss rate could thus be reduced from five per cent to a level of between four per cent and two per cent; an absolute improvement of between one per cent and three per cent of volume sold. This benefit is shared equally by this project and the Customer Service Excellence project; thus the financial contribution to the business offered by this project will be between a half and one and a half per cent of volume sold. The financial contribution of this benefit class will be based on the increased revenue, less the increase in cost of goods and distribution costs; that is, gross margin less costs of delivery.

As you can see, the key to the financial impact of this benefit class is the degree to which the rate of loss of customers to the competition can be reduced; something that requires subjective business judgement. The group has been sensible in suggesting that the loss cannot be totally eliminated and has perhaps been a little cautious over what it sees as the minimum improvement level. The resulting range of possible improvement values is acceptable at this stage; as a rule of thumb, a minimum figure that is no less than half of the maximum figure will give a full swing from the midpoint value of plus or minus about 30 per cent, which is within the allowable tolerance for the Feasibility stage.

Note that the wording has made allowance for sharing the benefit with a related project; something that we will discuss further in the next chapter. The wording also includes a specific reference to the financial baseline to use; in this case gross margin less delivery costs.

Now let us look at a completely different piece of business logic based on the benefits classes illustrated at Figure 13.7.

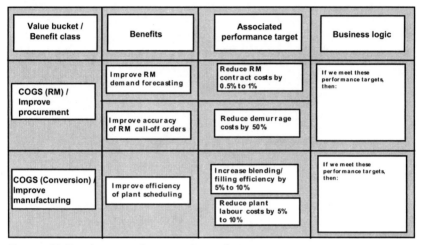

Figure 13.7 – An easier business logic derivation

We will look at the business logic for both of these business classes. In both cases the business logic is largely a matter of 'numerical algebra' rather than logic and will need little in the way of business judgement. There are two exceptions:

- In the first benefit case, there has to be some sleight of hand to come up with the target reduction in raw material (RM) costs. The table in the business logic (in the panel opposite) would, on reflection, have been better worked out when measures and targets were being addressed during the benefits workshop; the way it has been done looks a little like putting the cart before the horse. However, it illustrates that deficiencies in target setting can be addressed during this session and retrospective changes to the benefits case made later.

- In the second case, delegates need to ensure no double counting between the two identified performance targets.

Business logic for the 'Improve procurement' benefit class is:

Raw materials comprise base oils, additives and packaging. The region cannot directly influence the costs of base oils, which are subject to global negotiations conducted from the centre. However, improved forecast accuracy at the regional level will help our regional suppliers of additives, and particularly of packaging materials, to reduce their costs, thus providing us with a lever for price reductions during contract negotiations.

The value of achieving improved medium and long-range demand forecasting will be a reduction by 1 to 2 per cent of regional additive costs and 2.5 to 5 per cent of regional costs of packaging material.

	Proportion of overall value	Percentage reduction in cost	Weighted reduction in cost
Base oils	65%	Nil	Nil
Additives	25%	1% to 2%	0.25% to 0.5%
Packaging	10%	2.5% to 5%	0.25% to 0.5%
Total	100%		0.5% to 1%

Thus the overall value of RM cost reduction will be 0.5 to 1 per cent of total RM costs.

The value of a reduction in demurrage costs will be 50 per cent of the total current annual cost of demurrage.

Had there been separate targets set for the reductions in additives and packaging costs during the benefits workshop then this piece of business logic would have been very much shorter.

The business logic for our third example benefit class, 'Improve manufacturing', might look like this:

> If we improve blending/filling efficiency we can increase throughput in each plant by the same proportion without adding to plant fixed costs or significantly adding to plant variable costs. Savings in variable costs for a constant throughput would be slightly less than the proportional increase in efficiency.
>
> Variable plant costs make up 40% of total manufacturing costs. Of these variable costs, 60% are labour costs. The main value driver for this benefit class is a 5% to 10% reduction in labour costs. The balance of value will come from a smaller decrease in other variable costs (such as power consumption), estimated as a 2% to 4% reduction.
>
> The value of this benefit class is therefore the sum of a 1.2% to 2.4% reduction (labour cost reductions) and a 0.3% to 0.6% reduction (other variable cost reductions) in total manufacturing costs; giving a total benefit class financial contribution of 1.5% to 3% of total manufacturing costs.

If time allows, and you have managed again to arrange some slick stage management, it would be worth sending the delegates off to tea while you complete the financial contribution section in the benefits case spreadsheet. You can then finish the workshop, after tea, by showing the complete benefit case, class by class, to the delegates before they leave.

This may not be possible, in which case the output should be sent to delegates as soon as it is complete; in our case, by the end of the following day.

In either case, the benefits case (or part of one class of it) should look like Figure 13.8 opposite.

Benefit	Outcome	Responsible role	Performance measures and targets	Business logic
Support customer intimacy: - collaborative forecasting - VMI implementation	Introduce collaborative forecasting and/or Vendor Managed Inventory (VMI) for our key customers, linked to the internal APS demand forecasting, supply programming and inventory management systems		For those customers who accept collaboration offer: - Improve customer forecast accuracy from ~ 45% to 70 to 80% - Reduce customer inventory by 3 to 5% p.a.	Our customers in this region generally perceive us as a company that provides expensive, high quality products but that our level of service tends to let us down; we are difficult to do business with and our deliveries are not as reliable as those of our competitors. We know that, for a significant proportion of our customers, service levels are as important as product quality. There has been a constant loss of these customers to our competitors at a rate of about five percent per annum by volume of product sold, which has eroded efforts to grow our customer base. If we improve the way we engage with customers to take orders, our delivery reliability and our ability to give prior warning of delivery issues then we will improve the level of satisfaction held by most of our customers. On top of this, if we offer collaborative forecasting tools and vendor managed inventory to those customers that would benefit from these facilities, we will provide an enhanced level of intimacy and satisfaction for these customers
Enable better offer to the customer	Provide a clear picture to sales teams of inventory: incorporating stock held, stock already promised, stock resupply dates and customer prioritisation algorithms; taking into account stocks at all potential resupply points for each order. Achieved by i		Provide promise within 1 hour of customer request	
Deliver in full, on time, every time	Improve our ability to deliver in full, on time, through improved visibility of forthcoming promotions and their impact on demand, stock level planning, plant scheduling and control of secondary transportation (optimised and integrated secondary transport	Customer services manager	- 33% over base case - Reduce number of IFOT related complaints by 50%	Meeting the targets of this benefit class will bring our service levels at least up to the level of the best of our competitors and will stem the loss. The loss rate could thus be reduced from five percent to a level of from four percent to two percent; an absolute improvement of between one percent and three percent of volume sold. This benefit is shared equally by this project and the Customer Service Excellence project; thus the financial contribution to the business offered by this project will be between a half and one and a half percent of volume sold. The financial contribution of this benefit class will be based on the increased revenue, less the increase in cost of goods and distribution costs; that is, gross margin less costs of delivery
Inform customers of delivery delays	Use associated APS functionality to improve tracking of transport and provide alerts and visibility to customer service teams		100%	

Figure 13.8 – Example of part of a benefits case at the end of the financial impact workshop

▶ After the workshop

The one remaining scheduled task before the regional visit is over is to brief the leadership team. The briefing will have been arranged long before the visit and may include a number of topics. The most obvious, which were included in the leadership briefings of our example project, are:

- A short overview of the project.

- A proposed preferred regional implementation option.

- A summary of regional costs and benefits.

- Regional timescales and resource requirements for the next stage of the project.

The leadership team will not want to see project benefits in great detail at this stage. I suggest that just two slides should suffice:

- A bulleted list of the main project performance improvement drivers for the region.

- The summary of minimum and maximum project financial contribution to the region by financial category.

You have a day to prepare for your part of the briefing. The main preparatory work is to take the output from the last workshop session and plug in the financial baseline figures to produce the actual range of regional project financial contribution. A word here about financial baselines. These will have been produced by the finance function against a consistent baseline. A good baseline to use is the statement of actual annual financial performance for the year before the one in which this project stage is being conducted. If the Feasibility stage is finishing towards the end of the year, it may be better to choose the forecast out-turn for the current year. Either way, it will be for the finance function to decide this; you have merely to ensure that all the figures used are from the agreed baseline.

A possible format and content for these two slides are shown at Figure 13.9.

Principal performance improvement drivers

- Better forecasting and supply planning will:
  - Reduce RM purchase and storage costs
  - Enable a reduction in stock levels
- Better scheduling will:
  - Improve manufacturing efficiency
  - Improve delivery reliability
- Better offer promising, selective introduction of collaborative forecasting and VMI and more reliable deliveries will:
  - Improve customer satisfaction and
  - Increase sales volumes
- Regionally based planning tools and processes will reduce management overheads

Benefits summary

| Financial Value Buckets | Benefit value ($USM) | | | |
| | Minimum | | Maximum | |
	Annual	WC	Annual	WC
Sales	1.37		4.13	
COGS (RM)	0.86		1.62	
COGS (Conversion)	0.30		0.75	
COGS (Regionalisation)	0.60		1.20	
Cost to deliver	1.95		3.91	
Inventory	0.16	3.16	0.39	7.89
Total	5.24	3.16	12.00	7.89

Figure 13.9 – Benefits slides to support the leadership team briefing

Contributing to the business case

Introduction

You have now reached a point, probably at least half way through the Feasibility stage of the project, where you have completed a steady-state benefits case for at least one of the sub-projects – regions in our example. As was explained in Chapter 8, there are a number of additional things that you need to do before the end of the project stage to allow the benefits work to contribute fully to the stage business case. These are listed in Table 14.1.

Further activities to support the business case
1. Develop full-project value case
2. De-duplicate benefits with other projects
3. Add granularity to support option selection
4. Add time element to support NPV calculations

Table 14.1 – Additional benefits management tasks for the Feasibility stage

This chapter deals with these activities in turn and takes you to the end of the Feasibility stage.

Developing a full project benefits case

In Chapter 10, while talking about planning considerations, I mentioned that in an ideal world you would hold sufficient workshops to get a realistic picture of benefits in all sub-projects areas; thus, in our example, you would have held benefits workshops in each of the four geographic regions of the business. However, I also suggested that this would not always be possible – due mainly to time and cost pressures or non-availability of key personnel – and that alternative methods would be needed to assemble a global benefits case. There are two methods that come to mind, which are described below.

▶ Top-down method

The first method is to take the financial impact figures derived during the benefits workshops of one region and extrapolate them across the other regions using multiplier ratios from the top-down benefits case produced at the end of project Start-up.

You will recall the discussion in Chapter 10 about creating a tailored top-down benefits case by benefit class to support the 'go or no go' decision process at the end of project Start-up. I have reproduced that value case here at Table 14.2.

Benefit class	Asia Pacific	Americas	Europe	Rest of World	Total
Improve customer satisfaction	$1.3m	$1.8m	$1.7m	$0.8m	$5.6m
Improve procurement effectiveness	$9.0m	$9.0m	$12.0m	$7.0m	$37.0m
Improve manufacturing efficiency					
Improve logistics efficiency	$1.0m	$0.6m	$1.0m	$0.3m	$2.9m
Total annual value	$11.3m	$11.4m	$14.7m	$8.1m	$45.5m
Reduce inventory (one-off)	$8.0m	$1.9m	$6.0m	$6.1m	$22.0m

Table 14.2 – Top-down benefits case, by benefit class and region

In the example project, workshops were held in Asia Pacific and the Americas. The Asia Pacific supply chain model was more representative of those in the two regions (Europe and Rest of World) where workshops were not held. Had we used this method, the benefit class values for Europe and Rest of World would have been calculated by taking the Asia Pacific workshop-derived financial contributions and multiplying them by the ratios implicit in the Start-up top-down benefits case.

For example, the workshops resulted in an Asia Pacific financial contribution from improved customer satisfaction of $US2.75m (unusually, considerably larger than the financial contribution claimed for this benefits class at the end of Start-up). The calculated value of the same benefit class in Europe would have been $US2.75m multiplied by the ratio 1.7:1.3, or $US3.60m.

The main advantage of this method, assuming that such a top-down benefits case was developed during project Start-up, is that it is quick and easy to produce. It does, however, have two major disadvantages:

- In the Start-up benefits case, inaccuracies in the individual top-down financial contribution figures mean that the relative size of contributions between regions may be heavily distorted. Thus, the inaccuracies of the top-down benefits case are fed through to the Feasibility stage case through incorrect regional multipliers, which will make it very difficult to claim a plus or minus 30 per cent accuracy.

- Key personnel in the 'other' regions are not consulted. This will make buy-in from these regions difficult to achieve. There is likely to be further resentment as one of the options to be decided in this project stage will be the order in which the regions should be implemented; thus, regions will have a keen interest in relative project contributions between regions and will want the opportunity to make their individual cases.

▶ Consultation method

The second method, and the one we actually used in the example project, is one where the 'other' regions are asked to propose their regional benefits against the benchmark of the benefits case of one of the regions where workshops have been held. The Asia Pacific benefits case was used as the benchmark against which to elicit quantified benefits propositions from the Europe and Rest of World regional business units (BUs).

The Asia Pacific benefits case (in the form shown at Figure 12.12) was sent to the TDMs and Lead SMEs (roles defined in Chapter 11) of the two remaining regions, along with the questionnaire shown in Figure 14.1 opposite.

This consultation method overcomes the problems associated with the top-down method but inevitably requires more time. The TDMs and Lead SMEs will almost certainly need to consult with their regional colleagues before being able to send the questionnaire back; even then, there will need to be some challenges and responses by email or telephone between you and the regional representatives before a regional value is agreed between both parties. I would allow an elapsed time of three weeks for all this to be completed.

Once these negotiations with the regions have been completed, it is a simple exercise to combine the regional inputs to create a single steady-state summary of the financial contribution view of the project's benefits case. In our example, this looks like Table 14.3.

Benefit class	Project financial contribution by benefit class and region ($USm)				
	Asia Pacific	Americas	Europe	Rest of World	Total
Improve customer satisfaction	2.75	1.72	3.20	1.36	9.03
Improve procurement effectiveness	1.24	0.32	1.36	0.88	3.80
Improve manufacturing efficiency	0.53	0.40	0.26	0.46	1.65
Reduce cost of overheads	0.90		0.22		1.12
Improve logistics efficiency	2.93	2.55	2.82	0.36	8.66
Total annual value	8.35	4.99	7.86	3.06	24.26
Reduce inventory (one-off)	5.58	2.84	4.24	5.72	18.38

Table 14.3 – Steady-state global Feasibility stage benefits case

Note that, using this method, a smaller total annual financial value of the project was achieved than would have been the case with the top-down calculation method. Disappointing perhaps, but much closer to reality.

	APS Project - Asia Pacific benefits case			APS Project - ....BU benefits case			
Benefit class	Benefits	FI	FI	Key assumptions	Key differences	Business logic	
Improve customer satisfaction	•Improve customer intimacy •Enable better customer offers •Improve deliveries •Inform customers of delivery delays	2.75					
Improve procurement	•Improve RM demand forecasting •Improve accuracy of RM orders	1.24					
Improve manufacturing	•Improve efficiency of plant scheduling	0.53					
Reduce overheads	• Reduce the need for country-based managers	0.90					
Improve logistics	•Improve transportation scheduling •Reduce cost of invoice processing	2.93					
Reduce inventory	• Improve inventory planning and optimization	5.58					
	Totals ($USm)	- Annual	8.35				
		- WC	5.58				

Notes for completion – please complete all the shaded boxes:

1. Based on the Asia Pacific benefits case, provide an estimate of the financial impact of each business class in your BU
2. List all the financial assumptions (current volumes, stock days etc) upon which your values are based
3. Provide a list of key factors for your BU which are different from those that apply in Asia Pacific
4. Provide any variations from the business logic used to derive the financial impact of improvements in the Asia Pacific benefit classes

Figure 14.1 – Questionnaire for regional extrapolation of benefits case

You are now in a position to carry out the remaining Feasibility stage benefits management activities, all of which will have the effect of distorting the financial impact of the benefits case that you have so carefully created. However, these will be distortions towards, rather than away from, reality.

De-duplicating benefits

This section is somewhat different from the others in Part 2 of the book; partly because benefit de-duplication sits outside the sequence of activities that make up the end-to-end benefits management process and partly because it discusses the one major benefits management activity that is conducted mainly from the programme office rather than from within individual projects; or not at all, if the programme design had been benefit-driven from the outset. Let me first explain these two unique characteristics in a bit more detail.

▶ Sequencing

De-duplication of benefits is not an activity that is completed with a number of sequential and conjoined steps. Certainly, most of the steps will occur during the Feasibility stage but they are likely to be spread over the entire stage, interleaved with other benefits management activities. This is because:

- De-duplication is an iterative process, with flagrant conflicts between projects being detected and eliminated at an early stage (pre-workshop) but with more subtle conflicts waiting for the availability of more detail (post-workshop or, at least, post-strawman). If this multi-step process is not followed there is the danger of a lot of wasted work being done on benefits definitions that will have to be changed or deleted after finer-grain de-duplication takes place.

- The projects that have to be de-duplicated are not necessarily all at the same stage of development. A long de-duplication catchment period is therefore needed to be able to include as many projects with the required level of detailed information as possible.

▶ Accountability level

Your primary responsibility as benefits manager, prior to the completion of the PID, is to deliver an honest, accurate and representative project benefits case and this responsibility includes ensuring that all benefits are fairly claimed by the project, which implies that they are de-duplicated with other projects. However, if all project benefits managers have this responsibility within their own projects and were left to their own devices to fulfil it, then de-duplication would be an extremely inefficient process involving a myriad of bilateral meetings between the benefits and project managers of all the projects concerned. This approach would also leave open the question of who would arbitrate when projects could not agree the resolution of a benefits conflict between them. (Of course, if you are the benefits manager for a tranche of projects within a correctly structured change programme, then the issue should not apply.)

For these reasons it is almost essential that de-duplication of benefits between projects be directed from the programme level; by the programme benefits manager, if such a role exists.

At the programme level there are two main questions that de-duplication is designed to answer:

- Are there any unwanted overlaps between projects and their benefits?

- Is the sum of benefits claimed by all of the projects within the programme or portfolio realistic and achievable?

These are not easy questions to answer, particularly when there are many interdependent or complementary projects involved. To be able to do so with any degree of certainty, the programme benefits manager needs the help of a defined process and some specific tools.

De-duplication process

The benefits management method is not prescriptive about the de-duplication process to follow; details will probably differ according to the organisation's structure and culture. The main point is that there should be a process laid down and it should be followed by benefits managers at all levels within the programme or portfolio.

Figure 14.2 opposite illustrates the process in place in the company that initiated the supply chain project that is providing our example.

This diagram, and the process it represents, may look complicated at first. In fact, I have combined or deleted some of the steps from the process diagram that I developed for the company, in order to simplify it. From the programme benefits manager's viewpoint, there are really only two main activities within the overall process:

- Conducting an initial audit of all projects to eliminate gross overlaps and identify further potential areas of project activity overlap, benefits conflict or overstated benefits.

- Examining the potential problem areas more closely once the projects concerned have the level of detail available to do so.

Programme and project benefits managers alike have work to do to prepare for these two stages of benefits de-duplication and these activities are also shown on the process diagram. I will walk through these various steps on the assumption that the initial inputs to the process, shown on the diagram, are already in place.

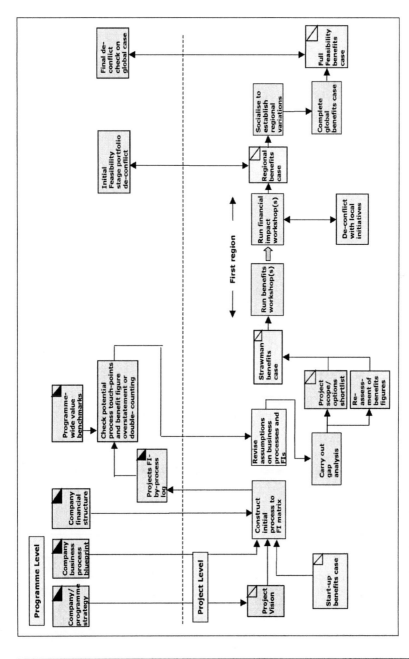

Figure 14.2 – Example of a programme-level de-duplication process

▶ Initial audit

The first step is for each project benefits manager to construct a matrix in which the financial contribution of each benefit class is shown against the business process that is being improved and the financial category that will receive the benefit. The matrix for our example project is shown below.

Business process	Benefit class	Revenue	COGS (RM)	COGS (Conversion)	Cost to deliver	Inventory
Order Fulfilment	Improve customer satisfaction	$3.0m				
	Improve logistics				$3.5m	
Procurement & Materials Management	Improve procurement		$1.5m			
Manufacture	Improve manufacturing			$1.0m		
Inventory Management	Reduce inventory					$7.5m

Table 14.4 – Financial contribution matrix for APS project

Of course, the financial contribution figures here are fairly approximate, being based on the top-down benefits work done during the Start-up stage.

The financial contribution matrices of all projects are then collated onto a single projects value-by-process log maintained by the programme benefits manager. There are at least two ways of doing this, which we will discuss in the next section on de-duplication tools and techniques.

The programme benefits manager's preparatory work is to create a view of the maximum potential financial value available to projects from improving business processes. This is an extremely difficult exercise to get right but it need not be done with precision as it is only going to be used to provide a sanity check of combined project forecasts of financial contribution. This view may well have already been created by the company while developing its strategy. If not, the programme benefits manager would be well advised to call in some specialist help from an external consultancy, who will probably use industry benchmarks coupled with a SWOT analysis of the company to derive an envelope of maximum achievable financial improvement by financial category, business process or both.

The initial audit is completed by the programme benefits manager:

- Identifying gross overlaps between the improvements being made by different projects to the same business process.

- Checking that the combined forecast financial contributions of all the projects do not exceed the maximum envelopes; I suggest by financial category.

- Flagging potential areas of overlap or benefits conflict to the appropriate project benefits managers.

Part of this initial audit may result in one or more projects having to modify their scope in order to avoid the identified gross areas of overlap. This should be negotiated between the programme benefits manager and the programme manager or project managers concerned. If this group cannot resolve the issue it may be necessary to refer the matter to the programme director and the respective project boards.

Having resolved the obvious conflicts there is little further that can be done until the projects have a better understanding of how they will be achieving the business process improvements and of the real financial impact that these improvements will have. This level of detail is unlikely to be available until at least strawman benefits cases are produced. However, the projects will now know where there are potential areas of conflict and they should keep talking to each other while their respective shapes firm up.

▶ Detailed de-duplication

There is not much process involved in the last stage of de-duplication but there are a couple of useful tools that we will discuss in the next section. The process diagram suggests that detailed de-duplication is itself done in two steps. This will not always be possible – due to timing differences between projects – and not always useful. The ideal circumstances in which to use both steps is when two or more global projects are closely in step and both (or all) use the same approach of running benefits workshops in one region and socialising workshop output with the other regions to obtain a global benefits case. This may seem a rather unlikely set of circumstances but it has happened; indeed, it will be designed to happen in a well-designed formal change programme. This two-step part of the de-duplication process also works when, for some projects, workshops are held in all regions, as long as there is a gap between the first and subsequent regional visits.

The purpose of this part of the process is to examine all the previously identified potential problem areas in more depth by comparing the detailed benefit definitions from the two or more projects involved in each problem area. This examination will confirm whether or not there is a benefit overlap and the details now available should make it easier to resolve the conflicting claimed benefits. The second step is mainly to check that the sum of global financial contribution figures claimed by all the projects still does not exceed the total value available in any one financial category.

There are some tools and techniques that are used solely to support the de-duplication process. The techniques supporting the two main de-duplication steps differ considerably.

▶ Techniques for the initial de-duplication audit

I mentioned earlier that there are different ways of doing the initial de-duplication audit. The two main methods available to the programme benefits manager are:

- To hold a de-duplication workshop with the benefits managers of all projects concerned.

- To collate and analyse financial impact matrices separately received from project benefits managers and discuss any apparent issues with the projects concerned.

Of the two methods, the workshop is preferable but only works when most of the projects in the programme are at a similar stage of development; roughly from towards the end of the Start-up stage to about half way through the Feasibility stage. The main advantages of the workshop method are:

- It presents a good opportunity for the benefits managers to get together and learn about each other's projects.

- It allows some emerging project overlaps, or other conflict issues, to be nipped in the bud very quickly.

- Benefits managers leave with a good overview of all the identified issues across the programme, as well as a closer understanding of the issues that affect them directly.

The projects still need to submit their financial impact matrices; the programme benefits manager needs them a few days before the workshop to allow time to prepare some brown paper sheets. The sheets will represent an expanded version of the project matrices but covering all the business processes and financial categories impacted by the projects. Availability of project matrices will allow the programme benefits manager to mark up the brown paper sheets without having to include any non-impacted processes or categories – giving a bit more useful space for the workshop exercise.

Gathering all the project benefits managers together provides the programme director with the opportunity to introduce a number of sessions into the workshop but the programme benefits manager's agenda should be given priority. There are really just two items that must be covered:

- A presentation by each benefits manager on the objectives, shape, status and issues of his or her project.

- The brown paper exercise, including identification of duplication issues and resolution of as many as possible.

The exercise is simple and can be very revealing. The benefits managers are asked to write each of their project benefits on a separate post-it, or something similar, and stick them in the appropriate cell on the brown paper. When the exercise is completed it will look something like Figure 14.3 overleaf; a real example from the programme within which our example project sat.

The result looks a bit chaotic. This is partly because of the large number of projects involved and partly because around a third of the projects were at a very early stage of development and there was a tendency for their benefits managers to scatter their unformed thoughts on benefits around the matrix.

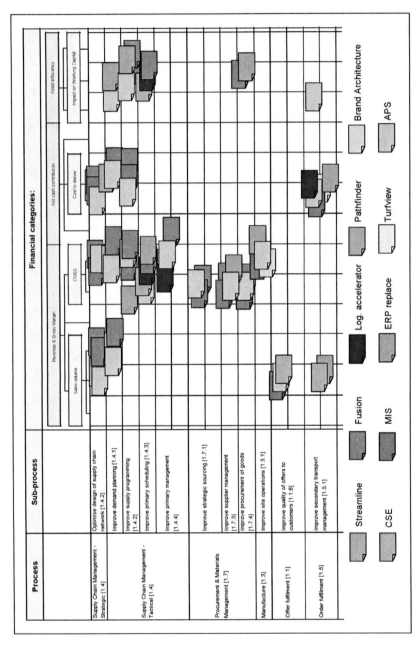

Figure 14.3 – Example of the de-duplication brown paper exercise

A quick examination of the nature of all the benefits placed within the same cell on the matrix reveals whether there are any major issues or merely areas of potential overlap of activities or benefits that need to be monitored and revisited later. Any major or flagrant overlaps should be discussed during the workshop and resolved where possible. If immediate resolution is not possible, the respective project managers will be contacted straight after the workshop and the matter resolved or escalated until resolution is achieved. The remaining, non-urgent, potential overlap issues are registered in a log maintained by the programme benefits manager, who will monitor and encourage progress towards their resolution until the next formal de-duplication stage.

▶ Tools for final de-duplication

Workshops are not a good way of resolving difficult or subtle duplication issues; these are better addressed in bilateral meetings between the projects concerned, possibly with the programme benefits manager in attendance. It helps all concerned if outstanding issues are resolved as soon as possible; if necessary, one at a time as the details become available from both projects.

Where two projects have a number of touch points they should maintain a shared log of the issues and their status. An example of such a log, in this case between our supply chain APS project and a global customer service excellence (CSE) project, is at Figure 14.4 overleaf.

There are three main causes of duplication of activities or benefits between projects:

- They are both attempting to re-engineer the same parts of the same process.

- They are re-engineering, or otherwise improving, different parts of the same process without the interface between their complementary activities having been formally defined.

- One project is providing enabling support to the other project.

The first of these possibilities may seem like the result of a very poorly structured or managed programme. However, it can happen when both

Srl.	CSE project opportunities	APS project activity	Comment
1	@ Incentive scheme to help customers accept changes in delivery and collection offers ... Promotion management tool è Track customer needs using web personalisation and tracking tools	@ Customers provided with post-event feedback on impact of promotions	APS project needs to provide more clarity around how this is enabled. Can then see whether these are complimentary activities
8	@ Create role of demand planner @ Demand planning & Forecasting training @ Cross functional coordination for demand planning & inventory management @ Formal process & protocols for stock allocation è Demand planning & forecasting of leads/prospects	è Implement collaborative forecasting/CPFR and VMI with selected customers - as adjuncts to Demand Forecasting and Supply Planning modules è Provide the analytical engine (Offer fulfilment module) to enable a promise to customers based on dynamic stock	Optimised solution may require interface between CRM and APS tools. Will need close cooperation between the two projects Current Americas view is that there is no need for the Offer fulfilment module, as more and more customers are expected to turn to
9	@ Standard process and protocols for delivery and collection @ Standard process and protocols for handling damaged stock @ Training for external suppliers £ Electronic confirmation that delivery matches original order placed by customer (bar code re	£ £- Deliver in full, on time, every time - including offering and meeting time-slots for delivery and recovery. Combination of better forecasting (Demand Forecasting module), better supply planning (Supply Planning module) and optimised secondary transpor	APS project will not be providing support for secondary transport optimisation in Europe and Americas, as this covered by the Logistics Accelerator.
10	@ Systematic approach to root cause analysis - returns @ Standard process and protocols for returns management @ Clarify etc ownership, roles & responsibilities for returns @ Training for CS on products, emergency response procedures and root caus		Support for returns execution not specifically addressed in APS project footprint but optimisation of secondary transport in AsPac and Transcon will implicitly support improvements in this area.

@ BPI opportunities

£ BPR opportunities

... other opportunities, not relevant to de-duplication with WCSC

Figure 14.4 – Example of a status log for projects with duplication issues

projects are implementing new systems and there is an overlap between the full functionality of the two systems. A case in point is the order promising functionality of some APS and CRM systems. Any duplication issues under this category should be identified and resolved during the initial de-duplication workshop.

The other two categories of potential duplication do not necessarily represent problems; merely areas where the respective project activities and benefit claims need to be well understood and carefully defined and documented. The techniques used to ensure that this is done differ between the two duplication categories.

Complementary benefits

Two projects appear to be addressing different aspects of the same process. But are they? How can we be sure that the activities are complementary and, if they are, that they will interface seamlessly where necessary?

The first step is to draw up a swim-lane diagram of the part of the process around the interface between the two projects at a sufficient degree of granularity that there can be no ambiguity over which project is doing what. An example of such a diagram is shown at Figure 14.5 overleaf.

This is our example of two projects, each implementing new systems and re-engineering the impacted processes. One is concerned with supply chain planning and the other with customer service support, and one of the touch points between the projects is the sub-process of making offers to customers in response to spot requests for goods. Both of the systems being implemented, the APS and CRM systems respectively, provide functionality to support the customer offer sub-process.

It was agreed that the supply chain project would deal with the back-office aspects of the process; primarily providing the data and allocation engine needed to be able to make near-real-time, firm, delivery promises. The customer service project would deal with the front end of the process, namely supporting the transaction between customer service staff and the customer.

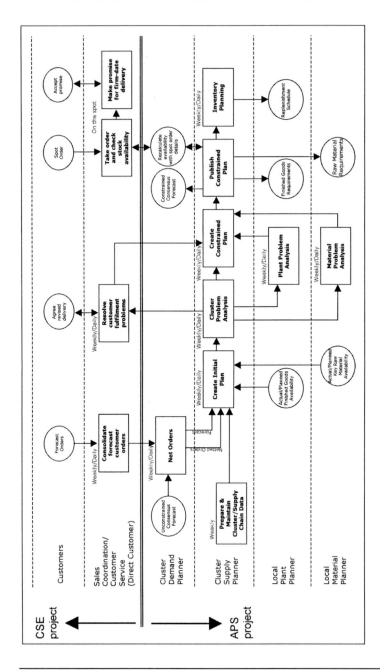

Figure 14.5 – Example of a swim lane diagram to identify the interfaces between activities of two projects

The diagrammatic view of this decision provides a focus for those points where systems and processes need to inter-communicate, and this is a matter for the respective project design teams to pursue. For the benefits managers, it provides the basis on which to agree the respective contribution of each project to process improvement and thus the share of resulting financial contributions. There are several ways of determining this share. Directly assessing relative contribution is perhaps subjective, and therefore more difficult, and an alternative method is to base relative contribution on the relative cost for each project to implement its share of the process improvement. Whichever method is used, the resulting agreement needs to be explicitly included in the relevant business logic in each project.

Enabling benefits

The other main duplication category differs from complementary benefit duplication in that the project providing enabling support to another project is not directly involved in the process that its support is helping to improve. It tends to address more general relationships between projects rather than the close focus needed to deliberate over complementary benefits. An example of this was the relationship between a global MIS project and a supply chain transformation programme. Two of the improvements made by the MIS project were to make tactical data (such as daily production and sales figures by product) available across the company in a consistent fashion and to make KPIs available to globally agreed standard definitions. The supply chain transformation programme conceded that most of its projects could only be implemented successfully if globally consistent MI was available to feed them and that this consistent data would be responsible for a significant proportion of the financial contribution that the transformation projects were forecast to generate. Once the enabling contribution was agreed it was, again, enshrined in the benefits case documentation of both the MIS project and the supply chain programme.

It would be appropriate for these more general project inter-relationships to be identified, examined and documented at the programme level. To do so is a bit more complex than separately addressing bilateral project relationships but will take less effort overall and will provide a valuable overview of what we might call the programme 'benefits stack'. An understanding of these relationships is best achieved through a schematic such as that in Figure 14.6.

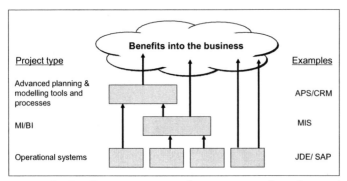

Figure 14.6 – Generic version of a programme benefits stack

A real programme benefits stack diagram would show all projects within the programme and consequently would be much busier than the diagram here. However, the generic diagram serves to illustrate its uses. It shows that:

- There is a benefits hierarchy of projects within a programme and this hierarchy tends to indicate an increasing level of process and systems sophistication. At the lowest level are the ERP systems that support basic operational transactions; at the next level are MI systems that support decision-making processes; at the top level are advanced planning and modelling tools to support optimised business processes.

- All projects contribute to the business (or they would not be there). Some contribute directly and others contribute by enabling a higher-level project. In many cases a project will contribute both directly and indirectly as an enabler for another project.

Of course, identifying these contributory relationships is only part of the story. The natures of the relationships also need to be defined, qualitatively and quantitatively. As was discussed in the first paragraph of this section, there are several ways of doing this – some more difficult than others. Even if the whole exercise is being conducted by the programme benefits manager, it is probably best left to the projects and their benefits managers to work out these details; the programme benefits manager will want to be satisfied with the agreement and may, anyway, have to intervene if the projects cannot reach agreement between themselves. I think it is well worth capturing a summary of the various bilateral agreements on the programme benefits stack diagram, as well as recording them in the business logic of the respective project benefits cases. The details would look like Figure 14.7, which shows a part of a benefits stack diagram with enabling contributory or complementary sharing instances superimposed.

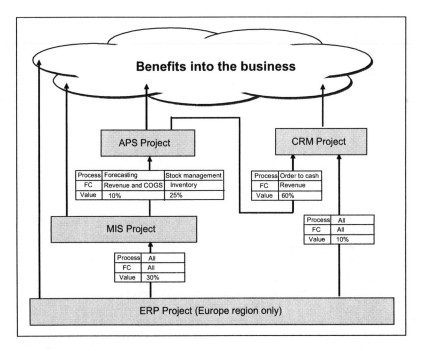

Figure 14.7 – Contribution sharing details on part of a benefit stack diagram

Figure 14.7 tells us that:

- An ERP replacement and consolidation project in the European region will avoid a need for the MIS project to install mapping software and procedures at the interfaces with a number of disparate ERP systems. This will reduce implementation costs for the MIS project by around 30 per cent in this region; this was the driver for an agreement that the ERP project contributes the same percentage of the MIS project's European regional value in all processes and financial categories.

- The ERP project is making a similar, but smaller, contribution to the CRM project. Smaller because the CRM project is less dependent upon consistent data standards across the region.

- The MIS project is providing essential consistent data to the APS project. The APS project manager has conceded that this data represents 10 per cent of the value of its annual benefits and 25 per cent of the value of its ability to enable stock reductions.

- In our example in the previous section of the complementary improvements made to the offer promising process by the APS and CRM projects, we allocated the benefit share by considering the relative impact of improvements made to the back office and front end aspects of the process. The agreement reached, that the APS project provided 60 per cent of the process improvement in value terms, can also be represented as shown on the diagram.

We now move on to the last two activities to support the business case: option selection and input to the NPV calculations.

Option selection

There are two ways in which a benefits case needs to be enhanced to support option selection:

- It must be decomposed to the same level at which options variations are being considered.

- It should be organised in a way that makes it quick and easy to derive the forecast financial contributions of options as they emerge.

Before discussing the details of how to do this, we will look at these characteristics of the enhanced benefits case in more detail.

▶ Level of granularity

This is best explained by looking at an example. In the APS project there was a strong push to maximise ROI while minimising the project investment costs. This meant that full implementation of the system, with associated re-engineered processes, in all areas of supply chain operations was unlikely to be a shortlisted option. The project had to decide the parameters that could be flexed to produce acceptable options; the decisions were:

- Not implementing at all in any one region was not an option.

- Within a region, the variations were at country and system module level – which parts of the system should be implemented in which countries or country clusters.

- The final variation, within and between regions, was implementation timing – which countries and modules to implement before others.

Once these parameters had been set it followed that the benefits case should be constructed by region and, within each region, allow for implementation variations in terms of which modules should be implemented in which countries and in which quarter.

▶ Medium for financial model of benefits

The financial model needed to support option selection is fairly complex in this example. An ideal way of representing this would be in a relational database (such as MS Access, which I introduce later in the book) but this requires a comparatively heavy up-front effort to construct. In the example project a spreadsheet was used, which was quickly put together and was reasonably easy to manipulate to derive the contribution of successive options.

▶ Elements of the financial data model

Bear in mind that for this exercise we are only concerned with the value aspects of the benefits case. So data elements such as benefit descriptions, measures and targets, although directly related, are not included in the financial data model. The elements we need are shown in Figure 14.8.

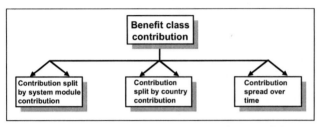

Figure 14.8 – Elements of the financial data model

The first step taken is to assess the relative impact of system modules and country operations to the regional financial contribution of each benefit class and to create spreadsheet matrices to record these assessments. At the same time, if not already done, a profile of the build-up of financial contribution over time is developed for each benefit class. We discussed these apportionment matrices, and how to create them, in some detail in Chapter 8. The baseline value table and apportionment and build-up tables used for our example project are reproduced here for convenience in Tables 14.5 to 14.8.

Financial category	Annual ($USm)	Working Capital ($USm)
Revenue	2.8	
COGS (RM)	1.2	
COGS (Conversion)	0.5	
NCC (Regionalisation)	0.9	
Cost to deliver	2.9	
Inventory	0.6	5.6
Total	8.9	5.6

Table 14.5 – Benefits summary for APS project in the Asia Pacific region

Proportion of financial value contributed by each APS module						
Financial bucket:	Revenue	COGS (RM)	COGS (Conversion)	NCC (shared service)	Cost to deliver	Inventory
By improving:	Customer satisfaction	RM purchasing	Manufacturing	Management structure efficiency	Logistics	Stock levels
Demand planning	0.17	0.75	0.17	0.25	0.17	0.4
Supply chain planning (master planning)		0.25	0.17	0.25		0.2
Supply chain planning (distribution planning)	0.17			0.25	0.17	0.2
Plant scheduling			0.67			0.1
2y transport scheduling	0.33			0.25	0.67	0.1
Demand fulfilment	0.33					

Table 14.6 – System module value contribution matrix for APS project

	Allocations by benefit class/financial category				
	Revenue	COGS (RM)	COGS (Conversion)	Cost to deliver	Inventory
China	0.16	0.16	0.36	0.11	0.18
Australia	0.25	0.17	0.29	0.51	0.22
New Zealand	0.03	0.04	0.04	0.07	0.06
Malaysia	0.14	0.17	0.06	0.04	0.14
Singapore	0.02	0.14	0.04	0.01	0.01
Thailand	0.12	0.12	0.05	0.06	0.10
Vietnam	0.10	0.08	0.03	0.02	0.12
Philippines	0.02			0.01	0.04
Indonesia	0.05	0.04	0.03	0.03	0.04
Taiwan	0.02			0.01	0.03
Japan	0.04			0.11	0.02
Korea	0.05	0.08	0.10	0.03	0.04
Sum check	1.00	1.00	1.00	1.00	1.00

Table 14.7 – Country financial contribution matrix for APS project in Asia Pacific region

APS module	% benefits released after "go live"			
	Q1	Q2	Q3	Q4
Demand forecast		0.3	0.7	1.0
Supply master plan		0.3	0.7	1.0
Supply distribution plan	0.5	1.0	1.0	1.0
Factory planning		0.5	1.0	1.0
Transportation scheduling	0.3	0.7	1.0	1.0
Demand fulfilment	0.3	0.7	1.0	1.0

Table 14.8 – Benefits release timeline for APS project

The other tools needed are the 'toggle switch' matrix, is shown at Figure 14.9 and an option implementation timeline such as that shown at Figure 14.10.

	Control - full regional implementation				
	Demand Planning	Supply Chain Planning	Plant Scheduling	Secondary Transport Scheduling	Demand fulfilment
China	Spoke	Hub 2	Yes	Yes	Yes
Australia	Spoke	Spoke 1	Yes	Yes	Yes
New Zealand	Spoke	Spoke 1		Yes	Yes
Malaysia	Hub	Hub 1	Yes	Yes	Yes
Singapore	Spoke	Spoke 1	Yes	Yes	Yes
Thailand	Spoke	Spoke 2	Yes	Yes	Yes
Vietnam	Spoke	Spoke 2	Yes	Yes	Yes
Philippines	Spoke	Spoke 1		Yes	Yes
Indonesia	Spoke	Spoke 1	Yes	Yes	Yes
Taiwan	Spoke	Spoke 1		Yes	Yes
Japan	Spoke	Spoke 2		Yes	Yes
Korea	Spoke	Spoke 2	Yes	Yes	Yes

Figure 14.9 – Module distribution matrix

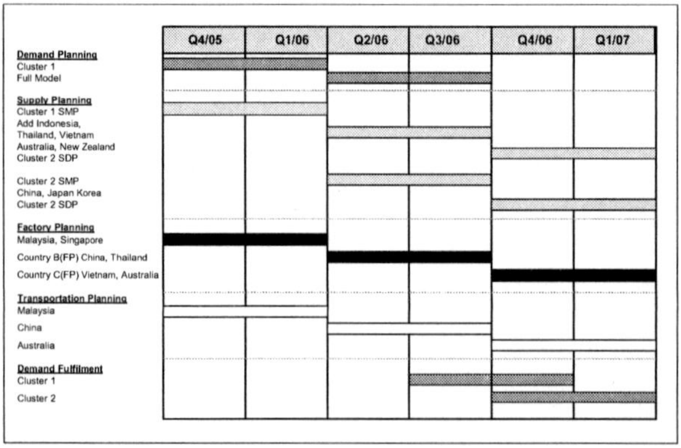

Figure 14.10 – Timeline for one implementation option in Asia Pacific region

▶ The composite financial model

The elements of the financial data model are linked to allow calculation of the regional financial contribution over time for any option that is created by varying the proposed implementation of system modules geographically or by time. This functionality of the composite data model can be automated to a greater or lesser degree. If there are likely to be many options sprung on you then it is worth investing in a fairly advanced level of automation. The way this was achieved in our example project was by building a number of linked spreadsheets that would give a build-up financial contribution by country or cluster for every considered geographical option by just toggling on and off which modules were to be implemented in which countries. Making changes to module go-live dates was not automated, as the effort needed to do so was not considered justifiable; however, it could have been done. Either way, manipulating the time element of implementations gave a regional project value over ten years for each option considered. An overview of the linked spreadsheet pages is shown at Figure 14.11.

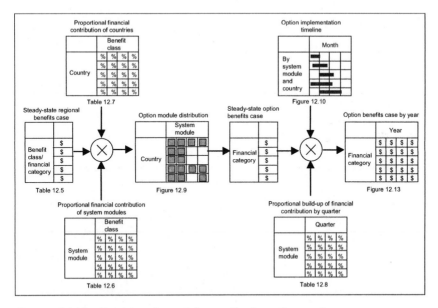

Figure 14.11 – Deriving financial contribution of an option

▶ Applying the financial model

There are many ways of linking the separate tables of the financial data model in practice. I shall show you one partially automated example but any competent spreadsheet operator would be able to construct a more fully automated model if this was considered necessary. Remember that more automation means more up-front work offset by reduced effort every time you want to derive the financial contribution of another project option. The balance can be a fine one; my only piece of advice is that you will almost certainly end up doing more option evaluations than you anticipate and some of them will be required in a hurry, so it may be better in the long run to build in more automation than you think is strictly necessary.

I explained earlier that financial modelling is best done against a quarterly timeline, whereas NPV calculations are usually done using an annual timeline. The way I have overcome this in this example is to produce each option evaluation in two steps. The result of the first step is shown in Figure 14.12 opposite.

Let me take you through the spreadsheet.

The steady-state regional benefits case and module attribution table are shown at the top of the spreadsheet. The main table below shows the build-up of financial contribution of the first of the system modules – Demand Forecast Management in this case. For this option a decision was made to implement the Demand Forecast Module twice in the region, each supporting demand forecasting for the clusters of countries shown. Similar tables exist below this one for each of the system modules with a final table summing the contributions for all modules in the same format as the one you can see.

The relative contribution of each cluster, for each financial category, is shown under the column headed 'Country cluster %'. The figures in this column were calculated manually from the base data shown at Table 14.7; here is an instance where further automation could have been added to the model. Another aspect of manual intervention is the start quarter for each cluster and the value build-up rate for the module. The value figures in each cell are then calculated automatically by applying a formula that multiplies

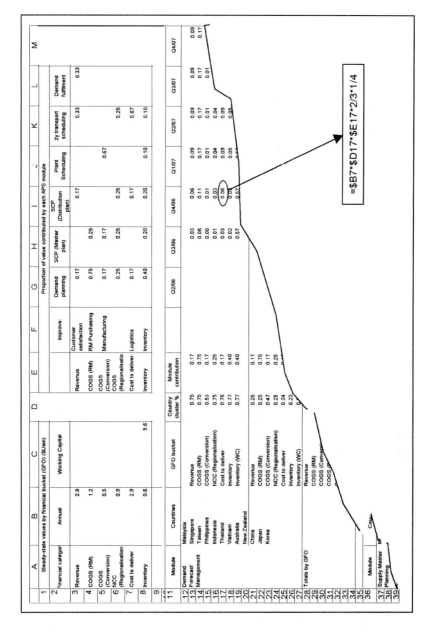

Figure 14.12 – Spreadsheet for calculating option financial contribution

the regional steady-state total for each financial category by module and cluster weighting figures and the build-up rate for the quarter concerned. You will see at the end of the formula illustrated a '2/3' and a '1/4'; these are respectively the build-up multiplier for the quarter and a factor to reduce the annual value '$B7' to one for a quarter.

With further manipulation the total for all individual module values is converted to a flat-rate 10-year value table. Part of such a table for one option is shown at Figure 14.13. This can then be fed into the NPV calculator, along with cost calculations, to calculate the ROI for the option.

Total value case for AsPac	Q2/06	Q3/06	Q4/06	Q1/07	Q2/07	Q3/07	Q4/07
Revenue	0.02	0.07	0.14	0.26	0.46	0.64	0.70
COGS (RM)	0.00	0.07	0.13	0.23	0.27	0.30	0.30
COGS (Conversion)	0.00	0.01	0.02	0.06	0.09	0.12	0.13
COGS (Regionalisation)	0.00	0.03	0.05	0.09	0.15	0.21	0.22
Cost to deliver	0.01	0.05	0.12	0.19	0.41	0.80	0.73
Inventory	0.00	0.03	0.05	0.09	0.12	0.15	0.15
Total RCOP	0.03	0.25	0.52	0.92	1.60	2.02	2.23
Inventory (WC)	0.00	0.91	0.96	1.33	1.19	1.06	0.13

Annual value case for Aspac		2006			2007	2008	2009
Revenue		0.23			2.07	2.79	2.79
COGS (RM)		0.20			1.10	1.20	1.2
COGS (Conversion)		0.03			0.39	0.53	0.5
COGS (Regionalisation)		0.08			0.68	0.90	0.9
Cost to deliver		0.18			1.93	2.90	2.
Inventory		0.08			0.50	0.60	0.
Total RCOP		0.80			6.67	8.92	8.
Inventory (WC)		1.87			3.73	0.00	

Figure 14.13 – Option contributions summary for 10-year NPV calculation

▶ Input to the business case

You will be asked to provide input to the business case, assuming that one is required for the end of the Feasibility stage (your governance rules may not require a formal business case until the PID is produced at the end of the Define stage).

Apart from the input to NPV calculations described in the previous section, I have suggested a list of textual inputs at the end of Chapter 8.

The Define stage

Introduction

On the face of it, there is little difference between the benefits management activities carried out in the Feasibility and Define stages of the project. Define stage activities are simpler – no strawman to create and no need for benefit de-duplication or options assessment – but the core activities of running workshops with the business to define the project's benefits are the same. Not exactly the same, or there would be no need for this chapter; they are the same activities but carried out in different ways to allow for the completeness and greater accuracy needed at the end of the Define stage.

A second reason for including this chapter is to introduce my second example project, which I will use from now to the end of the book.

▶ The second example project

The second example project is the implementation of the global management information system (MIS) that I touched on in Part 1. The same international lubricants company that produced our first, supply chain project, example perceived a need for radically improved management information (MI). The reason behind the need lay in the way that the company had been formed and then grown over the previous five years or so; it had been formed through the merger of two previously competing lubricants companies and then grown rapidly through a succession of acquisitions. As a result, although the company's organisational structure had been rationalised to optimise the way it served its customer base and manufactured and delivered product, it was hampered by the legacy of a large number of disparate country-based ERP systems. This scenario meant that it was extremely difficult for the company to be managed above country level, with central and regional leadership teams being presented with incomplete, inconsistent and delayed management information that had taken an army of analysts to assemble. The company recognised that in the long term it would need to replace its current ERP inventory with a new rationalised and integrated ERP network. In the meantime, it felt that a shorter-term project to enable consistent and timely MI throughout the organisation would reap the benefits of better operational efficiency and management decisions at all levels. The main elements of the project were to:

- Create a glossary of globally standardised definitions for all company KPIs and the individual data elements that contributed to the KPIs.

- Implement interconnected central and regional data warehouses, with data extracted daily from ERP systems and translated to the new data standards through an automated mapping process.

- Provide user-friendly access to the data via pre-formatted reports and the capability to drill down into the reports and to compose new reports as required.

The project provides a useful second example for the book because it differed significantly from the supply chain project in two ways:

- It covered four different business functions (marketing, sales, supply chain and finance & control)

- The benefits management method was introduced relatively late in the project; halfway through the Feasibility stage.

- As the benefits case developed, it was recorded and maintained in a Feasibility database rather than on spreadsheets.

▶ The data model

You will recall the benefits schema that was introduced in Part 1 (Figure 5.2). For this MIS project, the schema was emulated in a relational database, where each of the elements of the benefits case was defined – with all relevant parameters – and the relationships between elements were modelled. A view of these elements, parameters and relationships is illustrated in Figure 15.1.

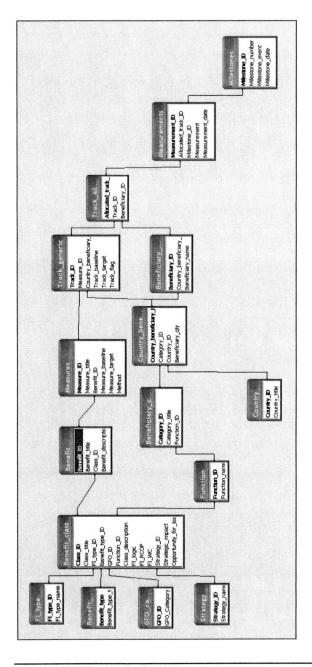

Figure 15.1 – Relationship diagram for a benefits case database

This is not the place to discuss the characteristics and merits of relational databases in general or to describe this relationship diagram in particular. However, a few points are worth making:

- The relationship diagram does not map directly onto the benefits schema of Figure 5.2. Nevertheless, all the elements of the benefits schema are present in the relationship diagram, which represents a more accurate but also more complex view of the components of a benefits case.

- There are additional files shown to the right of the relationship diagram that represent the data elements associated with the recording of benefit tracking measurements.

- Some relationships may appear to be over-specified but this is done deliberately. For instance, three files are used to describe beneficiaries to reflect first the list of beneficiary role titles, then the roles applicable in each country and finally the named beneficiaries associated with benefit tracking. The files are organised in this way to allow information to be recorded as it becomes progressively available during benefit case development.

Why should you saddle yourselves with this level of complexity when you know that the simpler solution of a workbook of spreadsheets will do the job adequately? There are two main reasons, both of which come into their own when the benefits case itself reaches a significant level of complexity:

- Data entry is quicker and error free. Any unique piece of data – such as a beneficiary role title – is entered only once and referred to, rather than the multiple entries needed in a spreadsheet.

- There is a more flexible report production capability in the database, such that reports with different fields and new formats can be designed and produced quickly when required.

For those like me who are even less of a database expert than spreadsheet expert, the question still remains whether it is sensible to embark on a database solution to the requirement for benefits case recording. To give a feel for the feasibility, the only non-trivial databases that I had built – before the one for this project – were to do the accounts and a three-day-event scoring system for a saddle club and to produce a catalogue of categorised Italian recipes for a website. Despite this, I did not run into too many problems building this one. The most useful tips I can give to database novices who decide to take the plunge are:

- Get a good book on the subject. There are plenty on the market for the more popular database applications.

- Keep the design – particularly the input/output user interface – simple. I found that coding problems increased exponentially the cleverer I tried to get with interface design.

Define stage planning

▶ Overview

Define stage planning is simpler than that required for the Feasibility stage. Under normal circumstances the activities to be planned are a repeat of the Feasibility stage activities with the following differences:

- The activities of gap analysis, strawman production and option selection are not required.

- De-duplication of benefits should have been largely completed but there may be some follow-up work with other projects that had not reached sufficient maturity during our project's Feasibility stage.

- The focus of attention during workshops turns towards preparing the ground for benefit tracking.

▶ The starting point

The first thing to do, of course, is to take detailed stock of progress to the end of the previous stage. How far did you get, where are the gaps, how broad is the target range for performance improvements? This understanding is needed to be able to assess the amount of work to be undertaken during the Define stage.

Our example project provides an interesting deviation from the norm. The benefits management methodology had been introduced after the start of the

Feasibility stage, at which point it was new to the company. Consequently, there was little time or local appetite to hold full-blown Feasibility stage benefits workshops. Instead, a series of workshops was conducted remotely, via teleconference links, between the benefits team in UK and the regional leadership team in Singapore. The resulting stage benefits case was fairly sketchy; a regional summary is shown below in Table 15.1 and the more detailed functional benefits case for Sales and Marketing is shown at Table 15.2 opposite. There were similar benefits cases for the Supply Chain and Finance & Control functions.

Beneficiaries	Srl	Benefit	Target	Financial Impact ($M)	
				Annual	WC
Top-line Growth					
Marketing/Sales	MA01	Improve margins (optimise pricing, productivity, brand, customer)	Increase GM/litre by $0.005 (70% MI project)	1.58	
Sales	SA10	Reduce lost sales	Reduce value of CNs etc by 10%	0.30	
Business Efficiency					
Marketing/Sales	MA02	More effective resource allocation (ASP)	Improve ASP/GM ratio by further 0.3%	0.15	
Sales	SA11	Improve return on trade loans		0.30	
Supply Chain	SC20	Improve portfolio management	Increase trade loan ROI by 1%		0.90
Supply Chain	SC21	Improve product management	Reduce stock days	0.54	
Supply Chain	SC22	Optimise logistics – transport, distribution, performance & control	Reduce SKUs and stock	0.81	
			Reduce stock and cash costs		1.60
Commercial	CM30	Reduce overdues	Reduce O-Dues by 12%; D-Days by 0.8D	0.21	
Commercial	CM31	Reduce bad debts	Reduce bad debts by 8%	0.42	
Commercial	CM32	Improve cost visibility	Improve cost ratio by 0.5 points		
People					
All functions	GE40	Reduce manual effort required to produce reports	Reduce effort by 80%	0.31	
				4.61	2.50

Table 15.1 – Feasibility stage benefits summary for Asia Pacific region

You can probably detect that this Feasibility stage benefits case still has a heavy top-down bias, even though an honest attempt was made to describe, at a high level, the project drivers that would lead to performance and financial improvements.

I now have an apparent dilemma. Do I continue to describe the planning and execution of Define stage activities such that they tie in with the example project and its previous deliverables or do I describe a more normal follow-on to the Feasibility stage activities discussed earlier? In fact, there is little difference in the planning and the main difference in the execution is that

SRL	BENEFIT	HOW ACHIEVED	NATURAL MEASURE	PARTIAL/ SURROGATE MEASURE	TARGET	FINANCIAL IMPACT
1	Improve margins by optimising pricing, product profitability and brand and customer management	Use MI data to focus market testing activity and understand better the relationship between brands, product prices and volumes sold in different segments. Use this understanding to optimise product prices in different markets, to enable better marketing	Sum of product GMs in each market segment		Improve GM per litre by $0.005 - of which 70% is attributable to MI project	1.575
2	Reduce lost sales	Using finer-grained and consistent data on lost sales and their causes, sales staff will focus on lost sale causes and initiate appropriate remedial action.	Number and value of Credit Notes, return orders and cancelled orders		Reduce volume and value of Credit Notes, return orders and cancelled orders by 10%	0.3
3	More efficient resource allocation (Advertising, sales support and promotions - ASP)	Use MI data to analyse the sales impact of marketing spend and thus make more informed decisions on future marketing spend	ASP per GM		Improve current ASP saving plans by a further 0.3% of Plan 2003 ASP	0.148
4	Improve return on Trade Loans	MI data will provide greater visibility of trade loans by customer, improving our understanding of the profitability of this customer sub-sector and allowing trade loans to be qualified more accurately - e.g. provisos on locations, product mixes, volumes	Trade Loan ROI		Improve ROI on Trade Loans by 1%	0.3
5	Reduce effort required to produce sales reports	Use MI to automate production of routine reports and ad hoc queries that are currently collated manually, including snapshots, sales incentives, trade loan reporting etc.	Man-hours expended in production of reports		80% reduction from current man-hours spent in report production	0.2

Table 15.2 – Feasibility stage benefits case for Sales & Marketing functions

the Define stage benefits workshops of our example project were a lot tougher because there was a great deal more ground to cover than would have been the case had we run on-site Feasibility stage workshops. So I will just describe those activities that would have been covered had we a more typical Feasibility stage benefits case as our starting point.

▶ The planning process

- Planning follows along much the same lines as that for Feasibility stage work, as described in Chapter 10. In fact much of the Feasibility material, such as the work breakdown structure and the Gantt chart, can be adapted for Define stage planning, thus saving considerable time and effort. The main difference is that there are really only two pieces of significant benefits work during this stage; preparation for, and conduct of, the benefits workshops. Having said that, there are a few matters that need bearing in mind:

- Workshop preparation should begin soon after the start of the Define stage, even though the workshops will be held towards the end of the stage. Reasons for this are that:

  - The project will be generally busier in this stage than during Feasibility and so it will be more difficult to fix dates for benefits workshops that do not clash with other project activities.

  - It is important to secure the commitment of a good proportion of the same delegates that attended the Feasibility stage workshops; this means giving them plenty of warning. I say 'a good proportion' because in fact it is useful to have some new faces with fresh ideas among the delegates. I suggest you should aim for between 50 and 70 per cent of the delegates being from those who attended the Feasibility workshops.

- The benefits team should spend a fair proportion of the lead time before workshops contacting delegates and other specialists from the business to discuss issues that remained unresolved at the end of the Feasibility stage. These issues will typically concern benefits for which measures could not be identified, or targets could not be set, for one reason or another.

- Bear in mind that you will need to leave headroom among the benefits team to deal with unplanned requests for benefits data, discussions and presentations from a variety of directions including the programme office, project board, user groups and the project manager. In my experience these will appear to be never-ending during Define.

▶ Preparing for the workshops

When considering the preparation for Define stage benefits workshops there is little that I would add to, or take away from, the discussion in Chapter 11 on preparing for Feasibility stage workshops. Apart from the fact that they have different start points (strawman benefits case for Feasibility workshops and Feasibility benefits case for Define workshops) and that the delegate list is largely known, there are very few things that we need to change. I would certainly recommend that a similar amount of time is allowed for each workshop and for the total time spent on site by the benefits team.

You may ask why we need to spend so much time on Define stage workshops, given that we are just filling the gaps that we left in the previous stage. A list of the differences between the two stages provides some of the answers:

- We are now focusing on the benefits from implementing just one project design; the selected option from the previous stage.

- The emphasis of benefits management work switches from a financial focus to a benefits tracking and realisation focus.

- A major portion of the benefits work will now be spent on defining the details of each benefit: outcome details, who will be responsible for the change, how will changes be measured.

- This stage benefits case will derive project benefits to a greater degree of accuracy and assurance; typically, from the plus or minus 30 per cent of the previous stage to plus or minus 10 per cent.

- A certain degree of reaffirmation will also be necessary; it may be several months since the previous benefits case was produced.

In summary, only a little time is saved on those aspects of the benefits case that need to be reviewed rather than created and this saving is soaked up by the extra time needed to develop missing information on outcome measures and targets; in other words, in completing the empty elements in the chains of events subject to change.

Workshop preamble

▶ Workshop objectives

Remember that these workshops have two main purposes:

- To review the Feasibility stage benefits case and revise it where necessary.

- To complete the gaps in identification of outcome measures and targets and associated beneficiaries.

The gap-filling task is fairly straightforward but you need to be clear what you are looking for in reviewing the benefits case:

- Is the list of benefits still relevant? Are there any that should be deleted or added?

- Does a deeper understanding of the project's design and capabilities alter our perception of the extent of resulting outcomes?

- Are the performance improvement measures still appropriate? Can we set a more accurate improvement target or reduce the gap between minimum and maximum improvement targets?

- Are there any factors, internal or external to the project, which might alter the business logic? Do any of these changes impact the forecast financial contribution of each benefit class?

Assuming that 50 to 70 per cent of the workshop delegates also attended the Feasibility stage workshops, the atmosphere will be more relaxed this time round and the facilitation techniques need not be so formal. There is a balance to be maintained throughout the workshop that will allow a more reflective response from delegates while keeping the energy levels high enough to keep them engaged; this balance is particularly at risk during the reviewing sessions of the workshops. However, in my experience, the reviews always throw up changes to be debated and agreed and this is usually enough to keep energy in the room at a productive level.

▶ Workshop schedules

The workshop schedules need to change slightly from those for the Feasibility stage workshops (Table 12.1) to reflect their revised objectives. The schedule for both workshops might look something like the one in Table 15.3.

Benefits workshop	Workshop briefing
	Session 1 - Reviewing benefits
	Refreshment break
	Session 2 - Qualifying change measures
	Lunch
	Session 3 - Setting change targets
	Tea
	Session 4 - Reviewing performance targets
Financial impact workshop	Benefits workshop wash-up
	Refreshment break
	Session 5 - Reviewing business logic
	Lunch
	Session 6 - Reviewing benefit class value

Table 15.3 – Example schedule for Define stage benefits workshops

The main change in the benefits workshop is that I have allocated more time to the gap-filling sessions (Sessions 2 and 3, identifying change measures, targets and beneficiaries) at the expense of time spent reviewing benefits and performance improvement targets. In the financial impact workshop you do not need to revisit allocation of the financial impact of benefits to financial buckets, but you do need to review business logic and financial impact of performance improvements on benefits classes.

Conducting the benefits workshop

▶ Workshop briefing

There is no need to repeat the full benefits management briefing given at the beginning of the Feasibility stage workshops, but remember that you probably have a proportion of delegates who are new to the method. I suggest a cut-down method briefing but with emphasis on the area dealing with the chains of events, which was not fully covered fully in the Feasibility workshop briefing.

▶ Session 1 – Reviewing benefits

I suggest that you do not use brown-paper-based facilitation for the review sessions. The tools you will need are a projected PC and flip charts. This is not a rubber-stamping exercise; it is more than likely that there will be changes to the list of benefits, as things will have moved on since the previous workshops were held. Go through the benefits one by one, by benefit class and record any agreed changes on the flip chart. There is typically a tendency for delegates to want to delete benefits from the list, particularly where these involve their accountability for delivery of improved performance, but these suggestions should be dealt with robustly unless there is a genuine reason for the change. At the end of each benefit class review, ask if there should be any new benefits within the class; if there are, the delegates will discuss a working description of the benefit, which a member of the team will need to record on the flip chart.

Once the session has finished, the delegates retire for refreshments. The team then has two tasks to complete before the start of the next session: transferring agreed changes from the flip chart to the database on the PC, and sticking pre-prepared brown paper onto the wall. If there are not enough team members to complete both tasks then concentrate on the brown paper and keep the flip chart sheets for transference after the workshop has finished.

The example I am using is taken from the Sales and Marketing function workshop. Their benefits list at the end of Session 1 is shown at Figure 15.2.

MIS project – Sales and Marketing benefits	
Benefit class	**Benefits**
Improve product margins	Improve profitability of sales Negotiate cross-region deals Improve price management Proactively manage distributor performance
Reduce lost sales	Better focus sales effort to problem customers More proactively manage IFOT problems Manage the causes of credit notes better Manage demand planning better Reduce the number of cancelled orders
More efficient sales resource allocation	Better allocation of sales resources More efficient use of training resources
Improve return on trade loans	Better adherence to trade loan Ts & Cs Better trade loan investment decision
Reduce effort to produce sales & marketing reports	Improve productivity of S&M data analysts Improve productivity of S&M data gatherers
More efficient marketing resource allocation	Better responsiveness of marketing resources More effective allocation of ASP spend

Figure 15.2 – List of Sales and Marketing benefits

▶ Session 2 – Identifying change measures

You will recall that, during the Feasibility workshop session to identify measures, delegates were asked to draw out the chain of events for each benefit as an aid to defining the benefit performance metrics (Figure 12.9). We will use these drawings as a starting point for a brown paper exercise to identify measures for each of these outcomes and knock-on changes and nominate associated beneficiary roles and, in a later session, targets for the measures. However, for this exercise, the chains are drawn vertically, rather than horizontally, as shown in Figure 15.3 overleaf.

Bear in mind that, while this workshop is for just one function (well, two actually, as we lumped Sales and Marketing together in one workshop), there are still likely to be about eight sheets of brown paper on the wall, representing 17 benefits in six benefit classes. Therefore, neither a centrally directed exercise with delegates remaining seated, nor a free-for-all with delegates milling around the brown paper in an unstructured way, would be appropriate ways of running this session.

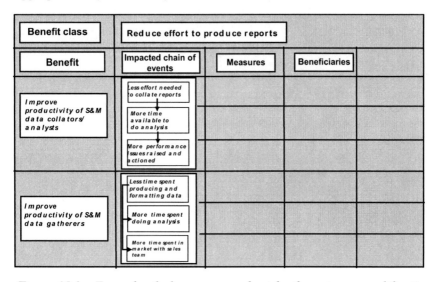

Benefit class	Reduce effort to produce reports		
Benefit	**Impacted chain of events**	**Measures**	**Beneficiaries**
Improve productivity of S&M data collators/ analysts	Less effort needed to collate reports		
	More time available to do analysis		
	More performance issues raised and actioned		
Improve productivity of S&M data gatherers	Less time spent producing and formatting data		
	More time spent doing analysis		
	More time spent in market with sales team		

Figure 15.3 – Example of a brown paper sheet for the outcome qualification exercise

I suggest that the best way to run the session is to divide the delegates into three groups and ask each group to post their suggestions for measures and beneficiaries for two of the benefits classes. Ideally, the groups should each include some delegates who are directly involved with the operations behind the benefits they are addressing and some who are less familiar with them.

Having set the group their tasks, the facilitation team (ideally, in this case, you plus two others) will need to help the groups achieve them. As I explained in Part 1, defining measures is a complex business. Although delegates have been briefed on the different types of measure, deciding which to use may not be straightforward. A facilitator should be on hand to remind delegates of all the considerations discussed in Chapter 7. They should be guided towards the simplest solution available – always use a direct or natural measure where one is available.

Once this part of the exercise is complete, the groups come together and post their suggestions for measures and beneficiaries for each outcome and knock-on change that they have been working on. Finally, you should quickly review each group contribution with the whole workshop and resolve any dissentions.

Completion of the review and achieving final agreement on all measures and beneficiaries is a good cue for lunch.

▶ Session 3 – Setting targets

When the delegates return from lunch the brown paper sheets will look like the example at Figure 15.4.

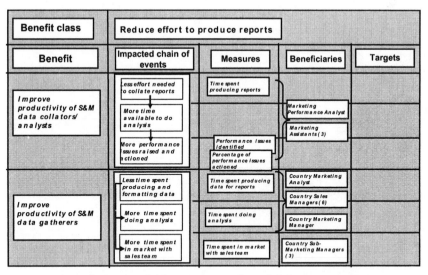

Figure 15.4 – Example of a brown paper sheet for the outcome target-setting exercise

The next exercise is to set a target for the degree of change to be achieved for each of the measures defined in the morning. This is a very important exercise as its findings will strongly influence any potential changes to performance improvement targets in the following session. I suggest that the same groups are used as for the previous exercise; it is certainly essential that each group should have one or two delegates who have intimate knowledge of the operations being changed and have a feel for their potential for improvement. Again, the groups should be guided by a facilitator who has good knowledge of the target-setting factors discussed in Chapter 7. The same procedure is followed as was used in the previous session. The groups post their suggested change targets on the brown paper, which are then reviewed by the whole workshop. You will have in mind what are understood to be realistic targets and should challenge any that appear to be significantly understated or overstated.

This can be a slightly tetchy session and it is a good idea to release delegates for a break once it is finished. The brown paper part of the day is now over and in its final form the sheet looks like Figure 15.5.

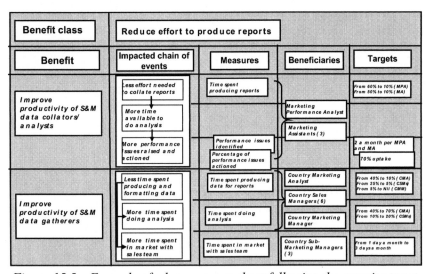

Figure 15.5 – Example of a brown paper sheet following the exercise to set targets for outcomes and knock-on changes

It is worth noting that the diagram illustrates that these exercises are rarely entirely straightforward:

- The workshop felt that it was not worth defining measures for all of the changes associated with the first benefit. Probably because the second change in the chain of events was seen to be explicitly covered by the third change.

- However, this third change warranted two measures because the change itself indicates two outcomes (more performance issues raised and more performance issues actioned) in which the second would not necessarily follow as a direct consequence of the first (more issues might be raised than are actioned).

- There is not a simple one-to-one mapping between measures and beneficiaries; in several cases, more than one beneficiary role is associated with a single measure.

- The same measure may have different targets for different beneficiary roles.

▶ Session 4 – Reviewing performance targets

The final session of the day is to review performance targets.

Our example project does not work so well in illustrating this stage, as MIS project benefits tend not to result in specific measurable operational performance improvements; rather, they produce changes in activity that lead to better management decisions that have business value. Thus business logic is sometimes derived from measured changes on the ground rather than measured improvements in operational performance. To a certain extent this is just semantics, as there can be a very fine line between a knock-on change from an output and a performance improvement.

Despite the above, I recommend that you revert to the procedure used during the Feasibility workshops, as described in Chapter 12, and ask the responsible delegates to present their performance targets, benefit by benefit, in front of the whole workshop. The same considerations and techniques as described in Chapter 7 should be used. The main differences that will apply in this Define stage workshop, compared with the same session in Feasibility, are:

- The project is closer to implementation, thus making delegates more sensitive to their responsibility for delivering performance improvement.

- You now have a much clearer view of the extent of the outcomes and knock-on changes that will lead to performance improvements through the work of the previous two sessions.

The main objective of this session is to obtain performance improvement targets that are more accurate than those resulting from the Feasibility stage workshops. This will most likely be achieved by narrowing the gap between what are agreed as the maximum and minimum possible extents of performance improvement. Your role here, again, is to lead the workshop away from understating or overstating the targets; honesty and realism are more important than attempting to pump up the value of the project but, equally, no one is well served if the targets are too timid.

There is no need to use more brown paper for this exercise. Instead, the benefits with their performance improvement targets can be projected, while the measures and targets for changes on the ground are still on display on the brown paper from the previous session. Changes to performance improvement targets can be made on a flip chart as they are agreed.

▶ Revising the benefits case

After the workshop is over, the various changes and additions agreed need to be incorporated into the benefits case database (or spreadsheet, if this is what you are using). As an illustration of what I see as the one of the advantages of the database solution, the input screens used to update the change measures, beneficiaries and targets are shown at Figures 15.6 and 15.7 and one of the benefits case report formats is shown at Figure 15.8. Of course, the content of reports in all formats is automatically updated when changes are made via input screens.

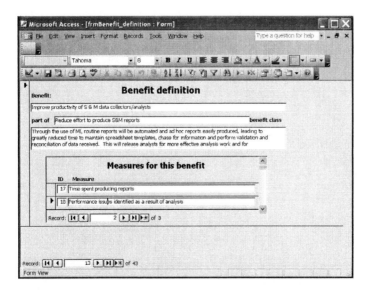

Figure 15.6 – Database input screen for measures

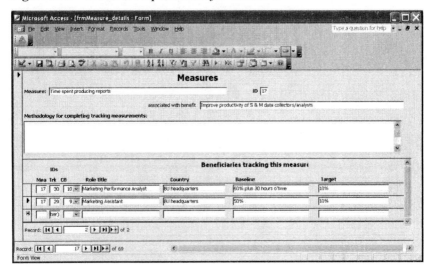

Figure 15.7 – Database input screen for beneficiaries and targets

Benefit class: **Reduce effort to produce sales/marketing reports**

Benefit:	***Improve productivity of S&M data collators/analysts***
Description:	Through use of BIGS, routine reports will be automated and ad hoc reports easily produced; leading to greatly reduced time to maintain spreadsheet templates, chasing for information and performing validation and reconciliation of data received releasing them for more analysis work and performance discussions with functional and Market Space leaders

Measure: **Time spent producing reports**

Beneficiary details for this measure:

Title	*Country*	*Number*	*Baseline*	*Target*
Marketing Assistants	BU headquarters	3	50%	10%
Marketing Performance Analyst	BU headquarters	1	60% plus 30 hours o'time	10%

Measure: **Performance issues identified as result of analysis**

Beneficiary details for this measure:

Title	*Country*	*Number*	*Baseline*	*Target*
Marketing Assistants	BU headquarters	3		2 a month
Marketing Performance Analyst	BU headquarters	1		2 a month

Measure: **Percentage of performance issues actioned**

Beneficiary details for this measure:

Title	*Country*	*Number*	*Baseline*	*Target*
Marketing Assistants	BU headquarters	3		70% uptake
Marketing Performance Analyst	BU headquarters	1		70% uptake

Figure 15.8 – Example of a database report on one project benefit

▶ Conducting the financial impact workshop

The financial impact workshop comprises the relatively straightforward exercises of reviewing the findings of the benefits workshop and amending, where necessary, the business logic and financial contributions of the Feasibility benefits case. There is not much to add to the coverage given in Chapter 13 on the same exercise conducted during the Feasibility stage.

▶ Reviewing the benefits workshop

There should be little to do in this session. There may be one or two issues remaining and the gap between the workshops will have given each responsible delegate the opportunity to discuss possible resolutions with colleagues or appropriate specialists so that they can present the suggested answer during this session. The review also gives you a last chance to challenge any of the target figures that appear wrong, having marshalled appropriate facts and arguments beforehand.

▶ Session 5 – Reviewing business logic

The bulk of the workshop should be spent on this session which, despite the suggested schedule of Table 15.3, may spill over into the afternoon. The reasons for needing extra time and care here are that:

- It is the part of the benefits case that is most likely to need some tightening up to take it to the required degree of accuracy for this stage.
- Changes made to measures and targets in the benefits workshop may cause changes to the logic.
- Some of the logic – particularly in this type of project – includes an element of subjective judgement that needs to be carefully debated.

Again, there is no need to veer from the procedures followed for the same session in the Feasibility workshops, except that we can dispense with the brown paper. Let the delegates debate business logic in groups and then present their findings, with the previous version of business logic for the benefit class under discussion projected as a backcloth. Any proposals can then be debated with the whole workshop and agreed changes recorded on a flip chart or, if relatively minor, directly into the PC.

▶ Session 6 – Reviewing benefit class value

The last session reviews the formulae and baseline data that are applied to the business logic to calculate a financial contribution for each benefit class. The task is quite mechanistic and does not really need input from the delegates. However, it will be their first chance to see how this process works, as it was not covered in the equivalent workshop during the Feasibility stage, so is a valuable exercise for cementing buy-in to the benefits case.

After the workshop

The final tasks before leaving the region are to update business logic and financial impacts in the benefit case and to complete any necessary leadership team briefings. The update screen for a different benefit class is illustrated in Figure 15.9 and the resulting benefit class report in Figure 15.10.

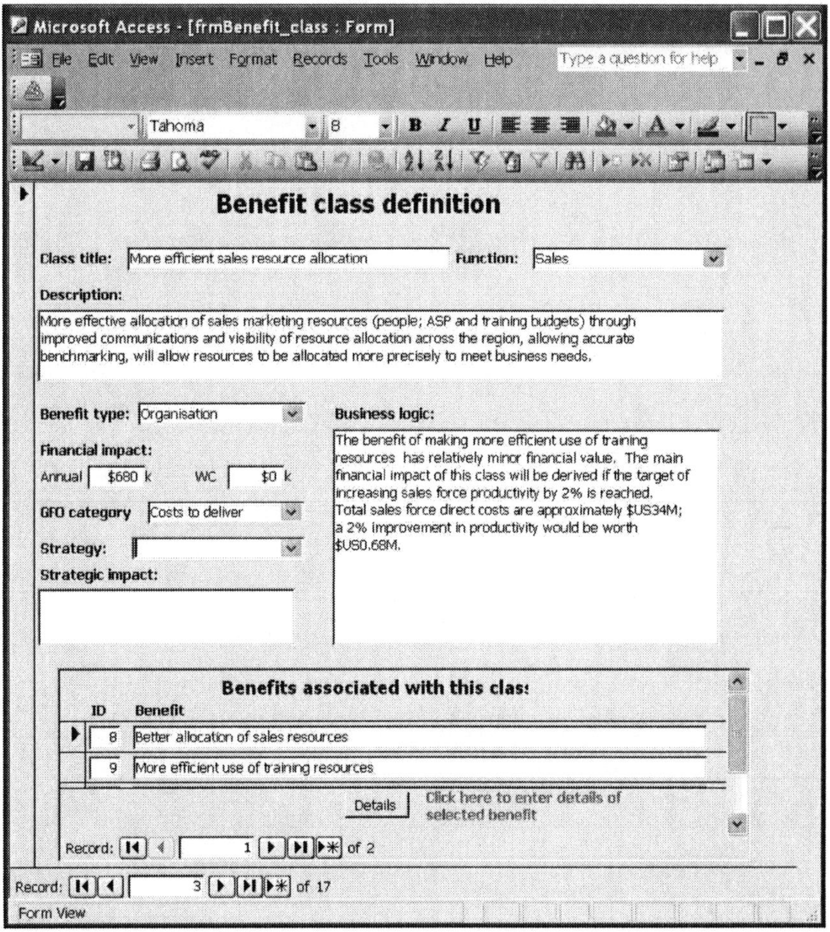

Figure 15.9 – Database input screen for benefit class business logic and financial impact

Benefit class: *More efficient sales resource allocation*

Benefit: *Better allocation of sales resources*

Description: Detailed analysis of fine-grained sales data will be possible, allowing some further centralisation of planning and control functions and consequent headcount reduction.

Measure: Sales force productivity

Beneficiary details for this measure:

Title	*Country*	*Number*	*Baseline*	*Target*
Regional Sales Director	BU headquarters	2		2% improvement

Benefit: *More efficient use of training resources*

Description: Analysis of training plans and actuals across all countries will provide possibility of rationalised training, reducing overall regional training costs

Measure: Reduction in region-wide training costs

Beneficiary details for this measure:

Title	*Country*	*Number*	*Baseline*	*Target*
Regional Sales Operation Manager	BU headquarters	1		

Logic to derive financial impact of this benefit class:

The benefit of making more efficient use of training resources has relatively minor financial value. The main financial impact of this class will be derived if the target of increasing sales force productivity by 2% is reached. Total sales force direct costs are approximately $US34M; a 2% improvement in productivity would be worth $US0.68M.

Financial impact:

Annual $680 k

WC k

Figure 15.10 – Example of a database report on a benefit class

Managing opportunities for loss

Introduction

We now move on a few weeks or months. The project was approved at the end of the Define stage and has started to be designed, built and delivered in the Implement stage. This stage can be dangerous for benefits management and for any other activities, such as change and transition management, which is are not directly associated with implementing the project's main deliverables. The reasons for this possible danger are twofold:

- Any overruns in time or budget that have built up since project initiation tend to squeeze the resources available for the Implement stage.

- The traditional measures of project success, delivery on specification to time and budget, still tend to prevail. Thus any resource squeeze will be on those activities that do not contribute directly to these success criteria.

This attitude is extremely short-sighted because it is the three softer activities mentioned – change, transition and benefit management – that are needed to ensure real rather than perceived project success. Part of your role then, during this stage, is to defend robustly the resources needed to complete benefit management activities. You should also make allies of the change and transition managers (if these roles are independent of your own) because, as we shall see, many of the problems associated with release of project benefits are to do with poor change and transition management.

Apart from the usual manipulation of benefits data to satisfy continuing requests from various quarters for different views of the benefits case, there are two main activities for the benefits team during the Implementation stage:

- Starting the creation of a network of benefits coordinators and inducting individual coordinators.

- Preparing for, and running, the final set of benefits management workshops in the first few countries to be implemented. These workshops are to create a benefit risk register and benefits tracking plan for each country. Note that the workshops in this stage are run at country rather than region level.

The benefits coordinators

▶ Organisation and numbers

For a small, single-function project with limited geographical spread, one benefits coordinator may suffice. Our example project, a global MIS implementation across four regions and impacting four business functions, needed an extensive network of coordinators, as illustrated in Figure 16.1.

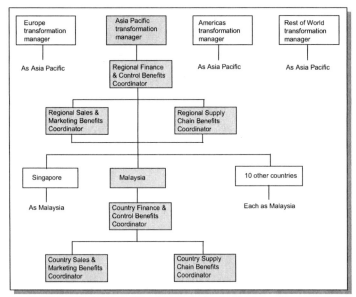

Figure 16.1 – Hierarchy of benefits coordinators for a global multi-function project

In this example, there are three functional benefits coordinators for each country, with the Finance & Control coordinators taking the lead in cross-functional issues and upward reporting. Similarly, at regional level, the regional Finance & Control benefits coordinator is responsible for collating a regional tracking report and submitting it to the regional transformation manager. However, at each level, the primary reporting line for each benefits coordinator is his or her function leader.

This may seem a complicated organisational structure that soaks up a lot of people. It is done in this way to ensure that:

- Benefits coordinators are close to, and have a good understanding of, the benefits whose tracking they are coordinating.

- Benefits coordinators need spend no more than 10 per cent of their working hours in the role.

I suggest that if you are operating within a formal change programme structure as described in Chapter 4 (possibly as a tranche benefits manager or business change manager) you will need a similar network of benefits coordinators, albeit with a different reporting structure.

In our example project, benefit coordinators were drawn almost exclusively from the performance analyst community. Apart from the fact that these members of staff were ideally suited to the role, there was the added advantage that the project itself freed up much of their time previously devoted to manual preparation of monthly and quarterly performance reports.

If a network of coordinators is required, it need not be created at a stroke. Typically, global projects such as our example are implemented a region at a time and, within each region, country by country. A just-in-time policy works well here and, for the first country implementation, only the coordinators for that country, and for the region in which it sits, need be in place. Others are added as subsequent country implementations are started.

▶ Recruitment and induction

The start of the Implement stage is the point at which input from the business community mushrooms from a small number of regionally based subject-matter experts to a more general management involvement at regional and country level. For strategic projects, such as our example, it is essential to get engagement and buy-in from the country leadership teams as their countries prepare for project implementation.

Before you start to engage at the country level, it will be essential to have the lead regional benefits coordinator on board. Chapter 9 tells you all you need to know about regional and country benefits coordinator roles and the skills and characteristics needed by coordinator appointees. The regional appointment is a more demanding and responsible role than that of the country benefits managers because of the added responsibility of inducting and guiding the benefits coordinators of later implemented countries (after you have moved on to the next region to be implemented).

The regional transformation manager will already be aware of benefits management and its importance, so need not be briefed on the subject at this stage. However, he or she needs to be involved in the nomination, selection and briefing of the lead regional benefits coordinator, as the two will work closely together during the Operate stage of the project.

For you, two key sets of country relationships are with the local project manager and the function leaders. The project manager needs to understand the importance and details of benefits work during this stage so that he or she deals sympathetically with resource and scheduling clashes between benefits management and other project activities. Function leaders need to understand what their responsibilities will be towards delivering business benefits following project implementation; this understanding will focus their minds towards the need for capable and appropriate benefits coordinators as these roles, carried out successfully, will help them considerably in meeting their responsibilities.

You will need to brief function leaders early in the stage; either alone or as part of a wider leadership team induction briefing. I suggest that the function leaders' briefing be supported by a shortened version of the benefits management presentation plus three specific slides shown below in Figure 16.2.

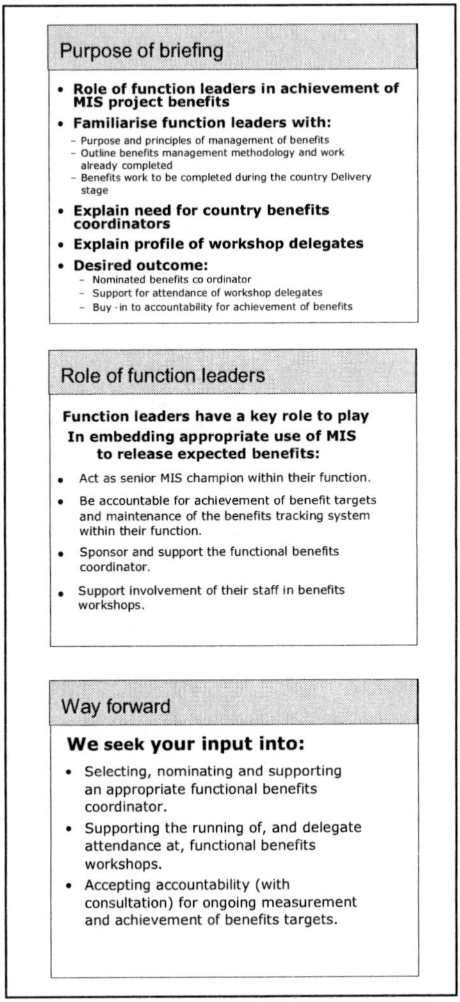

Figure 16.2 – Specific slides to be added to the presentation pack for function leaders' briefings

Induction of benefits coordinators, apart from an initial briefing, is largely achieved on the job. You will probably conduct the benefit risk and benefit tracking workshops for the first two or three countries and these workshops should be attended by the lead regional benefits coordinator and the appropriate country benefits coordinators. I say 'attended by' but the best way for the coordinators to learn will be for them to participate actively in workshop facilitation. The same process will apply for subsequent countries, except that the workshops will then be led by the regional benefits coordinator, or coordinators from countries that have already been through the Implement stage. After the benefit management workshops have been completed, the country benefits coordinators will need further training on their responsibilities during the Operate stage; I will cover this latter aspect in the final chapter of the book.

Stage planning and scheduling

▶ Outline scheduling

Benefits management activities during this project stage are fewer and simpler than those for the previous stages but have the added dimension of being repeated in each country being implemented, rather than the single regional instance of workshops. This begs the question of why you should not develop one OfL register and benefit tracking plan and distribute them to all countries for execution. The reason that this is not done is that conditions vary between countries to a degree that means there may be significant differences in the OfLs, in the selection of benefits to track and in some measurements and targets. However, there is no doubt that results from the first one or two countries make benefit management work in subsequent countries very much easier.

The cross-regional scheduling of benefit management activities will depend very much on the time needed for each country implementation and the gap between successive country implementation start dates. In our example project there were three country implementation teams; implementations overlapped, starting at one-month intervals with each taking an average of three months to complete.

Individual country schedules were planned with the engagement and benefits coordinator selection activities at the beginning of the implementation and coordinator induction and running of workshops towards the end. Figure 16.3 illustrates this. The large gap between the first and second group of activities is needed to ensure that detailed workshop scheduling and engagement of delegates go smoothly.

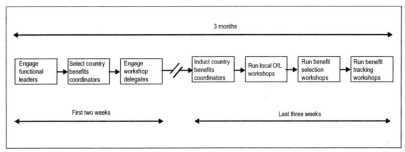

Figure 16.3 – Benefits management Deliver stage schedule for a single country

Benefits management activities across countries have to be interleaved to keep in step with the general implementation plan. This can be slightly tricky because there is one of you trying to keep up with three implementation teams. Thankfully, the benefits work within a country does not take up anything like the three-month elapsed time for implementation and so, while you may get a bit tired of airport lounges, a working schedule is possible, given that you are unlikely to engage directly beyond the third country implementation. The schedule is shown in Figure 16.4.

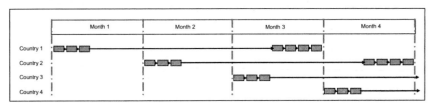

Figure 16.4 – Benefits management activities scheduled across multiple country implementations

▶ Scheduling the workshops

In our example project, separate workshops were held for each of three function groups, making nine workshops in all. Figure 16.5 shows that it is just possible to cram all activities into a two-week visit to the country.

In this diagram, the abbreviations mean:

- SM: Sales & Marketing

- SC: Supply Chain

- FC: Finance & Control

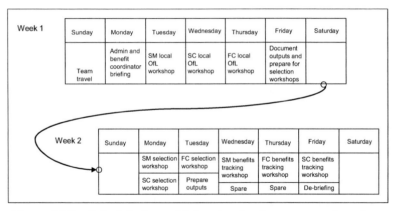

Figure 16.5 – Schedule for multi-function Implement stage benefits workshops

This is a very tight schedule – which is why, in the previous two diagrams, I have allowed a three-week period for these activities rather than the two weeks shown here. The reason for this is that, while it is possible in ideal conditions to complete in the time shown, local circumstances will almost certainly dictate that workshops cannot be packed this tightly. Also, there is a fair amount of preparation work for you to do in the two gaps between workshops and the allowance I have made for this is not generous. While writing this chapter I am planning a similar exercise for the ERP consolidation project in North America and have scheduled two and a half weeks to complete all activities, not including travelling time.

Points to note from the schedule include:

- Little time has been allowed to brief benefits coordinators. However, you will have sent them a preliminary briefing pack so this session is more about answering their questions and making them comfortable about supporting workshop facilitation.

- OfL workshops can take a full day and should be scheduled as such. Each benefits selection workshop will be a half day's work or less. Benefits tracking workshops typically take four to six hours to complete; it is too risky to schedule more than one of these per day.

- The debriefing is mainly for the benefit of the transformation manager and country function managers.

Running the benefit risk workshop

The objectives of the OfL workshop are very similar to those for a more traditional project risk workshop. These are to:

- Identify all possible opportunities for loss of project benefits.

- Rank the OfLs in terms of severity and probability.

- Decide which OfLs have sufficient potential impact to require active management and define how they should be managed.

▶ Introduction session

The number of delegates for this workshop should be similar to that for previous workshops (eight to 12) and I am assuming that many of them will have been involved in benefits workshops during the Feasibility and Define stages of the project. In this case the introduction session can be limited to a short reminder of the methodology and the regional benefits case, a briefing in greater depth on the method that applies to this stage and a schedule for the day. A suggested schedule is shown in Table 16.1 overleaf.

Morning	Introduction
	Session 1 – Identifying OfLs
	Refreshment break
	Session 2 – Ranking OfLs
	Lunch
Afternoon	Session 3 – Selecting OfLs for management
	Tea
	Session 4 – Defining OfL controls

Table 16.1 – Schedule for a functional OfL workshop

▶ Session 1 – Identification of OfLs

For the first country to be implemented, OfL identification may start with a blank canvas; I say may, because the early work on high-level OfLs (probably conducted by the group benefits manager) could provide an input to this exercise. For subsequent countries there is a completed template to follow; however, I recommend that for all countries you start the session as if there is a blank canvas. Not to do so risks the session becoming a rubber-stamping exercise during which no fresh ideas will materialise.

I suggest that this session be run as an almost unstructured brainstorming exercise. I say 'almost' because it can help to provide delegates with a framework of OfL categories within which to brainstorm; the framework helps to ensure that aspects of risk do not get overlooked and will make it easier for you to organise the OfLs once the session is finished. The list of categories used for our example project is shown at Table 16.2 opposite:

This is the category list that was used to frame the session. As we shall see, the list of categories became longer and more refined when the OfLs were analysed after the workshop (see Table 9.1, Chapter 9).

OfL categories
System issues
Data integrity issues
Usability issues
Change management issues
Behavioural issues

Table 16.2 – Initial OfL categories for an MIS implementation project

Ideally, to run this session in the way I suggest you will need three facilitators; two will do but it would be difficult to run it with just one person. This should not be a problem as, even if you are the sole member present from the central team, you should be able to call on the services of the regional and country benefits coordinators.

In our example project we were lucky enough to have electronic whiteboards available but, failing this, three flip charts will suffice. These should be prepared before the session starts, by drawing a line across the middle of each and writing an OfL category at the top of each half of the paper; thus three flip charts will accommodate up to six categories. In our example the last half chart would (had we not been using a whiteboard) have been reserved for miscellaneous OfLs that did not fit into any of the five predetermined categories.

There are many ways of conducting this session. One that works is to split it into three parts:

- Start with a true brainstorming, with delegates calling out ideas for OfLs and facilitators writing them onto the flip charts. There should be no challenging here except to seek clarification where necessary on which category each OfL fits into. Finish when the ideas from delegates start to dry up.

- The second part is to clean up the OfL list achieved so far. Taking a category at a time, seek consensus on elimination of inappropriate or duplicate OfLs, combining of overlapping OfLs and clarity to convey the true meaning of vaguely worded ones. All agreed changes are made on top of the flip chart lists from the brainstorming session. If there is a lot of editing as a result of this exercise, it is worth transposing the remaining OfLs onto fresh flip sheets; another instance where it helps to have three facilitators.

- The final part of this session is for you to suggest OfLs that have not so far been exposed. If time allows, it is better that missing OfLs be teased out of the delegates rather than just presented to them. Of course, this presupposes that you have done your homework before the workshop and have a good feel for what the OfL list should include. As new OfLs are agreed they are added to the flip charts under the appropriate category.

As a result of this session, how many OfLs should you be satisfied with? This is a 'how long is a piece of string' type of question and equally difficult to answer. However, there are some factors that should be borne in mind when assessing whether or not enough has been achieved in the session:

- If the project is multi-functional, as in our example, there will be one or two more similar sessions during which more OfLs are likely to emerge. Experience has shown that, although the workshops are run on a functional basis, many of the OfLs identified in each are applicable to all functions.

- Quantity is not as important as quality. The important point is that all the most relevant OfLs to release of project benefits are identified.

- Despite the above, it is good to have more OfLs identified than the organisation will wish to manage, if only to inject some realism into the decision-making in subsequent workshop sessions.

In our example project, each workshop identified between 23 and 28 OfLs which, when rationalised into a consolidated list, resulted in a total of 66 OfLs.

At the end of this session the flip charts should look something like the example shown in Figure 16.6.

Usability issues

Misunderstanding of the data presented

Accessibility of data to field sales force (lack of equipment, slow downloads etc).

Some users may misinterpret self-help reports through innumeracy

Timeliness is not good enough to stick with both report developers and users

Inappropriate comparisons of data between countries leading to erroneous decisions

---

Change management issues

Lack of change management and training to ensure new business processes stick

Insufficient skill level of users to get full benefit from the system

Lack of widespread availability of coaching to help optimize use by web users

Lack of channels to share good ways of using MIS data

Figure 16.6 – Example of a flip chart from the OfL identification session

▶ Session 2 – Ranking OfLs

The second session is to assess, for each OfL on the list, at what level of the organisation the risk exists, how likely is it to happen and how severe the impact of its occurrence would be on the release of project benefits.

The assessment of level (whether the OfLs apply at country level, regional level or both) is straightforward but assessments of the impact of likelihood and severity need a reference framework to ensure consistency. The framework needs a scale and boundary conditions.

- **Scale**. There are two traditional ways of setting a risk assessment scale: numerically (typically 1 to 10) or stepped (typically Low, Medium and High). There are advantages to both: the numerical scale allows a more accurate assessment that is easier to manipulate when selecting risks to manage because of the more granular differentiation between different impact levels; the stepped scale has the advantage of simplicity. In our example project the stepped scale was used.

- **Boundary conditions**. Delegates need to know what are the definitions associated with 'Low, Medium or High' impact (or associated with the numerical scale, if that is being used) both for OfL likelihood and severity.

Delegates to the first functional workshop get the privilege of setting the reference framework for the whole project but you will need to talk them through the process. Having chosen the scale (stepped in this case) they need to discuss the meanings of likelihood and severity. Likelihood is relatively easy to define but severity should be scaled to the project. I suggest that, knowing the forecast country and regional financial value of the project, OfL severity should be assessed against the potential loss of project financial contribution to the business.

In our example project, the forecast annual financial contributions of the project for the first country and the first region implemented were eight hundred thousand dollars and six million dollars respectively. The delegates agreed on the reference framework shown at Figure 16.7 opposite.

Note that both qualitative and quantitative boundary conditions have been expressed. I would encourage this approach as, intuitively, I feel that some delegates would be uncomfortable with one or other type of boundary condition on its own; the qualitative boundary is a bit vague while the quantitative boundary can be perceived as too prescriptive.

The same framework was used for subsequent functional workshops and subsequent countries, except that the boundary values for the severity of country-level OfLs were changed to reflect the different forecast project financial contributions of the individual countries.

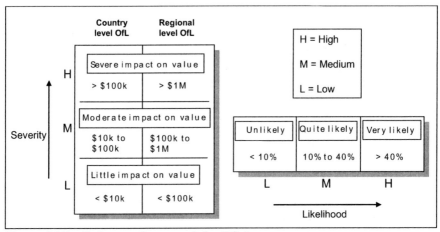

Figure 16.7 – Reference framework for OfL impact assessment

Having created the reference framework, the workshop can get on with the main objective of the session – to qualify each OfL. This is very much a consensus exercise, best done with all delegates together. You lead the workshop through each OfL in turn and the appropriate level, likelihood and severity marking is discussed, agreed and recorded. Once each OfL has been addressed, it is worth quickly reviewing the results to ensure that the boundary conditions have been applied consistently throughout the list.

There are two ways of physically conducting the session: either continuing with the flip chart or transferring to a projected PC spreadsheet template. The latter option is probably more convenient but it will mean some swift work by one of the team members during the refreshment break to type the agreed list of OfLs into a pre-prepared template. If this course is taken, the results will look something like Table 9.2 but with a single value given for each characteristic. If flip charts are used again, the way that the final OfL list is recorded during the previous session will be slightly different, leaving room for the characteristics to be recorded. The end result will look like Figure 16.8.

Usability issues	Level	Likelihood	Severity
Misunderstanding of the data presented	B	H	L
Accessibility of data to field sales force (lack of equipment, slow downloads etc).	C	H	H
Some users may misinterpret self-help reports through innumeracy	C	M	M
Timeliness is not good enough to stick with both report developers and users	C	L	L
Inappropriate comparisons of data between countries leading to erroneous decisions	R	L	M
Change management issues			
Lack of change management and training to ensure new business processes stick	B	H	H
Insufficient skill level of users to get full benefit from the system	B	H	H
Lack of widespread availability of coaching to help optimize use by web users	B	H	M
Lack of channels to share good ways of using MIS data	B	L	M

Figure 16.8 – Example of a flip chart from the OfL ranking session

▶ Session 3 – Selecting OfLs for management

The final session of the day may take a while to complete, so I suggest that this first session after lunch be completed as quickly as possible. The quickest way is for you to spend a good proportion of the lunch break preparing material for the session, which will leave very little to do during the session itself. The material can be presented in two ways and, if time allows, it might be worth preparing both:

- The OfLs are projected from the PC-based spreadsheet, with high-impact OfLs highlighted in colour (I suggest yellow): deep yellow for OfLs with double High characteristics and light yellow for OfLs with one High and one Medium marking (see Table 9.2).

- The risks are plotted on a value risk impact matrix drawn up on a flip chart (Figure 9.3).

With either or both types of presentation it is an easy task to select the high-value OfLs that should be actively managed. Considerations to be taken into account during this exercise are discussed in the text accompanying Figure 9.3 in Chapter 9.

▶ Session 4 – Defining OfL controls

The last session of the day is to establish how risks to project benefits and value are going to be managed. The types of control that can be used to manage OfLs were discussed in the section 'Establishing OfL controls' in Chapter 9. As I said there, we need to concentrate on the OfLs defined as high impact in the previous session but, if time allows, it is worth addressing all risks in the list; they can change from being of low impact to medium or high impact as circumstances change during project operation.

I suggest that a different method be used to facilitate this session. Firstly, the different types of control are explained to delegates and then they split into, say, three groups. Each group is given one or two OfL categories and asked to propose the most appropriate control for each OfL under the categories allocated. A danger here is that groups become over-zealous through enthusiasm and come up with controls that would be costly or otherwise impractical to implement. Groups should be allowed around an hour to complete the exercise so that they can give it proper consideration. During this time you and the other facilitators should circulate among the groups and offer guidance. Each control includes a description of what it is, who should be responsible locally for implementing it and, where necessary, who on the central team should monitor the control and provide support. The groups should complete the first two elements of the control definition (see Figure 9.2); they will probably not be in a position to say which central role need be involved and this part can be completed by you later. The groups record their proposals on a flip chart.

When the hour is up, the groups come together again and each presents its proposals to the rest of the workshop delegates. Even when proposals are accepted by the whole workshop there are likely to be minor changes to the wording. A good way of dealing with this is to have the OfL spreadsheet template projected alongside the flip chart and enter the wording for each OfL control as it is agreed; a good job for a second facilitator – perhaps one of the benefits coordinators. Figure 16.9 shows a section of the OfL register that results from this session.

▶ After the workshop

If the project does not require separate functional workshops then you will have just one task to do to prepare for the next workshop (the second of the two tasks listed below). However, if two or more functional workshops have been held then there are two tasks to be completed:

- Rationalising workshop outputs

- Mapping OfLs onto benefits

Rationalising outputs

This task involves merging the benefit risk registers from all functional workshops, deleting duplicates while choosing the most appropriate controls from the duplicated risks and showing the range of impact scores awarded by the different functions. This is done to allow each function to benefit from the work of the others in subsequent workshops. The exercise is best carried out by you and the function benefits coordinators working as a team. The simplest way of doing the merging is by cutting and pasting from the functional benefit risk spreadsheets onto a consolidated country spreadsheet. A section of a benefit risk register, after rationalisation, now looks like Figure 16.10.

| OfLs - Malaysia/Singapore Sales & Marketing function | | | | | | |
OfL	Level	Likelih'd	Impact	Controls	Local responsibility	Central responsibility
Organisational and marketing structural changes make MIS reports irrelevant until they can be re-engineered - leads to need for manual intervention to provide reports	B	H	M	Impact of changes should be assessed when planning major organisational changes	BULT	
Accessibility of MIS data to field sales force (lack of equipment, slow downloads etc)	C	H	H	Investigate potential more robust/quicker access mechanisms. Audit essential needs for sales force reports and ensure these reports are available in suitable format for iPacs	Malaysia DCT	
Sales force don't use the system - not sufficiently user-friendly, lack of confidence, fear of visibility of data entry errors, computer-phobia	C	M	H	Training, support, recognition, reward, performance management	Sales Director	Project team
Inappropriate use of system by sales force (too often, not often enough, looking at the wrong reports)	C	H	M	Training, support, recognition, reward, performance management	Sales Director	Project team
Misunderstanding of the data presented	B	H	L	Appropriate case studies in training	MIS Training	
Continued duplication of analysis - erosion of effort-saving benefit	B	M	M	Peer group to set up appropriate inter-function processes	Peer Group	
Timely availability of order delivery issues to sales force	C	M	M	Monitor and institute process improvement if found necessary	SOM	
Perception that MIS is not better than current systems	B	L	M	High profile launch (centrally funded) - sell the benefits	Project Governance Board	
Continuous availability of MIS data disrupted by planned outages and technical problems	B	L	M	Effective communication of planned outages.	Malaysia DCT	
Lack of on-going support to effect changes to the system, carry out continuation training, update training modules etc	B	L	H	Refer to project team to ensure this is being catered for	Malaysia project manager	
Over-analysis by vested-interest parties, leading to questions being asked and effort to answer them	B	H	H	Challenge value of requests 'why are you asking the question?'	Peer Group	
Requests for trend analysis using historic data not held in MIS (ie pre 2003)	B	L	M			

Figure 16.9 – Section of an OfL register after control definition

Mapping benefit risks

The second task, undertaken by the same team, is laborious but will ensure that the benefits selection workshop is kept short and sharp. The task is to take the benefits case and assess and record which benefit risks will impact each benefit. I suggest that this mapping can be limited to the risks that have been declared of high impact (double High or one High and one Medium category). This is not necessarily the same shortlist of benefit risks as those selected for active management, as a different selection threshold may have been used for that exercise (as explained in Chapter 9).

In carrying out this exercise, the format of the benefits case needs to be changed from that shown at Figures 15.8 and 15.10 in the previous chapter. You will recall that these reports were generated from the benefits case relational database but this medium and format are not best suited to the tasks of selecting benefits to track and developing a benefits tracking plan. That is to say, the database that I designed is not suitable; I am happy to concede that a greater database design expert than myself could do better. From the database used in our example project it is a relatively easy task to transform the list of benefits with associated targets and measures into a spreadsheet.

Note that the OfLs need to have been given serial numbers to be able to carry out this task; serialisation is reset when the merged and rationalised OfL list is produced. The task can be carried out in one of two ways:

- Take each high-impact OfL in turn and see which benefits it would impact.

- Take each benefit in turn and see which high-impact OfL would affect the benefit class financial contribution that the benefit is forecast to contribute towards.

It really does not matter which method is used; data entry into the spreadsheet template is slightly easier with the second approach. The important point is that whichever method is chosen is used consistently until the exercise is completed.

Srl	OfLs - All Malaysia/Singapore functions — OfL	Level	Likelih'd	Impact	Raised by	Controls	Local responsibility
	Usability and interpretation						
38	Larger number of people using self-help reports will increase misinterpretations through lack of numeracy	C	M	M	Commercial	Training and monitoring by line management	Peer Group
39	Inappropriate comparisons of data between countries leading to erroneous decisions	R	L	M	Commercial		
40	Accessibility of MIS data to field sales force (lack of equipment, slow downloads etc). / Usability is not good enough to stick with both report developers and users in terms of Accessibility	C/B	H	H	S & M LSC	Investigate potential more robust/quicker access mechanisms. Audit essential needs for sales force reports and ensure these reports are available in suitable format for iPacs. / UAT testing	Country Project Manager/ Malaysia DCT
41	Misunderstanding of the data presented	B	H	L	S & M	Appropriate case studies in training	MIS Training
42	Timely availability of order delivery issues to sales force. Usability is not good enough to stick with both report developers and users in terms of Timeliness	C	M/L	M/L	S & M LSC	Monitor and institute process improvement if found necessary	SOM
43	Usability is not good enough to stick with both report developers and users in terms of User friendliness	B	M	M	LSC	UAT testing. User training. Check adequacy of on-line help once established. User surveys and channel for providing feedback.	Project Team
	Super Users						
44	Report requestors ask for the same data presented in many different ways	B	H	M	Commercial	Escalation procedure for conflict between requestor and super-user. Training of super-user.	Commercial Function Leader
45	Super-users may end up spending too much time being application administrators/developers	B	H	H	S & M	Ensure superuser responsibilities are defined and understood by all. Superusers recognised as empowered to challenge requests for new reports	Project Change Management
46	May have too few super users/OLAP users (could apply particularly to Marketing support, who would need analysis capability)	B	H	M	S & M	Ensure superuser responsibilities are defined and understood by all. Superusers recognised as empowered to challenge requests for new reports	Project Change Management
47	Over -restriction on number of super-users may limit flexibility of system	B	H	M	LSC	Gain initial input from user community and check within function after a period of use.	Team leaders
48	Erosion of capability/flexibility through turnover of super-users	B	H	H	LSC	Ensure succession planning. Recognise need for on-going training, incl cross function training. Well documented procedures. Informal super-user network.	Project Team
	Maintenance						
49	Organisational and marketing structural changes make BIGS reports irrelevant until they can be re-engineered - leads to need for manual intervention to provide reports with impact on maintenance resources	B	H	M/L	S & M Commercial LSC	Impact of changes should be assessed when planning major organisational changes / One-time check on cost of changing BIGS mapping following reorganisation	BULT / Regional LSC LT
50	Continuous availability of MIS data disrupted by planned outages and technical problems	B	L	M	S & M	Effective communication of planned outages.	Malaysia DCT
51	Lack of on-going support to effect changes to the system, carry out continuation training, update training modules etc	B	L	H	S & M	Refer to project team to ensure this is being catered for	AsPac Project Manager
52	Ongoing maintenance insufficient to keep mappings etc up to date	B	M	H	LSC	Check use of Streamline to ensure rigorous mapping of new products etc	Data Manager

Figure 16.10 – Section of an OfL register after rationalisation

A part of the template, prepared for one of the next functional workshops, is shown at Figure 16.11 opposite.

Note that there are, as well as the 'OfL mapping' column, five new columns added that have not been used before. These are all transitory columns that will not be included in the benefits tracking plan; their use will be to assist the facilitation of the next workshop. I will summarise their purpose here; we will discuss how they are used in the next chapter.

- **Risk to benefit**. This will be a summary, single value, expression of the risk to the benefit from those OfLs identified as potentially able to affect its associated financial contribution. Risks will, as before, be registered as High, Medium or Low (or on a scale from 1 to 10 if the numerical approach is used).

- **Value of benefit**. This indicates the relative contribution of the benefit to the overall country-level financial value of the project. The same scale is used as for the risk column and the boundary conditions are those used in assessing the severity of OfLs (Figure 16.7).

- **Decision point 1**. Selecting the benefits to track is, as we shall see, a two-stage process. This column allows the first, provisional stage selection to be registered with a simple 'Yes' or 'No' entry.

- **Measure type**. This is used to qualify the way the measurement will be taken: automatically from the system, by questionnaire or needing an interview.

- **Decision point 2**. This records the final decision on whether or not the benefit will be included in the tracking plan.

Benefit	OfL mapping High/High	OfL mapping High/Medium	Risk to benefit	Value of benefit	Decision point 1	Measures	Measure type	Beneficiaries
Sales and Marketing								
Improve product margins								
Improve profitability of sales - trading up, cross-selling, increased volumes	40, 59, 62	9, 13, 14, 17, 18, 29, 63				- Number of customer sales ranking enquiries made of MIS - Number of attempts per customer to improve sales - Product lines per order		- Country sales managers - Country sales executives
Negotiate cross-region deals	62	20, 36, 49				- Number of potential cross-deals identified		- Regional sales directors
Improve price management to optimise customer operating margins	36, 59, 61, 62	9, 14, 20, 29, 49, 63				- Number of optimizing actions taken		- Country sales managers
Manage distributor performance more proactively	62	20, 36, 49				- Number of informed discussions with distributors		- Distributor account managers
Reduce lost sales								
Better focus sales effort to problem customers	29, 40, 59, 62	9, 13, 14, 17, 18, 63				- Number of wavering customers - Number of unwanted customers		- Country sales managers - Country sales executives
More proactive management of IFOT problems	7, 40	9, 14, 63				- % of IFOT instances where sales person can warn customers		- Country sales managers - Country sales executives
Manage the causes of Credit Notes better	7, 29, 36, 40, 59, 61, 62	9, 14, 18, 27				- Number of credit notes per invoice		- Country sales managers - Country sales executives
Manage demand planning better	7, 29, 36, 40, 59, 61, 62	9, 14, 18, 27				- Number of stock-outs		- Country sales managers - Country sales executives
Reduce the number of cancelled orders	7, 29, 36, 40, 59, 61, 62	9, 14, 18, 27				- Number of cancelled orders		- Country sales managers - Country sales executives
More efficient sales resource allocation								
Better allocation of sales resources	29, 35, 61	20, 27, 49				- Sales force productivity		- Regional sales directors
More efficient use of training resources	7, 29, 35, 61	20, 27				- Reduction in region-wide training costs		- Regional Sales Operations Manager
Improve return on trade loans								
Better adherence to trade loan T's and Cs	7, 29, 36, 40, 59, 61, 62	9, 14, 18, 27				- Number of loan customers with performance issues		- Country sales managers - Country sales executives
Better trade loan investment decisions	7, 29, 36, 40, 59, 61, 62	9, 14, 18, 27				- Transferred benefit		- Country sales managers - Country sales executives

Figure 16.11 – Spreadsheet form of benefits case with OfL mapping

Tracking to release benefits

Introduction

The last chapter is about the benefits management activities that lead to full release of project benefits; developing and executing a benefit tracking plan and taking appropriate remedial action where necessary.

The chapter starts with the development of a benefit tracking plan and follows closely on the heels of the last chapter, where we mapped OfLs against individual benefits in the country-level benefits case. The mapping was done in the gap between OfL and benefit selection workshops; you are now in a position to conduct the latter.

Running the benefit selection workshop

This workshop is different from any of the previous benefits workshops in this or previous project stages. The difference is that it is conducted more like a working meeting, around a table, with a peer group of informed attendees. A good number for the workshop would be six: yourself, the appropriate country functional benefits coordinator and four business delegates. Perhaps seven is better, with the regional benefits coordinator also in attendance. The business attendees should be selected from the delegate list of the previous workshop and be the same people who will attend the final workshop. The criterion for selection is that attendees should be in positions of wide but relevant operational knowledge and influence, such as a sales operations manager for the Sales and Marketing workshop. The reasons for this will become clear when we discuss the tasks undertaken in the final workshop.

You will have prepared carefully for this workshop, by doing the things we covered in the last section of Chapter 16, so that tasks remaining to be done in the workshop can be completed in a short space of time – less than four hours if you have planned for two such workshops in a day. The tasks are to:

- Review the benefits case and the mapping of OfLs to individual benefits that you completed before the workshop.

- Allocate risk and financial value scores to each benefit.

- Provisionally select benefits to track on the basis of risk and value.

- Review tracking measures for relevance and feasibility and identify measurement types.

- Make a final selection of benefits to track.

Note that the steps listed here, designed to complete the empty columns of Figure 16.11, are somewhat less formally structured than those described in the section in Chapter 9 entitled 'Selecting benefits to track'. Both approaches are valid; in the one described here, some of the Chapter 9 decision points are implicit rather than explicit but all factors are considered, whichever of the two methods you use.

▶ Initial review

This should be a short session to remind attendees of the benefits within the benefits case and explain the mapping of OfLs onto each benefit. I suggest that there is no need to justify the mapping, entry by entry. Rather, you should go through one or two examples and bring up any entries you are not sure about and discuss any challenges from attendees.

▶ Allocation of risk and value scores

Like all the score allocation exercises during this series of workshops, this is not an exact science and attendees should not get bogged down in detail or exactitude. Allocation of risk level is subjective and is based on the weight of OfLs – particularly double-High risks – impacting each benefit. The value score can be assessed more objectively by estimating the proportion of benefit class financial value contributed by each benefit and measuring that value against the agreed financial boundary conditions. An example in the panel opposite illustrates this.

The Asia Pacific benefits case includes a benefit class 'Improve product margins'. The benefit class is made up of the following benefits:

Benefit class	Benefits
Improve product margins	• Improve profitability of sales • Negotiate cross-regional deals • Improve price management • Manage distributor performance more proactively

The benefit class has a regional value of $1.575m, of which the Malaysia/Singapore contribution is $110k.

The great majority of this value at country level is contributed by two of the benefits within the class 'Improve profitability of sales' and 'Improve price management'. We therefore assume that each of these benefits is valued at greater than $50k and thus above the $50k 'High value' threshold (see Figure 16.7).

▶ Provisional selection of benefits

This is another exercise that can, and should, be quickly completed. The purpose here is to eliminate benefits that are either at negligible risk or contribute negligible financial value, or have a combination of only moderate risk and financial value. The emphasis here should be to delete only those benefits whose tracking would be emphatically non cost-effective.

▶ Review of measures and identification of types

This is perhaps the first exercise in this workshop that requires considered thought and debate; about an hour and a half out of the four should be allocated to this session.

The review should be completed first and consists of thinking through whether the measures previously selected are really appropriate as measurements of the forecast changes along the chain of events and whether they are feasible; by which I mean, will it be possible to obtain the measurement in practice. If any measure is found to be inappropriate for either reason, the workshop should delete it and, where possible, replace it with one that is appropriate.

The second step is to mark the type of each agreed measure: whether it will be derived automatically from a system (including the MIS being implemented, in this example), derived manually or obtained from responses to questionnaires or interviews. The purpose of this part of the exercise is to give a lead as to how costly or intrusive each measure may be.

▶ Final selection of benefits

The last exercise confirms the benefits and measures that will form the basis of the benefit tracking plan. Again, this is a somewhat subjective exercise but it should be run against a number of rules of thumb:

- Any benefit that contributes high financial value, or is at high risk and at least moderate financial value, should be included, however costly or intrusive the measures (within reason).

- Where a single benefit has a number of measures allocated to it, any that are costly or intrusive should be eliminated unless to do so would leave a dangerous gap in the ability to monitor the benefit.

- If a benefit had been deleted at the provisional stage, consideration should be given to its reinstatement if the associated measures are of negligible cost and are non-intrusive.

This session completes this workshop. The benefits selection template should now look like Figure 17.1

Benefit	Off. mapping High/High	Off. mapping High/Medium	Risk to benefit	Value of benefit	Decision point 1	Measures	Measure type	Beneficiaries	Decision point 2
Sales and Marketing									
Improve product margins									
Improve profitability of sales - trading up, cross-selling, increased volumes	40, 59, 62	9, 13, 14, 17, 18, 29, 63	M	H	Yes	- Number of customer sales ranking enquiries made of MIS - Number of attempts per customer to improve sales - Product lines per order - Number of SKUs per order [new]	- System - Decision log - N/A - System	- Country sales managers - Country sales executives	Yes
Negotiate cross-region deals	62	20, 36, 49	L	M	No	- Number of potential cross-deals identified	- Questionnaire	- Regional sales directors	No
Improve price management to optimise customer operating margins	36, 59, 61, 62	9, 14, 20, 29, 49, 63	M	H	Yes	- Number of optimizing actions taken - Volume of free oil [new]	- Decision log - System	- Country sales managers	Yes
Manage distributor performance more proactively	62	20, 36, 49	L	M	No	- Number of informed discussions with distributors	- Questionnaire	- Distributor account managers	No
Reduce lost sales									
Better focus sales effort to problem customers	29, 40, 59, 62	9, 13, 14, 17, 18, 63	H	H	Yes	- Number of waivering customers - Number of unwanted less desirable customers	- System - System	- Country sales managers - Country sales executives	Yes
More proactive management of IFOT problems	7, 40	9, 14, 63	H	M	Yes	- % of IFOT instances where sales person can warn customers	- System coupled with questionnaire	- Country sales managers - Country sales executives	No
Manage the causes of Credit Notes better	7, 29, 36, 40, 59, 61, 62	9, 14, 18, 27	H	M	Yes	- Number of credit notes per invoice	- System	- Country sales managers - Country sales executives	Yes
Manage demand planning better	7, 29, 36, 40, 59, 61, 62	9, 14, 18, 27	H	M	Yes	- Number of stock-outs - Number of cancelled orders [transferred]	- System - System	- Country sales managers - Country sales executives	Yes
Reduce the number of cancelled orders	7, 29, 36, 40, 59, 61, 62	9, 14, 18, 27	H	M	Yes	- Number of cancelled orders [amalgamated into benefit above]		- Country sales managers - Country sales executives	No
More efficient sales resource allocation									
Better allocation of sales resources	29, 35, 61	20, 27, 49	M	H	Yes	- Sales force productivity	- System	- Regional sales directors	No
More efficient use of training resources	7, 29, 35, 61	20, 27	H	L	No	- Reduction in region-wide training costs	- System	- Regional Sales Operations Manager	No
Improve return on trade loans									
Better adherence to trade loan Ts and Cs	7, 29, 36, 40, 59, 61, 62	9, 14, 18, 27	H	M	Yes	- Number of loan customers with performance issues	- System	- Country sales managers - Country sales executives	No
Better trade loan investment decisions	7, 29, 36, 40, 59, 61, 62	9, 14, 18, 27	H	L	No	- Transferred benefit		- Country sales managers - Country sales executives	No

Figure 17.1 – Completed benefit selection spreadsheet

Running the benefit tracking workshop

▶ Preliminaries

The final workshop of the entire benefits management method is designed to construct the benefit tracking plan. This is an extremely important workshop as the benefit tracking plan is the main link between all the benefits work conducted within the project stages and with what will happen in practice, on the ground, once the project goes live.

Before the workshop starts, you may want to complete one simple task, which is to partially populate a pre-prepared benefit tracking template with the agreed output from the previous workshop. This template will look like Figure 17.2 at the start of the workshop.

There is no need for a formal presentation at the beginning of the workshop. This is another working meeting with people who by now understand the methodology, the importance of the work and their contribution to it. The one thing to impress on all present is the need to inject realism and clarity into the tracking plan. This should not present much of a problem, assuming that a sensible delegate selection has been made; everyone present will have a personal interest in ensuring a watertight tracking plan.

▶ Running the workshop

For the first time, I am not proposing a session by session schedule for a workshop. The reason for this is that the best way to approach the workshop is to undertake all the tasks required on a single measure before moving on to repeat the tasks on the next measure. The tasks for each measure are to:

- Reconfirm or complete measure targets.

- Make a final decision on the beneficiary roles, numbers and names that will be involved in measurements.

- Set a measurement schedule.

- Define how the measurements will be taken.

Benefit	Tracking method	Confirmed measures	Target	Beneficiaries and/or trackers Title	Name	Schedule	Measurement definition
Sales and Marketing	**Benefits co-ordinator: Peng Ho Chin**						
Improve product margins							
Improve profitability of sales – trading up, cross-selling, increased volumes	- System	- Number of customer sales enquiries	- 1 a week				
	- Decision log/questionnaire	- Number of attempts to improve sales	- 30% increase				
	- System (possibly JDE, if not in BIGS)	- Number of SKUs per order (new)	10% increase				
Improve price management to optimise cust. margins	- Decision log/questionnaire	- Number of optimising actions taken	- Target not set				
	- System	- Volume of free oil (new)??	- 10% reduction				
Reduce lost sales							
Better focus sales effort to problem customers	- System	- Number of wavering customers	- Reduce by 50%				
	- System	- Number of less desirable customers	- Reduce by 30%				
Manage the causes of Credit Notes better	- System	- Number of credit notes per invoice	- Reduce by 50%				
Manage demand planning better	- System	- Number of stock-outs	- Target not set				
	- System	- Number of cancelled orders					
More efficient sales resource allocation							
Better allocation of sales resources	- System	- Sales force cost-effectiveness (cost per litre sold)	- Improve by 2%				

Figure 17.2 – Spreadsheet prepared for the benefit tracking workshop

The considerations to take into account for each of these tasks are fully discussed in the section 'Developing the tracking plan' in Chapter 9. You can introduce these considerations informally as each task is undertaken. By the second or third measure, delegates will be able to progress smoothly through the tasks without the need for interruptions for explanations.

Some of the measurements will need to be via responses to questionnaires. You may (should) have some generic questionnaire templates available but the workshop is probably not the place to tailor these to the requirements of the measures in question, even if time allows; questionnaire development is best done by you after the workshop. However, where a questionnaire, action log or decision log is required, workshop delegates should agree a specification for aspects of the questionnaire that need tailoring to the measure.

When all the tasks have been finished, the benefits tracking plan for the function is also complete and will look like the example in Figure 17.3.

▶ After the workshop

Despite the finality of the last workshop, there are still some tasks remaining for you to do. These are to:

- Fill any remaining gaps in the tracking plan.

- Draft associated questionnaires.

- Brief leadership team members and help with the drafting of changes to performance contracts.

- Complete baseline measurements.

Benefit	Tracking method	Confirmed measures	Target	Beneficiaries and/or trackers Title	Beneficiaries and/or trackers Name	Schedule	Measurement definition
Sales and Marketing	**Benefits co-ordinator: Peng Ho Chin**						
Improve profitability of sales - trading up, cross-selling, increased volumes	- System	- Number of customer sales enquiries	- 1 a week	- SOM	- Charles Tang (KL); Robert Smith (S'pore)	- Once a month from April	- Average number of enquiries per salesman for identified range of reports
	- Decision log/questionnaire	- Number of attempts to improve sales	- 30% increase	- Selected sales staff : Team leaders (5), Sales Managers (5), Sales execs (10)	- Sales staff selected by SOM after first stats re enquiries received	- Baseline - SOM to establish when sales staff selected. For one month, 3 months after go-live, repeated after further 3 months	- Av. no. of actions/successful actions recorded on decision log per respondent
	- System (possibly JDE, if not in BIGS)	- Number of SKUs per order (new)	- 10% increase	- SOM	- SOMs as above	- Baseline month before go-live, then quarterly	- Average number of SKUs per order over a month, by sales team
Improve price management to optimise cust. margins	- Decision log/questionnaire - System	- Number of optimising actions taken	- Target not set	- Selected sales staff as above	- Sales staff selected as above	- Monthly, after 3 months	- On questionnaire
		- Volume of free oil (new)??	- 10% reduction			- Baseline in month before go-live then monthly after 3 months	- Average ratio of free oil per total sales volume over a month, by sales team
Reduce lost sales							
Better focus sales effort to problem customers	- System	- Number of wavering customers	- Reduce by 50%	- SOM	- Charles Tang (KL); Robert Smith (S'pore)	- Baseline in month before go-live then quarterly	- Quarterly sales by customer down by 10% or more compared with same month previous year
	- System	- Number of less desirable customers	- Reduce by 30%	- SOM	- as above	- As above	- Customers with average quarterly margins below 50c per litre
Manage the causes of Credit Notes better	- System	- Number of credit notes per invoice	- Reduce by 50%	- SOM	- Charles Tang (KL); Robert Smith (S'pore)	- Baseline in month before go-live then quarterly	- Number of credit notes received per quarter, as ratio of total number of invoices, by sales team
Manage demand planning better	- System	- Number of stock-outs	- Set after baseline figure established	- Customer service	- Benjamin Zana	- Baseline in month before go-live then quarterly	- Number of instances of negative availability, by product, per quarter
	- System	- Number of cancelled orders	- as above	- as above	- as above	- As above	- Number of cancelled orders, by reason code, as ratio of total number of orders, per quarter (by sales team?)(from JDE?)
More efficient sales resource allocation							
Better allocation of sales resources	- System	- Sales force cost-effectiveness (cost per litre sold)	- Improve by 2%	- SOM	- Charles Tang (KL); Robert Smith (S'pore)	- Baseline in month before go-live then every 6 months for 2 years	- Cost of sales force per litre sold: total cost per country; cost (less central sales overhead) per sales team

Figure 17.3 – Section of a functional benefit tracking

Gaps in the tracking plan

There will have been some details in the tracking plan that could not be completed, or confirmed, during the final workshop. These remaining tasks should be controlled by adding development management columns to the tracking plan, as shown in Figure 17.4.

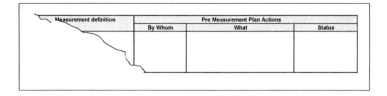

Figure 17.4 – Additional control columns for tracking plan

Use of these columns is as follows:

By whom. The name of the person tasked to complete the actions.

What. The action needed to complete the tracking plan for the measure concerned. For instance, against the first measure listed in Figure 17.3, there might be an entry:

> Check whether 'average number of enquiries per salesman' will be available to the sales operations manager from intranet statistics.

Similarly, against the first measure for the 'Improve price management.' benefit there will be an entry:

> Draft the decision log/questionnaire.

Status. A column in which the action status can be recorded. For instance, against the first measure, a typical entry would be:

> Emailed the question to George Smith, project intranet designer, on 25 April. He will check and give a response by 7 May.

Outstanding issues need to be resolved before the project go-live date in the country concerned. This will give little time for resolution, as the tracking plan workshop is normally held only a week or two before the go-live date.

Questionnaire drafting

This should just consist of tailoring some generic questionnaires to meet the specific requirements of a measure, or group of measures, in the tracking plan. The factors to take into account when drafting questionnaires are covered in Chapter 9.

Briefing leadership team members

Briefings need to be given to the regional transformation manager, particularly after the workshops for the first country to be implemented, and to the country leaders of impacted functions. These briefings will explain the details of the tracking plan, the way that execution of the tracking plan will be driven by benefits coordinators and their roles and responsibilities during operation.

Depending on the way that the organisation is run, there may also be a desire from the regional leadership team to amend the performance contract of impacted country function leaders. This is done to reflect their responsibilities in ensuring that benefit tracking takes place and that consequent recommendations to achieve project benefits are actioned. If this is the case, you will probably need to assist the regional transformation manager, whose responsibility this is.

Completing baseline measurement

The tracking plan gives details of which baseline measurements are needed and when they should be taken (the details are highlighted with underlined entries in the 'Schedule' column of the tracking plan – Figure 17.3). You should ensure, before leaving the country, that function benefits coordinators have these measurements in hand.

Executing the tracking plan

In this section we stay in the country in which we previously developed a benefit risk register and benefit tracking plan. Things have moved on since the end of the last section:

- The baseline measurements have been taken and targets that were dependent upon a missing baseline measurement have been set.

- Other missing or provisional elements of the tracking plan have been filled or confirmed.

- The project has been delivered and gone live in this country.

- You have moved on to the next country to be implemented and the country benefits coordinators are now in charge.

The last point may sound alarming (at least to the benefits coordinators) but you and the regional benefits coordinator are only a telephone call or email away if advice or support is needed.

The benefits coordinators all have day jobs. In our example project they were all performance analysts whose time had been largely occupied extracting and collating data into a variety of monthly and quarterly performance reports. A significant proportion of their time spent preparing reports was due to be saved following implementation of the MIS project whose benefit tracking they were to coordinate; however, it was expected to take up to three months before significant savings in their effort could be achieved and, in the meantime, they had also to coordinate benefit tracking from the day the project went live. This example demonstrates that if benefits coordinators are to carry out their responsibilities effectively while holding down their normal day-to-day duties they need a clear view of all the tracking to be undertaken – how, when and by whom – and what they have to do with tracking results, so that the time they spend on the role is used as effectively as possible. The benefit tracking plan goes a long way towards helping to control these activities but the coordinators will need additional tools to allow them to fulfil their responsibilities effectively.

▶ Benefit tracking

The tracking plan comprises measurements that need to be taken at different times; with different start dates for first measurements and a variety of periods between measurements. In some ways this is a blessing, as it will tend to spread the coordinators' workload. It is however an added complication and the first extra tool that coordinators should use is a simple calendar-based schedule, giving a week-by-week view of the measurements that have to be taken. This will provide a good overview of benefit tracking activities and avoid the possibility of a particular measurement getting overlooked.

Coordinators then need to establish a procedure that will ensure that all materials needed for measurements (for example instructions to beneficiaries and questionnaires) are available on time and all beneficiaries involved in taking measurements have been briefed before the event. It is advisable that the start date for each of these procedures, running up to the first taking of a measurement, be at least a week before the measurement itself is due.

The two main types of measurement are system readings and records of individuals' activities, actions and perceptions. There may be a third type – manual measurements.

System readings

These measurements are relatively straightforward; two things to say about them are that, although automated:

- They may need to be set up in the first place by, for instance, creating a specific MI report or giving access rights to restricted data to the person responsible for taking the measurement.

- You are unlikely to achieve the level of automation needed to populate a benefit tracking report automatically from system data without some human intervention (although such automation is possible if considered worthwhile). The measurements still have to be taken and recorded on the appropriate date, even if this merely involves downloading an MI report or interrogating an ERP system.

Logs and questionnaires

Log and questionnaire processing needs more intervention from benefits coordinators, to:

- Ensure that each log or questionnaire, with its accompanying instruction sheet, is ready to distribute.

- Distribute questionnaires to the selected beneficiaries and make sure, by way of individual briefings, that they understand all aspects of how to complete their questionnaire.

- Chase up beneficiaries for completed questionnaires after the due date.

If a questionnaire includes an activity or decision log that has to be completed over a period of, say, a month, it would be well worth the benefit coordinator checking, at a couple of points during the period, that beneficiaries are completing the log day by day. Some beneficiaries will, left to their own devices, leave the recording of the whole month's activities until the last day, thus introducing inaccuracy and bias into their log recording.

Questionnaires that require information about personal perceptions may, however clear the completion instructions, need follow-up interviews between benefits coordinators and some beneficiaries, to clarify the entries in their completed questionnaires. The discussion on targeted questionnaires in Chapter 9 gives further insight into the reasons for this need.

Manual measurements

There may be some measurements needed to calculate a KPI that cannot be provided automatically with the systems currently deployed in the organisation. An example of such a measurement could be the amount of fluid present in a storage tank, which requires a manual dip to measure. It may be that daily dip readings are taken and recorded anyway as part of normal procedures. In this and similar cases, the benefits coordinator needs to establish whether periodic recordings are available and, if not, take particular care to ensure that the reading can be, and is, taken on the date required in the benefit tracking plan.

▶ Reporting benefit tracking

A benefit reporting strategy will have been agreed between yourself, the regional transformation manager and the regional benefits coordinator. Country benefit tracking reports need to be synchronised with the regional reporting regime; in terms of timing, what is reported and in what format.

There are no hard and fast rules about how to set a reporting strategy but the following factors should be taken into account:

- In any upward reporting system there is a tendency to aggregate results at successive reporting levels. This should be avoided in the case of benefit tracking, where it is important to identify not only trends but also anomalies; aggregation can hide anomalies.

- The period between reports will be dictated largely by the frequency of measurements in the tracking plan. Reports are normally submitted from country to region quarterly, on the basis that a majority of measurements will have been taken once, but not twice, in each quarter.

- Whatever the regional reporting requirement, country benefits coordinators will collect and collate measurements as soon as they have been taken, so that there is no delay before analysis is done and any necessary remedial actions initiated.

Reports should be collated in a way that will help subsequent analysis. The example below demonstrates how this can be done.

As we have seen, one of the benefits from introduction of the MI system in our example project concerns performance analysts and their ability to spend more time doing their proper role (performance analysis) because the system has freed up most of the time they previously spent on producing reports. To track this benefit, performance analysts were asked to complete an activity log in the month before project go-live to obtain a baseline measurement and then again after three and six months of system operation. The activity log for one performance analyst at all three measure points is shown in Table 17.1.

Pre- Go-live

Activity (hours)	Mon 1	Tue 2	Wed 3	Thu 4	Fri 5	Sat 6	Sun 7	Mon 8	Tue 9	Wed 10	Thu 11	Fri 12	Sat 13	Sun 14	Mon 15	Tue 16	Wed 17	Thu 18	Fri 19	Sat 20	Sun 21	Mon 22	Tue 23	Wed 24	Thu 25	Fri 26	Sat 27	Sun 28	Mon 29	Tue 30	TOT
Data gathering	1	1	1	3	4	0	0	5	5	5	3	3	2	0	2	0	2	0	0	0	0	0	0	0	0	1	0	0	0	0	38
Report preparation	0	0	0	1	4	3	0	3	4	4	2	0	0	0	2	1	2	2	0	0	0	3	2	0	3	0	0	0	2	0	24
Analysis/investigation								2	4	4	2	4			4	5	4	5	4	0	0	4	3	2	1	2	0	??	0	0	46
Total hours spent in data-related activities	1			4	8	3	??	8	11	11	7	7	2	??	8	6	8	5	4	??	??	3	3	2	1	2	??	??	2	??	108
Total hours worked	7	7	7	7	9	3	0	9	11	11	7	7	??	??	10	7	9	7	6	0	0	7	7	7	7	??	??	??	7	7	173
Number of hours overtime				2	3			2	4	4					3	2						3									20

Month 4

Activity (hours)	Thu 1	Fri 2	Sat 3	Sun 4	Mon 5	Tue 6	Wed 7	Thu 8	Fri 9	Sat 10	Sun 11	Mon 12	Tue 13	Wed 14	Thu 15	Fri 16	Sat 17	Sun 18	Mon 19	Tue 20	Wed 21	Thu 22	Fri 23	Sat 24	Sun 25	Mon 26	Tue 27	Wed 28	Thu 29	Fri 30	Sat 31	TOT
Data gathering	1		0	0		3	0	4	3	0	0	0	0	1	1	1	0	0	0	0	0	0	1	0	0	0	1	1	0	0	0	20
Report preparation	0	0	0	2	2	2	1	2	3	0	0	0	1	1	2	1	0	0	0	2	2	0	1	0	0	1	2	1	1	0	0	19
Analysis/investigation	2	2	0	0	0	2	2	2	2	1	0	2	2	3	3	5	0	3	0	2	2	2	3	0	2	2	3	4	2	3		57
Total hours spent in data-related activities	3	3	??	??	7	7	5	5	8	1	??	3	4	4	6	6	??	??	3	2	2	2	4	??	2	??	5	5	3	3	??	96
Total hours worked	7	7	0	0	0	10	7	7	10	9	0	7	7	7	8	7	0	0	7	7	7	7	7	0	7	7	7	7	7	7	0	163
Number of hours overtime					3				3	2		1			1																	10

Month 7

Activity (hours)	Sat 1	Sun 2	Mon 3	Tue 4	Wed 5	Thu 6	Fri 7	Sat 8	Sun 9	Mon 10	Tue 11	Wed 12	Thu 13	Fri 14	Sat 15	Sun 16	Mon 17	Tue 18	Wed 19	Thu 20	Fri 21	Sat 22	Sun 23	Mon 24	Tue 25	Wed 26	Thu 27	Fri 28	Sat 29	Sun 30	Mon 31	TOT
Data gathering	0	0	0	0	0	0	2	0	0	1	1	0	1	0	0	0	0	0	0	0	1	0	0	0	0	0	0	0	0	0	0	8
Report preparation	0	0	2	2	2	0	1	0	0	1	0	1	2	1	0	0	0	0	0	0	1	0	0	0	2	1	1	3	0	0	2	12
Analysis/investigation	0	0	0	4	3	2	5	0	0	5	6	5	5	5	0	0	6	6	6	7	5	0	0	4	5	6	4	3	0	0	3	91
Total hours spent in data-related activities	??	??	2	2	5	2	4	0	0	6	7	6	8	6	??	??	7	6	6	7	7	0	??	5	7	6	6	6	??	??	3	111
Total hours worked	0	0	7	7	7	7	7	0	0	8	7	7	9	7	0	0	7	7	6	7	7	0	0	7	7	7	7	7	0	0	7	150
Number of hours overtime	0	0	0	0	0	0	0	0	0	1			2																			3

Table 17.1 – Activity log to track the benefit of reducing effort to produce reports

Timeline profiles for both the basic changes associated with this benefit – reduction in time spent producing reports and increase in time spent undertaking analysis – were produced (see Figure 9.6 and associated text) and from these the expected improvements at the measure time points can be read off; these are summarised in Table 17.2.

	Before go-live	After 3 months	After 6 months
Time spent producing reports	40%	25%	12%
Time spent undertaking performance analysis	30%	37%	58%

Table 17.2 – Forecast time-point improvements associated with benefit of reducing effort to produce reports

Now the results from all performance analysts are summarised and collated as shown in Table 17.3, which is the summary for the analysts in the Finance and Control function:

Name	Time spent producing reports			Time spent undertaking analysis		
	Pre go-live F'cast 40%	4th month F'cast 25%	7th month F'cast 12%	Pre go-live F'cast 30%	4th month F'cast 37%	7th month F'cast 58%
Wong Lee	42%	26%	10%	28%	33%	58%
Tom Anders	45%	28%	13%	25%	31%	55%
Nancy Lean	38%	24%	8%	32%	35%	62%
Roland Tang	49%	30%	15%	23%	30%	50%
Average	44%	27%	12%	27%	32%	56%

Table 17.3 – Collated results from tracking the benefit of reducing effort to produce reports

This summary is in sufficient detail to tell us all we need to know about progress against forecast improvements for this group of analysts. The average results indicate that progress is more or less as predicted, while details at the individual level suggest that Roland Tang's performance could be investigated further.

These results, along with those for other benefits being tracked, other functions and other countries, will be collated into a regional summary report – probably quarterly – by the regional benefits coordinator in one of three ways:

- Directly from each country function benefits coordinator.

- As country submissions, collated by lead country benefits coordinators.

- As function submissions, collated by regional functional benefits coordinators.

The method to use is a matter of local preference and subject to the benefits coordinator organisation that has been put in place. Whichever is chosen, it should not be an undue burden on the regional benefits coordinator as long as the format for submissions has been carefully designed to facilitate simple cutting and pasting into the required format for the regional summary benefit tracking report.

▶ Acting on results

Chapter 9 presented a detailed example of how to analyse an apparently poor set of results and act upon the issues identified from the analysis (Figure 9.7 and associated text). The example given was from the same project and concerned the same benefit of reducing the effort to produce reports as used in the previous section of this chapter. The difference in results between the examples illustrated respectively in Figure 9.7 and Table 17.3 is that they took place in successive country tracking instances, thus demonstrating that errors discovered through benefit tracking in one country can lead to more successful subsequent country implementations, if the lessons learned are used and communicated sensibly. Conversely, it does not pay to become complacent after success in one country; circumstances can be different in another country, leading to far less satisfactory results.

The whole strength of benefits management can become unravelled if the organisation does not have the staying power, after the project team has left, to continue tracking benefits, analysing the results and acting on identified blockages to value release. This is where the efforts made to create a benefit-centric environment, involving the transformation manager, function leaders and benefits coordinators, bear fruit. The key relationship here is the one between functional benefits coordinators and function leaders; the former to keep tracking going and identify value release issues, the latter to ensure that the issues are acted upon until they are resolved.

A P P E N D I X

Feasibility workshop briefing

This series of diagrams forms a generic presentation on benefits management, designed to introduce Feasibility stage benefits workshops. They can be modified, or combined with others shown in the book, to create presentations for most types of benefits management briefings.

Benefits Management Briefing
for workshop delegates

Benefits Workshop

Benefits agenda

Day 2
• An introduction to benefits management (this session)
• Identifying and qualifying benefits
   – Identify measures
   – Set targets
Day 3
• Building towards project value
   – Allocating financial buckets
   – Building business logic

2

This slide assumes the workshop scheduling of Figure 11.8. It could be replaced by the schedule at Table 12.1 and supplemented by the slide at Figure 12.3

Principles behind defining benefits

- Project benefits, and value, relate to what will change on the ground.
- All benefits can be measured, but not necessarily directly in financial terms.
- Benefits need to be defined such that they are separable from those claimed by other projects .

The presentation text behind these two slides can be drawn from the section 'Why this method?' in Chapter 1

Purpose and strengths of the method

- Builds the project value case on solid, defensible, foundations
- Gives confidence that project benefits will be achieved.
- Helps to identify any process/behaviour changes needed to release potential benefits.
- Provides a practical way of measuring achievement of benefits.

Management of Benefits is about taking action to make sure benefits are achieved when the project is delivered

Benefits management toolkit

We have a kit of tools used at various project stages to:
- Identify benefits and beneficiaries
- Define measures and set targets
- Derive financial value
- Identify and mitigate risks to benefits achievement
- Set up tracking plan
- Track benefits

You may feel that it is unnecessary to include this slide as well as the next one in the pack – however, it does make quite a nice introduction to the next slide.

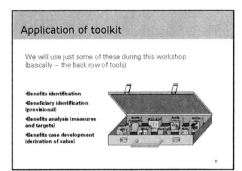

The same slide could be useful for Implement stage workshops but referring to the front row of tools. It took a bit of drawing – if you can track me down I could make it available to you.

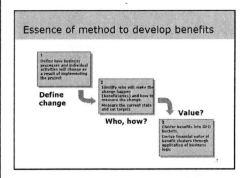

A useful slide to illustrate the balance between the main activities of the two workshops.

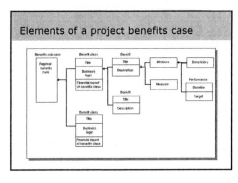

This slide introduces the details that will need to be completed during the two workshops. It is easier to see at Figure 5.2

The role of beneficiaries

- Beneficiaries are people who, by virtue of their position in the organisation, can deliver the benefit to the business. They will be the people who modify their activities as a result of project implementation.
- A beneficiary is:
  - Only sometimes a member of senior management.
  - Not normally a member of the project team.
- Beneficiaries are collectively responsible for achieving the benefits.
- Ultimate accountability rests with function leaders.
- Benefits tracking is the responsibility of the benefits coordinator but requires cooperation and involvement of beneficiaries.

This slide is slightly out of context in that it naturally belongs in a workshop session rather than the introduction. However, most delegates will be beneficiaries and it is important that they understand the concept from the outset.

Use of method at project stages

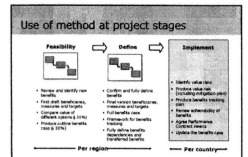

This is a useful slide for putting the whole process into context. It more or less combines the views of Figures 3.5 to 3.8, leaving out reference to de-duplication, which is a programme-led activity.

Structure of benefits sessions during Feasibility

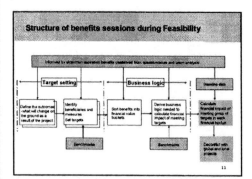

Use this slide to focus delegates' attention on the activities that are carried out in the two workshops, as opposed to the highlighted activities which may be carried out during the visit but outside the workshop environment.

References

1. *The definitive business plan*
   Richard Stutely   1999
   Prentice Hall   ISBN 0 273 63930 7

2. *Benefit Realisation Management*
   Gerald Bradley   2006
   Gower   ISBN 0 566 08687 5

3. *Managing Successful Programmes*
   Office of Government Commerce   2003
   HMSO   ISBN 0 11 330917 1

Project Manager Today
P U B L I C A T I O N S

Project Manager Today Publications specialises in books and journals related to project management. Titles include:

Managing Programmes of Business Change
Managing Risk for Projects and Programmes
Managing Smaller Projects
One Project Too Many – a novel approach to the management of projects, portfolios and programmes
Project and Programme Accounting – a practical guide for professional services organisations and IT
Right First & Every Time – managing quality in projects and programmes
The Programme & Project Support Office Handbook vol's 1 & 2
Using PRINCE2 – the Project Manager's Guide

and the flagship monthly magazine:
Project Manager Today

Publishers of *Project Control Professional* on behalf of
The Association of Cost Engineers

Full details from:
Project Manager Today Publications
Unit 12, Moor Place Farm, Plough Lane, Bramshill, Hook
Hampshire RG27 0RF
Tel: 0118 932 6665
Fax: 0118 932 6663
Email: info@projectmanagertoday.co.uk
Website: www.pmtoday.co.uk

Project Manager Today also organises topical conferences and seminars.